Relationships
in Social Service Practice:
Context and Skills

Relationships
in Social Service Practice:
Context and Skills

Thomas Keefe
University of Northern Iowa

Donald E. Maypole
University of Northern Iowa

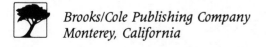
Brooks/Cole Publishing Company
Monterey, California

Brooks/Cole Publishing Company
A Division of Wadsworth, Inc.

Printed in the United States of America
10   9   8   7   6   5   4   3   2   1

Library of Congress Cataloging in Publication Data

Keefe, Thomas, date -
    Relationships in social service practice.

    Bibliography: p.
    Includes index.
        1. Social service—United States.   2. Social case
work.   I. Maypole, Donald, date -.   II. Title.
HV91.K4   1983   361.3'2   82-20693
ISBN 0-534-01322-8

Subject Editor: *Claire Verduin*
Manuscript Editor: *Barbara Burton*
Production Editors: *Sue Ewing, Jane Stanley*
Interior Design: *Jamie Sue Brooks*
Cover Design: *Terril Neely*
Illustrations: *Lori Heckelman*
Typesetting: *Graphic Typesetting Service, Inc., Los Angeles, California*

Preface

The human-service social services practitioner encounters two realities on entering practice. First, practice involves relationships—not just with clients but with colleagues, administrators, related professionals, and others. Second, practice is tied to formal organizations, the ubiquitious bureaucracy, public and private. Successful functioning in the second reality, in a way that preserves professional values and objectives, requires mastery of the first.

Many introductory social work, social service, and human-service practice texts focus on organizing practice frameworks and specific techniques, but the realities of practice require a further step. In addition to organizing framework and methodology, the authors believe there is a need to address the past and present context of practice relationships and the skills that enhance those relationships for the student and beginning practitioner.

Chapter 1 of this book therefore examines the social-historical and contemporary relationship contexts of practice, offering insights into the social and economic genesis of problems that people experience and clues to the historical antecedents of practice relationships. We want to ensure that students and beginning workers know where we have been because we believe this to be a unique and important component of the knowledge that is common to human-service practitioners. Chapter 2 examines the factors that shape practice and practice relationships, including theory, the realities of practice, values, and objectives. Chapters 3, 4, and 5 detail the key relationships skills that can enhance practice relationships, and offer illustrative examples and recent research findings that demonstrate their use and value. Chapter 6 sets forth communication principles and practice techniques useful in forming and sustaining practice relationships.

Each chapter includes extensive references of source material for further inquiry and research. Much of our source material is of an empirical nature. Many texts portray practice relationships as an art, but we have sought to support our portrayal of practice relationships on a scientific basis as well. Consequently, seasoned practitioners and faculty, as well as students, may find our sources from basic and applied social sciences and professions particularly valuable.

Because sexism and racism continue to plague our society, they are a part of human-service practice and the lives and relationship systems of social workers and related professionals. Indeed, they are at the heart of the social problems which we work to prevent, ameliorate, or repair. Chapters 7 and 8, written by experienced social workers, directly address these phenomena as they affect practice relationships.

Chapters 9, 10, and 11 discuss the realities of job burnout and bureaucracy in practice and look at how the bureaucratic environment affects practice relationships. We provide information and examples of research, theory, and our own experience to help deal with the bureaucratic context of our practice relationships.

Chapter 10, which deals with intraorganizational relationships, examines the distribution of power. Practitioners who wish to humanize and otherwise improve client services in their agencies must have a firm grasp on power theories and exercise skill in applying them to intra-agency and community development goals. Sometimes practitioners feel powerless in their work setting, but they often impose their own prison of bureaucratic controls before their supervisors and administrators do. Such behavior in their work place and in the larger society is self-defeating. Practitioners can develop power by applying techniques that we and other authors suggest.

Some notes on terminology: we use the word *client(s)* instead of *consumer, patient, recipient,* or other words denoting those who receive the services of practitioners. The term *human-service workers* is sometimes used synonymously with the term *social service workers* to denote social workers and related professionals. The newly renamed federal Department of Human Services no doubt gives impetus to this trend. To the extent, however, that the term implies or supports any declassification or diminution of professional social work or social service positions, we are cautious of its use. Political and fiscal expediency must not be allowed to replace professional commitment, values, or skills in the service of people in need. Hence, we use the term *practitioner(s)* to refer to social workers and related professionals, such as nurses, counselors, psychologists, psychiatrists, and others with formal codes of ethics and commitments to the service of the injured, handicapped, deprived, oppressed, or needy. These professionals are the practitioners for whom this book is intended.

About the authors: Thomas Keefe and Donald Maypole are social work educators. Keefe's practice was mostly in the mental health field, in psychiatric child guidance, in marriage and family counseling, and in correctional settings. He has worked with mental patients and groups; his clients have included people with drug and alcohol abuse problems; personal, marital, and family difficulties; legal problems; and members of a variety of consciousness-raising and counseling groups. He currently engages in a number of community advocacy activities. After earning his doctorate in social work, he coordinated a university social work program. His research activities have involved theory development and publications on the topics of empathy, meditation, social service practice, the effects on practice of social and economic change, their influence on stress and mental health, and their impact on social welfare and society.

Maypole has practiced in a variety of settings over a 15-year period: county social service departments, a settlement house, a state mental hospital, a state division of mental hygiene district and central offices, and a three-county community mental health center. The positions involved working with low- and middle-income people, minority groups, emotionally troubled persons, alcohol abusers, and developmentally disabled people. The spectrum of his responsibilities ranged from casework, group work, consultation, supervision, planning, program evaluation, and executive directorship duties. Maypole has conducted research in interorganizational relations theory, administration, group home development, alcoholism services, and sexual harrassment in work settings. In addition to these areas, his publications have included writing on management information systems and mental health/health services integration at the community level. The acting head of the Department of Social Work at the University of Northern Iowa, he is also a consultant to local health and social agencies and businesses.

Keefe and Maypole co-authored Chapters 1 and 12 of this book. Keefe wrote Chapters 2 through 6. Preliminary research for these chapters was supported by a University of Northern Iowa Faculty Summer Research Fellowship. Maypole wrote Chapters 9 and 10. Chapters on sexism, racism, and burnout were written by contributors. Dolores Niles, M.S.W., who wrote Chapter 7, has worked in a variety of mental health and alcohol abuse settings and participated in the development of a women's counseling center. She is currently the director of an alcoholism training center at the University of Wisconsin, Madison, and is working on a doctorate. Paul Keys, M.S.W., who wrote Chapter 8, has an extensive background in public social services. While pursuing his doctorate, he works as a management consultant. W. David Harrison, Ph.D., wrote Chapter 11. An assistant professor in the School of Social Work at the University of Tennessee in Knoxville, Harrison has a wide background in child welfare work both in the U.S. and in England. He has published materials on burnout and has conducted many workshops on how to combat it. Finally, Paula Keefe is responsible for the initial rendering of many of the illustrations that appear in the book, a task which required much patience and insight.

ACKNOWLEDGMENTS

We wish to thank our wives, Paula and Mary Jane, and our children, Chris and Kim; Nathan and Kristin, for their patience as we labored over this work. We wish also to thank our teachers—our own professors, clients, colleagues, and students—for their unknowing but substantive education of our consciousness and convictions.

Very able typing support was provided by Becky Hanssen and Carlene Burrichter, whose expertise and flexibility contributed considerably to the project.

We also wish to acknowledge the efforts of a number of reviewers whose comments and suggestions helped us improve our book. We particularly wish to thank Betty P. Broadhurst of Colorado State University, Nile D. Meservy of

Utah State University, Raul H. Solis of Pan American University, Ken Urich of Seattle Central Community College, Douglas Gauss of Freed Hardeman College, and Irene Glasser of Eastern Connecticut State College.

Thomas Keefe

Donald E. Maypole

Contents

Relationships
in Social Service Practice:
Context and Skills

1

Social-Historical Context

Relationships in social service practice are a part of a *context* of human relationships that has been shaped by cultural, social, and economic forces. Historically, these forces have affected the general character of human relationships. In Western industrial societies, they have created the need for service professions and have determined the nature of the practice relationships these professions maintain. A broad historical view is important to grasp the nature of practice relationships, though such a view is admittedly rare among practitioners.

Chapter 1 provides a historical account of the impact of changing social and economic forces on human relationships in Western society. After reviewing the effect of these forces on the history of practice relationships, the chapter examines the effects of social and economic forces on contemporary human relationships, particularly as they contribute to the human problems with which social service professions deal. We begin, then, with a look at the origins of the need for a helping profession.

HISTORICAL IMPACT OF SOCIAL AND ECONOMIC FORCES

Social service professions were created by Western industrial society. They arose in response to the character of human interaction and relationships in industrial society. These are quite different from the relationships among people in tribal or feudal societies, which had different social and economic arrangements or structures.

Tribal and feudal societies

Prior to the development of an industrial market economy, human relationships were sustained by rigid, highly specific economic, cultural, and social roles. In tribal societies, each person depended on another to carry out a particular function in sustaining the small community's social life. In addition, individuals identified one another by their roles and by the economic and social needs they filled. For example, the maker of pots relied on the cultivator for grain. The weaver supplied both with cloth in exchange for pots and grain. In essence, human relationships were economically *specific* and *interdependent*.

The pivotal human relationship in feudal society was between noble and peasant. Ostensibly, one provided protection; the other, food. In feudal society, people were identified by their production roles and, collectively with their peers, formed social classes. Their relative positions in society were determined by their class position in the economic order. Barbara Tuchman, in her history of the 14th century,[1] describes the economic gradations of peasant life at a time when society was shifting from a manorial system to a money economy.

> Possession of a plow, which cost 10 to 12 livres, and of a plow horse at 8 to 10 livres was the line between a peasant who prospered and one who just survived. Those too poor to afford a plow rented a communal one or turned the earth with hoe and spade. Perhaps 75 to 80 percent were below the plow line, of whom half had a few acres and some economic security while the rest lived on the edge of subsistence, cultivating tiny plots supplemented by paid work for the lord or for richer neighbors. The lowest 10 percent existed in misery on a diet of bread, onions, and a little fruit, sleeping on straw, living without furniture in a cabin with a hole in the roof to let out the smoke [Tuchman, 1978, p. 173].

The class relations of feudal society had for centuries been relations of mutual dependence. The welfare of the peasant was of genuine concern to his lord, whose own survival depended on the well-being of his charges. The peasants were the providers of food; in the 14th century they began to meet his need for larger armies (Tuchman, 1978). They were part of his land; they sustained him. He in turn collected tribute, redistributed goods, policed and defended the territory.

The mutual dependence of nobility and peasantry, however, did not generate mutual respect, as historians suggest in descriptions of each by the other.

> A deep grievance of the peasant was the contempt in which he was held by the other classes. Aside from the rare note of compassion, most tales and ballads depict him as aggressive, insolent, greedy, sullen, suspicious, tricky, unshaved, unwashed, ugly, stupid, and credulous or sometimes shrewd and witty, incessantly discontented, usually cuckolded. In satiric tales it was said the villain's [peasant's] soul would find no place in Paradise or anywhere else because the demons refused to carry it owing to the foul smell. In *chansons de geste* he is scorned as inept in combat and poorly armed, mocked for his manners, his morals, even his misery [Tuchman, 1978, p. 175].

At about the time of the Peasants' Revolt of 1381, the peasant revolutionary John Ball advocated that there should be no more vassals or lords.

> How ill they behave to us! For what reason do they hold us in bondage? Are we not all descended from the same parents, Adam and Eve? And what can they show, or what reason can they give, why they should be more masters than ourselves? They are clothed in velvet and rich stuffs, ornamented with ermine

[1]From *A Distant Mirror,* by B. W. Tuchman. Copyright © 1978 by Ballantine Books, a division of Random House, Inc. Reprinted by permission.

and other furs, while we are forced to wear poor clothing. They have wines, spices, and fine bread, while we only have rye and the refuse of the straw and when we drink it must be water. They have handsome seats and manors, while we must brave the wind and rain in our labours in the field; and it is by our labour they have wherewith to support their pomp [Gimpel, 1976, p. 218].

The revolution that Ball advocated was to fail; but the social-class structure had by the 1300s begun a slow change that would alter the character of human relationships at both class and at personal levels.

Emergence of new classes

With the gradual shift from feudalism to the guild and cottage industry system, the nature of relationships between individuals and between classes began to change radically. A new class of tradesmen and artisans owed less allegiance to the other classes because their source of subsistence depended only indirectly on the land, its cultivators and protectors. Members of the new class owned their own shops and tools—their own economic *means of production*.

As the new means of production became more organized, a fundamental duality developed in the social structure. On the one hand were those who owned the shops and tools and, on the other, those who could provide skill or labor but who had little economically productive property. When *owners* of economic means of production required *workers* to produce goods, they could hire those with only their skill or labor to sell. Out of this new relationship, two new social classes began to develop. The development probably began with mill owners and mill workers even prior to urbanization (Scull, 1977). First in England in the 1800s and later throughout most of Europe, new mechanized means of economic production began to draw people off the land and into cities where they took jobs in the burgeoning factories.

The new class of industrial worker began to develop concurrently with the new business- and factory-owning class. The struggles and victories of the new ownership class over the old noble or aristocratic class is the stuff of revolutionary history. Of chief concern here is parallel revolution in the nature of human relationships that made social service professions a necessity, for the industrial revolution engendered profound changes both in personal relationships and in social-class relations.

Changes in personal relationships.   First, the individual's relationships to other individuals lost their economically specific quality. There was no longer *a* potter or *a* weaver whose identity was tied to a socially unique role in the production of necessary goods. Productive roles lost their specific quality. Industrial workers were no longer artisans or craftsmen so much as employees, becoming increasingly interchangeable in their productive roles. Except in the family, where early vestiges of specificity and interdependence in relationships still persist, relationships began to undergo two processes of change that are still occurring today.

One is *atomization*—breaking extended relationships into smaller and smaller networks (Schneider, 1975). An example of this process is the fragmentation of the *extended family* that usually included three generations, cousins, and in-laws in frequent, close contact. Currently, the *nuclear family* with only two generations—parents and children—has supplanted the extended family. Moreover, single-parent families and singles make up an increasing percentage of households. Atomization also includes increasingly temporary and shallow relationships which require less long-term commitment and thrive on the economic autonomy of the relating parties.

The other process is *objectification*—people relating to one another more as *things* than as unique *persons*. In the interests of efficiency and profit, emotional and subjective responses to one another are subordinated to rational and objective or analytic responses. People and relationships are evaluated against other people and relationships. Indeed, people are even quantified as a basis for determining their worth to others or to the productive economy. For example, one's salary, IQ, sales record, or number of publications can supersede personal or other, more relevant qualities as measures of worth. The current fad of rating physical attributes on a scale of 1–10 forestalls and distorts natural subjective reactions and consideration of less visible qualities.

Changes in class relations.   Second, class relations underwent a *structural* change. As the old class structure of aristocracy and peasants was replaced with the new structure of ownership class and workers, the nature of class relations changed as well, in a most important way. Unlike the lord of the manor, who was responsible for, and depended on, the peasant's welfare, the owner's responsibility for his workers ended with the payment of a wage. The social welfare of the workers was not the employer's concern.

Traditionally, care of the indigent, old, and inept had been a matter for the family, residential community, and the local lord of the manor. With the structural shift from an agricultural-feudal society to an industrialized-urban society, pauperism became a general problem. Relief was now a vehicle by which the owning classes could maintain social order and the status quo. Means to manage the various kinds of indigent persons were needed to assuage the boom-and-bust economic reality.

Simply stated, people are thrown out of work in times of economic recession or depression; people are displaced in times of economic expansion and modernization. The chaos created by large numbers of people without means for subsistence must be controlled if the basic economic arrangements are to remain unchanged (for a synopsis of this phenomenon, see Piven & Cloward, 1971). People who were problematic to the new market economy—the poor, criminal, and inept—were segregated from the community in almshouses, subjected to forced work programs, imprisoned, provided limited outdoor relief (help provided to the needy in their own home as opposed to an alms-house), exiled, or executed.

Stresses on families.   Industrialization, urbanization, and migration to the cities began to exact a toll on families during the industrial revolution. As families could no longer meet all their members' needs in the areas of health, education, income, housing, employment, and emotional support, public and private agencies arose to fill the gaps.

In the early days of industrialization, the horrors of the factories, mines, and sweatshops, the 12- to 15-hour days, the 7-day work weeks, and the labor of children and women, necessitated by wages so low that no one person could support a family, manifested the exploitation of the lower classes (Thompson, 1963). With increasing mechanization, the worker increasingly became an extension of the machine of production. As workers were drawn into factories and then displaced by mechanization, or economic recession, the worker's plight was surpassed only by that of the chronically unemployed poor.

Moreover, the work of factory and unskilled laborers was less and less a source of gratification and identity as they were increasingly alienated from their work and their social roles. Unlike the peasants who controlled 50–70 percent of their products (Mandel & Novack, 1973, p. 22), industrial workers did not control the products of their labor. Daily they withstood the monotony of routinized, repetitive work that used only a fraction of their human potential, followed by a few scant hours of rest and recuperation with family. Beginning in the 1860s, the union movement in the United States accelerated, and after 75 years of struggle, many of the problems of the working classes—grueling hours, inadequate wages, child labor—were lessened.

With the rise of national and international market economies and increasing governmental power, local institutional care for problematic populations became the concern of the state. The poor, criminal, and inept were increasingly segregated from one another and from the general population in large, centralized, state-run institutions. The population of these institutions burgeoned, particularly in periods of economic recession (Scull, 1979; Brenner, 1973), as families with scanty economic resources lost the capacity to care for or tolerate nonproductive members.

Hence, the personal, specific relationships of people in small, self-sufficient communities began to give way to atomized and objectified relationships which—at first in the community and later in the family—could less ably tolerate the deviant, unproductive, problematic individual. Care shifted from the community to the large, centrally located institution and thereafter to the state, and troubled populations were increasingly differentiated. The criminal was segregated from the insane, the insane from the mentally handicapped, and so on. Not surprisingly, the people charged with the care, processing, and management of these populations themselves became differentiated from one another (Scull, 1977, 1979).

Social service professions began to emerge in the late 1800s in the United States (Federico, 1980, pp. 61–103). By tracing the history of their emergence, we can begin to trace the development of practice relationships in particular. As noted, client-practitioner relationships were mediated by trends affecting general human relationships in industrial society. Atomization, fragmentation, objectification, periodic severe economic hardship, and loss of control over work and its products are powerful forces that continue to stress human relationships and therefore to shape practice relationships.

In some ways, practice relationships have developed to compensate for, and to repair, problematic, inadequate, or destructive relationships in the lives of social service clientele. They have also been shaped by their utility in helping to deliver the information and material support needed by individuals and families to meet basic needs unmet by the economic system. Keeping in mind the general historic impact of social and economic forces on relationships in Western society, we may now focus on the history of practice relationships in particular.

HISTORICAL DEVELOPMENT OF PRACTICE RELATIONSHIPS

The historical antecedents of practice relationships lie in the relationship between society (and its government) and the poor, deviant, handicapped, unproductive, criminal, or other problematic individuals whose welfare is of general social concern. Hence, we find the beginnings of the history of practice relationships in the human-service professions.

Throughout history, how have poor or problematic people been regarded? Were they viewed as deserving human beings, as dependent consumers of society's wealth, or as potentially threatening political dissidents? As we shall see, each of these attitudes has had periods of ascendancy and to varying degrees persists in Western industrial societies today. Before discussing the United States specifically, let us briefly examine the history of individual welfare as exhibiting a consistent pattern of humanitarian concern and social control.

Biblical times

The Old Testament Hebrews manifested a marked *humanitarian concern* for the poor. In the Book of Ruth, the Hebrew farmers leave the corners of their fields unharvested so that the produce will be available for the poor. Likewise noted is the farmers' practice of filling central granaries so that their contents would be available to all in case of drought. Indeed, Joseph recommended this course to the Egyptian pharaoh to ward off the impact on his people of such a catastrophe.

In the Book of Mark, Jesus states that it is easier for a camel to get through the "eye of the needle" (in reality a pedestrian gate through the wall of old Jerusalem) than for a rich man to get into Heaven. In response to a rich man's question on how to get into Heaven, Jesus says that he must give all his possessions to the poor. Elsewhere in the New Testament, Jesus makes it clear, by feeding the poor, healing the sick, and relating to prostitutes, that he feels an especial affinity toward the common people. In this Hebrew society the poor were not stigmatized, and in Jesus' preaching that we are all our brother's keeper we see primarily a humanitarian concern for the poor and needy.

In discussing the Hebrew society of biblical times, however, we must not suppose that humanitarian concern was widespread throughout the Mediterranean area. The Middle East, North Africa, and most of Europe were under the political, economic, and military control of the Roman Empire, and there was little social justice for the common man and none for slaves after Caesar overthrew the republic in 49 B.C. As the Roman Legions conquered the forces in other lands and brought back loot and tribute, the wealthy expanded their farms by displacing free farmers and substituting slave labor. With no means of support, those displaced by slave labor migrated to the cities for work. Since there was no work for most of them, they became members of the city mobs.

Because the wealthy class viewed the mobs as both social and political threats, a system of public welfare was worked out to deal with them. Referred to as "Bread and Circuses," the system involved government officials doling out food, providing public work in constructing buildings and free entrance to the coliseums. In contrast to a humanitarian philosophy, then, the Roman system was built on a philosophy of *social control.* There was no real concern about the poor as people but only about the danger of their potential social and political actions.

Middle Ages

With the fall of the western half of the Roman Empire at about A.D. 450, the feudal system slowly evolved. Whereas the Roman plantation system had been based on slave labor (and was to be replicated in the United States 1200 years later), the feudal system was based on the labor of "free" serfs, and this system, involving an exchange of labor, loyalty, and service for protection and life maintenance, was to last for some 800 years because the social contract met the needs of both parties. Its primary philosophy was based on neither social control nor humanitarianism but on survival expediency. The Catholic church, as a social institution, manifested the humanitarian philosophy throughout the era. At this time, it helped the poor primarily by making the monasteries places to secure food, lodging, clothing, and such medical care as then existed.

The feudal system began to decline with the advent of the Renaissance in about A.D. 1200, with the great plagues that decimated medieval Europe, and with the development of strong central governments. The increased afflu- ence of the English aristocracy and wealthy classes and their change in farming practices, from labor intensive crops to sheep raising, lessened their need for serfs. Displaced from lands that their ancestors had farmed for ages, the serfs frequently sought work at the early mills. When there was not enough work, many turned for help to churches, to begging, or to crime.

In the mid–14th century, the first English law to restrict and regulate begging was implemented. Successive laws focused on forcing the poor to work. In 1601 the English poor laws were codified into one cohesive set. As it turned out, this law was to play the primary role in establishing a public welfare system in the United States and thus in shaping the nature of our practice relationships.

English Poor Law of 1601

Although the primary policy of the English Poor Law of 1601 was to force the able-bodied poor to work (reflecting the social control philosophy), its humanitarian features of providing help to the non-able-bodied poor must also be recognized. Essentially the law formally recognized the responsibility of the state for the nonproductive individual without means. Unlike the pol- icies of the Hebrews and the Catholic church, which helped all who sought help, the English Poor Law separated the poor into specific categories based on their being "worthy" (non-able-bodied) or "unworthy" (able-bodied). Mandatory, the law was implemented throughout England.

The poor were not viewed as needy human beings but as dependent creatures who needed to be forced to work or cared for at minimal expense if they couldn't work—which was preferable to having them begging in the streets. The pervasiveness of this belief continued among the English colonies in the New World. Indeed, it is the foundation for some contemporary policies relating to the poor.

WELFARE IN THE UNITED STATES

The colonial period (1608–1789)[2]

During the initial years of the Jamestown (1608) and Plymouth (1620) colonies, the focus was on sheer survival. Because of lack of resources, half the colonists in each place died within the first year. The religiously based colony at Plymouth practiced mutual aid from the beginning; but in the secular Jamestown colony, Captain John Smith had to impose a mutual aid approach in its second year (Pumphrey & Pumphrey, 1961).

After the initial survival period, each of the colonies imposed the public welfare system of the homeland—the English Poor Law of 1601. By the middle of the 17th century, all the provisions of the law were being implemented; the first almshouse and workhouse were developed in Boston in the 1650s–1660s. Thus, from the very beginning of our country, the primary aim of public welfare was to force the able-bodied poor to work. Concurrent with this social control philosophy, however, was the humanitarian approach to helping the non-able-bodied poor, who were cared for by their families or at public expense. In fact, doctors were provided monies to give medical care to the poor!

The care of the mentally incompetent (mentally ill or mentally retarded) poor was less enlightened. If families could care for a mentally incompetent member, they had to do so—if not in the house then in cages back by the barn or woodhouse or in cells in the attic. If there was no family, mental incompetents were placed in almshouses or taken into the forest and set free to wander. Of course, without residency, they could receive no help elsewhere. In the second half of the 17th century, the able-bodied poor were auctioned to the highest bidder for their labor. The non-able-bodied were contracted out to the lowest bidder for public funds to pay for their maintenance. These practices continued alongside the Poor Law programs until well into the 19th century.

In 1657 the first formal mutual aid association was formed—the Scots Charitable Society (Trattner, 1979). On a prepaid basis, families received assistance if a member became disabled or died. Other such associations were formed, including one for freed Blacks toward the end of the 18th century. No provisions were made for freed Blacks or Native Americans in any public program.

---

[2]Approximate time periods devised by Pumphrey & Pumphrey (1961).

The colonists' sense of social responsibility must be emphasized, however. By the beginning of the 18th century, all Overseers of the Poor were mandated to do needs assessments to locate poor people in their towns (New England) or counties (southern colonies). By the standards of the times, the colonial towns and counties (and to some extent the colonies' governments) spent large sums on the poor. By the 1750s, according to Trattner, towns were spending from 10 to 35 percent of their budgets on the poor alone. One reason for this was religious commitment. The 1720–1735 Great Awakening was a mass religious revival that emphasized the equal nature of all people—rich and poor—and the obligation to help the latter. Indeed, the 18th century has been described as the "humanitarian age" (Trattner, 1979).

Although the colonial governments were preoccupied with the Revolution toward the end of the colonial period, four developments should be noted.

1. The first children's orphanage, developed by the church and Governor James Oglethorpe, was established in Georgia in the 1740s.

2. The first general hospital appeared in the 1770s. Developed by Benjamin Franklin and Dr. Thomas Bond, the Pennsylvania General Hospital in Philadelphia was also notable for its partial capital subsidy from the Pennsylvania colonial legislature and for the admission of mentally ill and alcoholic people. Unfortunately, in the early 1800s, general hospitals closed their doors to these two groups, and they were not reopened until the 1960s and 1970s.

3. The first colonial (state) mental hospital was opened in Williamsburg, Virginia, in 1770, serving as the model for subsequent state mental hospital development.

4. The fourth development was the opening of the Walnut Street Prison in Philadelphia.

All these developments were movements away from the almshouse and toward differentiated care or rehabilitation for these groups (although social control was probably the primary reason for the prison). All were forerunners of the explosive institutional development that occurred in the early 19th century. With the development of institutions and of differentiated care, professional caretakers emerged who were the forerunners of today's social service practitioners.

First national period (1789–1854)

During the first national period, almshouses, state mental hospitals, prisons, general hospitals, and children's institutions were developed in each of the states. The last two institutions tended to be developed as private charitable endeavors; the first three tended to be developed by cities, counties, and state governments. In typical U.S. fashion, social control and humanitarian concerns are mixed in each of these developments.

During the 1820s, a short-lived upsurge of religious revivalism advocated the saving of poor people through missionary works and by meeting their material needs. Institutionalized children were forced to undergo rigorous, disciplined, daily moral, academic, and vocational training regulated by school bells. Although very difficult, such a life was far superior to what poor children experienced in almshouses. The reformers who developed the institutions believed that the answer to much of pauperism was to educate the children "morally" into becoming working, independent adults. Here the focus is on individual character as the source and solution of poverty and social discord.

At the same time, the public demonstrated growing concern about the economy of public expenditures, coupled with a desire for the most efficient forms of social control of paupers. Similar concerns are the subject of much politically motivated manipulation through the mass media today, as manifested in changes in the laws, policies, and procedures relating to poor and troubled families.

In 1821 the Massachusetts legislature issued a report named after the state committee chairman, Josiah Quincy (Breckinridge, 1970). Utilizing survey techniques very similar to those in use today, the committee was amazed at the poverty it found (the depression following the War of 1812 caused widespread suffering). Typical of the newly hardening attitudes toward the poor, however, the report's data were evaluated strictly in moral terms. Outdoor relief was described as a costly, unmitigated evil which caused rather than reduced dependency. Without the dread of want, what would motivate the poor to work? Also, the use of public tax monies for such a purpose would reduce private philanthropy. Accordingly, the abolition of public outdoor relief and the reliance on institutional care (almshouses and workhouses) were advocated. The "worthy" poor were to be housed in almshouses and the "unworthy" in workhouses.

In 1824 the New York legislature issued the Yates Report in which the public relief system was studied and the four main methods of providing public relief—indoor relief (in almshouses or other institutions), outdoor relief (in the home), contracting out, and auctioning—were evaluated at length. The commission concluded that the last two systems were inhumane and that home (outdoor) relief created idleness, dissipation, and crime. Such reports resulted in a diminution of contracting out, auctioning off, and outdoor relief, though the latter form of public assistance was never completely terminated. Indoor relief generally was seen as a public responsibility. The newly developing church and secular charitable organizations underlook outdoor relief to help the poor, whose ranks grew with the advent of our industrial revolution, as well as the flood of European immigrants. Additionally, these organizations responded to cyclical depressions.

As almshouses and prisons became more numerous, the mentally ill who could not be cared for at home were increasingly confined to them. In 1841, a former schoolteacher, Dorothea Dix, began to teach Sunday School in Massachusetts' East Cambridge jail and was appalled by the treatment of the mentally ill there (Abbott, 1941). In visiting other places housing the mentally ill, she found that many were kept in unsanitary conditions and treated cruelly. Well educated and sensitive, Dix decided to devote her life to crusading for humane care of the mentally ill. Ultimately she was responsible for the development of 32 mental hospitals in the United States and Europe (Leiby, 1978), and she pioneered the development of case studies and cost-benefit analyses to buttress her arguments for more humane care.

Borrowing from the English Quakers (who had built a mental hospital for Quakers exclusively), Dix advocated a *moral treatment* approach to treating the mentally ill. In this approach, staff treated their patients kindly, as dignified human beings, and engaged them in a variety of activities. This approach, which revolutionized care of the mentally ill, was adopted by state mental hospitals throughout the nation. The result was a high discharge rate. The moral treatment approach of this era epitomized the humanitarian philosophy. The moral courage of the 19th-century female reformers was remarkable.

Period of national expansion (1854–1895)

President Franklin Pierce vetoed a bill initiated by Dorothea Dix to secure federal involvement in care for the mentally ill. This, coupled with the exigencies of the Civil War, severely damaged the earlier optimism and promise for care of the mentally ill. At about the time of the Civil War, judges were given the right to commit people involuntarily to state mental hospitals, and the flood of poverty-stricken immigrants from Europe provided many candidates for such actions. The result was that state mental hospitals became too crowded for the exercise of the moral treatment approach, and they deteriorated into warehouses and worse.

In the public sector, the trend toward lessened outdoor relief and more indoor relief (as shown by the use of the state hospitals for community outcasts) increased. The need for public assistance augmented with immigration, the development of large cities, and growing industrialization. To meet mass needs, private church and secular organizations proliferated; all the large cities had numerous such organizations. The suspicion that certain of the poor were receiving help from more than one organization led to a reconsideration of proposals by the Society for the Prevention of Pauperism (1820s) and the Association to Improve the Conditions of the Poor (1840s) that outdoor private relief be centrally organized. Accordingly, in 1877, in Buffalo, New York, the first Charity Organization Society (COS) was developed (Leiby, 1978). The goals of the COS were to prevent welfare cheating (social control) and to serve the "truly needy" (humanitarian). In addition to providing cash or in-kind assistance, agency representatives gave clients liberal doses of moral exhortation to reform and become independent.

Initially, the COSs reflected the contemporary value judgment that the poor were poor because they refused to work. This belief, which had developed during the first national period, was supported by simplistic applications of Charles Darwin's (biological) theory of evolution to the social sphere. The philosophy of *Social Darwinism* claimed that the poor were responsible for their own poverty because they were weak, noncontributing members of society and that if they did not support themselves they should be permitted to perish. Competition was the law of life; hence, those who failed were by nature unfit. If allowed to multiply, they would become evermore dangerous to society (Bremner, 1956).

Is social Darwinism alive today?

The importance of values and ideologies is shown in the following: A nineteenth century listing of the causes of dependency highlighted individual character flaws and argued that the help given the poor by organized charity aggravated the problem. The dominant nineteenth century response to dependency was the organization of friendly services aimed at pushing the poor individual, and by extension, the family, above the need for relief. Alternatively, if people are considered essentially good (that is, ambitious), the response to need is more likely to be guided by the offer of incentives and the development of programs that provide opportunity for self-advancement [Axinn & Levin, 1982, p. 6].

Some 19th-century views of the needy persist today and still affect practice relationships. Nevertheless, other, competing views began to bring forth their own movements, also affecting the character of practice relationships.

Just a half-dozen years after the inception of the COS movement, the urban settlement house movement began. In contrast to the COSs, the settlement house workers believed that the poor were poor because of structural deficits in society, such as the exploitation of child and women labor, low wages, lack of jobs, and discrimination. Instead of patronizing or attempting to reform the needy individual, these workers provided assistance to the needy in overcoming barriers to employment, such as the inability to speak English, lack of job skills, and the absence of a suitable place for the children of working mothers. Major efforts were made to organize residents to better their neighborhoods and to deal with City Hall.

Although practice relationships for settlement workers were quite different from those for the COS visitors, both institutions reflect the beginning of the social work profession and its different areas of practice, casework (COSs), and group work/community organization (settlements).

Period of social work professionalization (1895–1937)

The professionalization of social work before World War I coincided with the rise of Populism, a resurgence of concern about the welfare of the common man, the poor, women, and children. According to Compton (1980), the forces for reform centered around the increasing prosperity of the United States, relative peace, great forward strides in applying the scientific method (in such areas as medical care), the leadership of women, and increasingly active social workers, especially those associated with settlement houses.

The focus on societal reform through social legislation reflected a deep humanitarian understanding of the role of the social structure and social forces in creating and sustaining poverty, oppression, exploitation, and discrimination against the poor and vulnerable. The punitive treatment of these groups, fully justified in Social Darwinism, was spotlighted by social workers and "muckraking" journalists. That the huge fortunes amassed by "captains of industry" were in stark contrast to the gruelling poverty experienced by one of every eight people in the United States (Hunter, 1904) led to the realization of disproportionate wealth. Reformers and labor unions called for decent housing, regulation of the work hours of women and youngsters, occupational safety, public health campaigns, prohibition of child labor (under 16), and worker compensation for involuntary unemployment, sickness, and old age. Labor unions pressed for a ten-hour day and later an eight-hour day.

The period of Progressivism saw broad-based advances against many social problems. The Pure Food and Drug Act promoted public health. President

Theodore Roosevelt implemented federal land conservation programs. Writers pointed out the need for federal government involvement in public welfare and social insurance programs. The latter were based on successful programs implemented by Count Otto von Bismarck in Germany in the 1880s; the former meant the federalization of programs related to the English Poor Law of 1601. Major advances were made in medicine, nuclear technology, manned, powered flight, radio communications, movies, and automobiles. It was a time of optimistic conviction that the application of reform measures and technology could solve fundamental societal problems and enhance the quality of life. It was clearly recognized that people could be poor or troubled through no fault of their own.

Compton (1980) indicates that social workers were deeply involved in the social movements and national politics of the time. In 1909 the first White House Conference on Children was held, which led to the development of the federal Children's Bureau in 1912. This bureau—a major advocate of services for children for the next 70 years—is currently slated for elimination.

Paul Kellogg, director of the Pittsburgh Survey (which studied the city's social problems in depth) and later the editor of *Survey* magazine, was a major advocate of social work reforms during the early 1900s. In addition, social workers had the ear of Theodore Roosevelt. The social welfare component of his 1912 Bull Moose party platform was written by social workers; indeed, it was Jane Addams who seconded Roosevelt's nomination at the national convention (Leiby, 1978).

Social workers dedicated themselves faithfully to the professionalization of their work. With the development of state boards of charities and corrections, charity organization societies, and settlement houses, workers became paid employees rather than volunteers. As time passed, the need for in-service training to enhance worker skills became increasingly apparent. The charity organization societies responded by developing summer training workshops and, at the turn of the century, a master's degree program, with many universities thereafter following suit.

The beginning of World War I dealt the death blow to the Progressive Era. The suffering and death of millions of Europeans and some Americans (an estimated 20 million soldiers and civilians died) and the seemingly unresolvable political issues led to a growing disbelief in governmental intervention in social problems and individual lives. Indeed, most of the social reforms sought had been attained. Women received the franchise (after 40 years of demonstrations). The misguided Prohibition endeavor, women and child labor laws, eight-hour work days, etc., were all implemented.

Pessimism and the belief that these reforms were sufficient led to a "pulling back" from further efforts to improve society, and in the forefront of those pulling back were the social workers. During and after World War I, they became enamored of Freudian psychology and therapy, both of which focused on the defined client, on the family as the source of emotional-behavioral problems, and on the value of the therapist-client relationship. A dwindling few continued to point out societal impacts on mental health and poverty, but the overall national humanitarian concern dissipated.

Period of federalization (1935–1969)

Social complacency terminated abruptly with the onset of the Great Depression in 1930. One-quarter of the work force became unemployed. Again, it became apparent that hard-working, self-reliant people could be poor through no fault of their own. Private and public (state-county-city) outdoor relief programs quickly used up their scarce resources in attempting to meet immense social needs. Mass deprivation and suffering, natural calamities such as the drought in the "dustbowl" states, and labor and political dissatisfaction contributed to political unrest and a sense of mounting urgency. The federal government alone had, or could create, the resources to alleviate desperate public needs and to stave off political turmoil.

Once again politically active, social workers helped to formulate the Social Security Act of 1935, but this act perpetuated many policies of the English Poor Law of 1601, such as residency requirements, categorization of the poor and differential programs, local administration, and a forced work policy (no outdoor relief programs were provided for the able-bodied). Social assistance to the blind, the aged, and to families without breadwinners, child welfare and maternal and child health, which had been funded by many of the states, now gained federal participation. The "revolutionary" new social insurance programs, such as retirement, survivors' and unemployment compensation, were to be based on insurance philosophies rather than on the English Poor Law philosophies in the social assistance programs. Workers and deserving recipients were to receive nonstigmatized benefits, both cash and, later, in-kind, such as health care and food stamps. The humanitarian philosophy was alive but secondary to the social control features of the actions by Franklin D. Roosevelt and Congress. Because of industrial challenges to the constitutionality of the 1935 act, it was not implemented until 1937 when the depression was practically over.

On balance, the 1935 Social Security Act's social assistance and social insurance programs have had a profound impact in the United States. It has served as the primary income-maintenance program, as well as a tool for control, through its policies and regulations of recipients' behavior. Examples of its use as a tool for control include the mandatory feature of relatives' responsibility for poor family members, the residency requirement which tied the poor to their poor geographic area, and the use of Aid to Families of Dependent Children (AFDC) to try to control female recipients' sexual behavior. Thus, the act projecting the federal government into the social welfare field finally broke the precedent of President Pierce's view that the federal government should "not be the great almoner." It laid the groundwork for the federal role in the Great Society program of the 1960s.

After World War II, the United States transferred billions of dollars to Europe by means of the Marshall Plan program, helping to better the lives of people devastated by the war. At the same time, Americans became slowly more aware of the continuing social problems in their own country. Some conscientious objectors had worked in various public welfare and social agencies, and now they, social services practitioners, and the media called for reforms in mental health and health and welfare programs. The social welfare policies of John Kennedy's New Frontier and of Lyndon Johnson's Great Society marked the next (and last) high-water mark in humanitarian concern for the needy, though Cloward and Piven (1971) have argued that the Great Society programs were related to growing political and social turmoil.

As the social turmoil diminished and local politicians perceived their lack of control over the Great Society's local programs, a process of dismantling began in 1969. Participation of the poor in designing and implementing programs to meet their needs, the funding of advocacy programs to increase their share of resources, and providing opportunities for them to better their lives—all showed a clear movement away from stigmatized income maintenance and social services. But the participation of professionally trained social services practitioners at the national level in conceptualizing the services of the Economic Opportunity Act was minimal.

Politicians and minority group personnel sought to avoid relying on the existing service-delivery systems and to "democratize" the provision of services. Some professionals were employed at the local level, but the general lack of professionalism may have contributed to several administrative and practice problems that were highlighted by the mass media. Still, one of the main strengths of the movement lay in "empowering" clients to overcome their social and environmental problems and to seek a more satisfying level of life. Clients were viewed as partners rather than as passive recipients of help in dealing with their problems.

The proliferation of federally funded local programs created a tremendous job market for social services practitioners in Great Society programs, such as in serving the aged and in community mental health. Professional social services workers supported the need for the development of paraprofessional career ladders, such as social services aides and alcoholism counselors. Development of an undergraduate social work curriculum occurred in the late 1960s and the 1970s. The proliferation of such curricula led to the development of accreditation standards, as had the proliferation of masters' programs during World War I.

Period of new federalism (1969–present)

In the late 1960s, with the heightening of vested interest and minority group pressure on the federal administration and Congress, with open revolts on some campuses and in some cities, with the United States embroiled in a controversial war in Vietnam, and the Great Society humanitarian philosophy coming unglued, President Richard Nixon adopted a new policy of federal-state-local-private industry relationships. Called the New Federalism, this policy emphasized returning power and responsibility from their centralized governmental location to the states and to the private-enterprise sector. Owing to his own political difficulties, however, Nixon's implementation of his new policy was limited to dismantling the major programs of the Economic Opportunity Act.

Now the poor and needy are viewed not as real people but as unproductive, endless consumers of public wealth. Poverty and social dysfunctioning are not the fault of societal defects but of flawed individuals. Rhetoric on balanced budgets and investment of capital for productivity proffers simple-minded economic schemes in the interest of corporate profit over the welfare of the needy and vulnerable. The definition of *truly needy* is manipulated for political ends rather than to provide a decent standard of living for the poor.

Now the problem of stigmatization reappears:

> When I first came on welfare, I was ashamed, because society has taught me to be ashamed of something like that. It's not something you go out and brag about, because you don't like to be degraded and humiliated. You already feel that way inside you because you are taught it from childhood. We were taught that welfare was begging, charity, and when you have a little pride, you don't do that [Calvert, 1972, p. 25].

Although this mother's statement focuses on securing income maintenance from Aid to Families with Dependent Children, how will her feelings affect her relationship with her caseworker and other helping practitioners? Will the caseworker empathize with her or understand the economic/social context of her situation?

President Reagan has implemented the New Federalism policy in its entirity. This philosophy and policy of returning to the pre-1935 federal involvement in welfare will have a major structural impact on the relationship of the federal government with the poor and other vulnerable groups as well as on shrinking the social services delivery systems. Now, with the states not able to tackle problems, such as poverty, unemployment, industrial manipulations of the economy, and environmental pollution, our social problems will increase; the need for social services will also increase. If private enterprise continues to perform as in the past (that is, relying only on the "trickle down" theory to create jobs for the poor and to transfer wealth), we will be unable to meet the mass needs of the poor. State and local governments will be unable to pick up programs previously funded by federal laws. The pressures on social services practitioners will increase and their need for enhanced understanding of their practice relationship networks (to meet client needs) will become even more critical.

The industrial state, with its increasingly institutional and universal forms of provision for human welfare, has generated a high degree of specialization in services and professional helping roles. The nature of social services practice relationships has taken on aspects of the personal and specific relations that were more universal in pre-industrial times. Thus, the emotional need-meeting character of some direct practice relationships with clients is a result of the social and economic character of the society that conditions human relationships. The contemporary societal factors conditioning human relationships in general and practice relationships in particular are extensions of the historical trends sketched above. A brief critique of the effects of these forces on contemporary relationships must supplement our historical introduction.

CONTEMPORARY RELATIONSHIP CONTEXT OF PRACTICE

A historical survey of professional social work relationships with clients would be incomplete without noting that the social and economic forces that have historically altered the nature of human relationships continue to condition them today. Through these relations, individual developmental histories are shaped; and through our individual backgrounds, the content and nature of our relationships are affected in turn (see Figure 1–1).

The impact of contemporary social and economic forces on relationships and development is not altogether beneficial. Indeed, forceful arguments to the contrary often underwrite the need for a social work practice that protects, nurtures, and rehabilitates the casualties of contemporary social and economic relations. *Change* is the amorphous catchword that is used to characterize the sources of stress on human relationships. But to understand socioeconomic forces, we must look deeper into the stream of social change.

At the structural-economic level of society, *work* and *work life* continue to condition contemporary human relations, either to enhance or to damage and alienate them. When the means of economic production in industrial society are privately owned or in the hands of a nondemocratic state—state capitalism—the wage worker does not own or control the product of his or her labor. This fundamental economic reality is a source of *alienation* (Torrance, 1977; Blauner, 1964).

In other words, the worker is often the human extension of some machine or system of production. Personal creativity, as expressed in the process and product of work, may be limited. When working, the worker may endure monotony, routine, and subordination of bodily, emotional, and intellectual needs to the work. Problems in social relationships with family and peers are exacerbated by the stresses of unemployment and poverty generated in boom-and-recession economic cycles. The stress of unemployment is related to human suffering and death. The Joint Committee on Economics reports that 1.4% unemployment in 1970 generated nationally 1540 suicides, 5520 mental hospital admissions, 870 cirrhosis mortalities, 26,440 cardiovascular–renal disease mortalities, and 1740 homicides (Brenner, 1976). Moreover, admissions

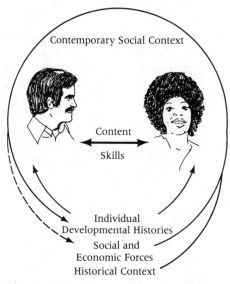

Figure 1–1.   Context of human relations

to mental hospitals are inversely related to employment, a significant relationship that has persisted since 1914 (Brenner, 1973).

The family, once a network of extended relationships, has become a small nuclear group, allowing a degree of intimacy and fulfillment for many in the industrial market economy. But the assaults of economic stress and of work alienation in industries have brought about further fragmentation and atomization in even this persisting institution. In 1910, for example, there was about 1 divorce per 1000 people; in 1940 there were 2 divorces per 1000 people; from 1970 to 1979 the divorce rate accelerated from 3.5 to more than 5 in 1000. While the divorce rate accelerated, the marriage rate increased only slightly. Hence, by 1979 the divorce rate was about half the marriage rate (Bureau of Labor Statistics, 1981). Of course, changing mores and laws accommodate this process, but the underlying economic element remains present.

Child and spouse abuse also reflects the stresses in this last domain of economically specific human relationships. Increasingly, the living wage or family wage is eroded by inflation. Mothers of 53% of all children under age 18 are now employed or are looking for work (Grossman, 1981) in order to sustain an adequate standard of living. When human creativity, sexuality, intimacy, and security are threatened as a result of alienating and sometimes dangerous work life, people must look to other areas of life and to other hours to fill their needs.

That leisure time should become yet another source of stress is ironic. Nevertheless, when happiness and fulfillment are defined in terms of consumer goods, these basic human values are diverted into support of the continually expanding production-consumption cycle. Often, the needs frustrated at work in goods production are frustrated again in leisure-time goods consumption. For success in sexual relationships, for example, evidently a new deodorant, shampoo, or cosmetic will do. When grieving over the death of a loved one, we are offered foam-padded coffins so that the deceased will rest easier (Mandel & Novack, 1973). Affiliative needs are to be filled in planned tours.

Youth is idealized in the interests of commodity consumption. Recently a university student counselor observed that a new common complaint of students was dietary disorder—especially anorexia nervosa, pathological undereating. The source of this problem seems to lie in the image of slim youth portrayed by the advertising media as the necessary condition for success in love, career, and life in general.

In ten thousand ways, our need structures frustrated at work are exploited, or *colonized* (Kovel, 1976) like a foreign land, to create new markets for nonessential goods in the interests of an economy that must expand to survive. In this circumstance of stressed relationships and of frustrated and exploited needs, it is not surprising that the more vulnerable among us seek help from social workers and related professionals. What do social service professionals provide in the way of a relationship that is valuable in restoring to the injured their capacity to cope, master, and meet their needs in an unhealthy social environment?

There have been many answers to this question: expertise in helping people to solve problems, in linking people to services, in reaching out to prospective clients, in advocating client needs to those that can fill them, in changing problematic behaviors, in organizing people to act in their own best interests, in restructuring personality, in creating preventive programs, in moving the system on behalf of people, and in providing nurturance, growth, and recuperation. Except when a client is coerced, hostile, unknowing, or unconscious, a formal or informal practitioner-client relationship is necessary for results to be realized.

But effective practice usually requires a variety of other formal and informal relationships as well. As Figure 1–2 illustrates, people with whom we maintain these relationships usually include, but are not limited to, supervisors, agency administrators, professional colleagues, paraprofessional workers, contact persons in agencies, city councils, agency or county board members, and political representatives. Each of these relationships has many variables. These include frequency of contact, power and authority differences, personality and background differences and similarities, the degree of importance of the relationship to the participants, and the degree of attraction between them.

CONCLUSION

Chapter 1 gives the reader (a) an acquaintance with the social and historical context of human relationships in Western industrial society; (b) a grasp of the history of practice relationships, and (c) a perspective on social and economic forces stressing and changing contemporary relationships. With these understandings one is better prepared to deal with the variety of relationships that sustain practice. But there is more to practice relationships than their context; they have unique features. They are affected by particular professional values and practice objectives. Client-practitioner relationships have features that distinguish them from other practice relations. Indeed, relationship skills that have been researched and developed as facilitators of client-practitioner relationships can enhance all practice relationships.

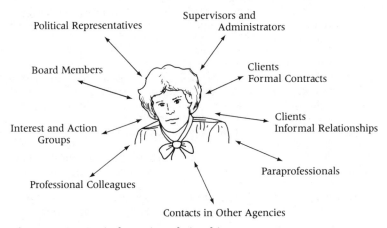

Figure 1–2. Typical practice relationships

Irrespective of one's theoretical approach to practice or one's field of practice, practitioner skills applicable to all practice relationships can be identified and examined. Chapter 2 will look at the unique features of practice relationships with clients and others and learn what elements of theory, practice, and values shape these features. Later chapters will identify and detail skills useful in all practice relationships, together with current research that refines and enhances them.

STUDY QUESTIONS

1. Human relationships in preindustrial societies were economically specific and interdependent. One social institution persists today in which human relationships have some of these qualities—the family. Does contemporary concern for the family and its problems suggest that it is losing these original relationship qualities? If you think so, why?
2. Some contemporary economists criticize the unwillingness of the jobless to move to where the jobs are to be found. What are the consequences for families and of practice with families, of increasing relocation?
3. This chapter cites some examples of how we *objectify* people—treating them more as things and less as persons. In what ways have you been so treated, and how have you done this to others?
4. Practice requires a variety of special relationships in addition to that between practitioner and client. What does this imply about how practitioners must allocate their time?
5. Having studied the history of practice relationships and a view of their socioeconomic context, what changes do you foresee in the social and economic context of practice?
6. Do the changes you anticipate agree or conflict with your values and beliefs about fulfilling human needs and maintaining affirmative human relationships?

REFERENCES

Abbott, G. *From relief to social security.* Chicago: University of Chicago Press, 1941.

Axinn, J., & Levin, H. *Social welfare: A history of the American response to need.* New York: Harper & Row, 1982.

Blauner, R. *Alienation and freedom.* Chicago: University of Chicago Press, 1964.

Breckinridge, S. P. *Public welfare administration in the United States.* New York: Johnson Reprint Corp., 1970.

Bremner, R. H. *From the depths: The discovery of poverty in the United States.* New York: New York University Press, 1956.

Brenner, H. M. Estimating the social cost of national economic policy: Implications for mental health and criminal aggression. *Achieving the goals of the employment act of 1946—Thirtieth anniversary review.* Joint Economic Committee of Congress. Washington, D.C.: U.S. Government Printing Office, 1976.

Brenner, H. M. *Mental illness and the economy.* Cambridge, Mass.: Harvard University Press, 1973.

Bureau of Labor Statistics. Divorce rates, vital statistics of the United States. *Monthly Labor Review.* Washington, D.C.: U.S. Center for Health Statistics, U.S.D.L., May 1981.

Calvert, M. Welfare rights and the welfare system. In T. H. Tarantino & D. Becker (Eds.), *Welfare mothers speak out: We ain't gonna shuffle any more.* New York: W. W. North & Co., 1972.

Cloward, R. A., & Piven, F. F. *Regulating the poor: The functions of public welfare.* New York: Random House, 1971.

Compton, B. R. *Introduction to social welfare and social work: Structure, function and process.* Homewood, Ill.: Dorsey Press, 1980.

Federico, R. C. *The social welfare institution: An introduction* (3rd ed.). Lexington, Mass.: D.C. Heath, 1980.

Gimpel, J. *The medieval machine: The industrial revolution of the middle ages.* New York: Holt, Rinehart & Winston, 1976. Secondarily citing Hassel, W. O. *They saw it happen, 55 B.C.–A.D. 1485.* Oxford: Basil Blackwell, 1973, p. 167.

Grossman A. S. Working mothers and their children. *Monthly Labor Review,* May 1981, 49–54.

Hunter, R. *Poverty.* New York: Grosset & Dunlap, 1904.

Kovel, J. Therapy in late capitalism. *Telos,* 1976, *30,* 73–92.

Leiby, J. *A history of social welfare and social work in the United States.* New York: Columbia University Press, 1978.

Mandel, E., & Novack, G. *The Marxist theory of alienation* (2nd ed.). New York: Pathfinder Press, 1973.

Pumphrey, R. E., & Pumphrey, M. W. *The heritage of American social work.* New York: Columbia University Press, 1961.

Schneider, M. [*Neurosis and civilization*] (Michael Raloff, Trans.). New York: Seabury Press, 1975. (Originally published, 1973.)

Scull, A. T. Madness and segregative control: The rise of the insane asylum. *Social Problems,* 1977, *24* (3), 337–351.

Scull, A. T. *Museums of madness: The social organization of insanity in 19th-century England.* New York: St. Martin's Press, 1979.

Thompson, E. T. *The making of the English working class.* New York: Random House, 1963.

Torrance, J. *Estrangement, alienation, and exploitation: A sociological approach to historical materialism.* New York: Columbia University Press, 1977.

Trattner, W. I. *From poor law to welfare state: A history of social welfare in America* (2nd ed.). New York: Free Press, 1979.

Tuchman, B. W. *A distant mirror.* New York: Ballantine Books, 1978.

2

The Shape of Practice Relationships

The historical and contemporary contexts of human relationships have shaped practice relationships. Social and economic forces, social problems, and the breakdown of primary human relationships have generated the need for social services and have also conditioned the nature of relationships that practitioners maintain. In addition, practice reladionships are shaped by theory, by practice itself, and by practitioner values and objectives (Figure 2–1).

The theories that shape practice relationships are both *basic* and *applied*. Basic theory is composed of perspectives on human behavior and the social environment. These perspectives underlie the applied theory, or *theoretical approaches*, to practice. Of course, practice itself—its respective fields, levels of intervention, and other factors—shapes the relationships we maintain. Though

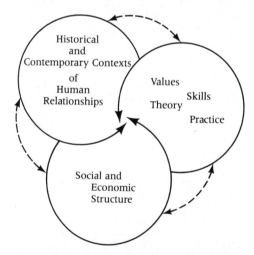

Figure 2–1. Factors shaping practice relationships

professional values and objectives vary, they, too, shape the nature of practice relationships in subtle but profound ways. To provide a full overview of factors that shape practice relationships, Chapter 2 begins by identifying predominant theoretical approaches. After outlining the aspects of practice that influence relationships, we will review professional values that shape practice relationships and suggest a set of practice objectives useful in advancing them.

Finally, although this book focuses on practice relationships, it neither generates a new theoretical approach nor provides a comprehensive or eclectic approach to practice (for books devoted to the latter, see, for example, Anderson, 1981; Goldstein, 1973; Siporin, 1975). The aim of this chapter is to provide an overview of factors shaping the practice relationship, which can be of value to practitioners regardless of their theoretical approach or other factors distinguishing their particular practice. Wisdom arises from the interaction of theory and practice. For social service practitioners, that interaction begins in their relationships.

THEORETICAL APPROACHES

An overview of predominant theoretical approaches to practice will suggest common themes related to practice relationships. Though the classification of approaches is necessarily artificial, it is useful in facilitating a grasp of the varieties of theoretical approach.

From basic theories

Social service practitioners draw from a vast array of basic theory about human behavior and the social environment. Psychoanalytic theory (Strean, 1979), ego psychology (Wasserman, 1979), sociobehavioral theory (Thomas, 1967; Stuart, 1979), existential perspectives (Krill, 1979), and ecology (Germain, 1979; Germain & Gitterman, 1979)—all have provided approaches to practice. Most of these approaches are fairly recent, but they enrich social service practice with their wide diversity.

Traditional approaches

The names of certain individuals have become associated with the approaches to practice that they founded. Because these approaches have engendered trends—particularly in social work practice—they might therefore be called *traditional*. Traditional approaches have been widely taught, elaborated, and extended over the years.

Problem-solving approach.   Helen Harris Perlman's pragmatic *problem-solving* approach focuses on clients' reality problems and minimizes the use of transference or unconscious factors in helping people to find solutions (Perlman, 1964). This approach helped to distinguish social work practice from the psychoanalytic school which has so greatly influenced practice. The problem-solving process, the core of the client-practitioner relationship, enables the client to solve immediate problems while at the same time developing skills applicable to other problems (Compton & Galaway, 1975). Some regard the *task-centered* approach (Epstein, 1980; Reid, 1978; Reid & Epstein, 1972; Reid & Shyne, 1969) as an extension of the problem-solving approach (Anderson, 1981, p. 163) which elegantly specifies goals, tasks, and time limits for the treatment process.

Class Irene's emphasis

Psychosocial approach. Florence Hollis set forth the basic premises of the *psychosocial* approach (Hollis, 1965), in which the client is diagnosed in a particular situational context (*person-in-situation*). The interrelationship of the personality with the environment is assessed in a psychosocial study. Then, a variety of treatment techniques foster support or change in the individual, the situation, or both. The practitioner-client relationship is preeminent in this approach, which emphasizes the potential for realistic and unrealistic attitudes, acceptance and communication (Hollis, 1965, pp. 149–164) in a paradigm influenced by psychoanalytic ideas. The psychosocial model has influenced current clinical approaches to practice (Strean, 1978).

Functional approach. Jessie Taft initiated the *functional* approach to practice (Taft, 1937); more recent contributions have come from Ruth Smalley (1967, 1971) and from Alan Keith-Lucas (1972). If the problem-solving model can be justly described as pragmatic and the psychosocial model as analytic, the functional model might be described as intuitive. The term *functional* derives from the function of the social service agency in which the practitioner is employed. Again, the practitioner-client relationship is primary. The practitioner listens to the client's feelings and provides this person an opportunity to take the risk of growth toward independence within the context of the agency's function.

Practice-focused approaches

A variety of theoretical approaches can be characterized by the particular clientele or social systems they address. Examples include family therapy or family practice (Janzen & Harris, 1980; Minuchin, 1974; Satir, 1967; Sherman, 1979); group treatment or group work therapy (Alissi, 1980; Coyle, 1948; Konopka, 1963; Northern, 1970); practice with racial and ethnic minorities (Devore & Schlesinger, 1981); administrative and organizational approaches (Brager & Holloway, 1978; Trecker, 1977; Weissman, 1973); community organization, social planning, social action approaches (Alinsky, 1946; Dunham, 1970; Kahn, 1970, 1981; Ross, 1967); and social development approaches (Hollister, 1977).

These approaches have their own coherent sets of principles and techniques; they are not merely practice at different levels of a social system. Each has different modalities of relationships—for example, group interaction or community-power group relationships. Although the practitioner-client relationship is usually central, practitioner relationships with other people (including informal relationships) are frequently very important for effective practice.

Generic and systems approaches

Some theoretical approaches to practice cut across basic theory and specific focus in order to provide practitioners with a common core of theory and technique. There are practitioners who work directly with clients as individuals, in families, and in groups. Those who work in planning, research, or administration may have infrequent contact with clients but maintain various other kinds of relationships.

To meet the daily realities of practice, some approaches are *generic*: they assume an integrated core of values and provide common principles and skills. Some of these focus on the individual or family (Fisher, 1978); others are useful to practitioners who work directly with clients and helpful to those who do not (Anderson, 1981; Goldstein, 1973; Siporin, 1975). These approaches also have an eclectic quality, drawing from a variety of sources. The *systems* approach (Hearn, 1969; Pincus & Minahan, 1973) provides a general systems theory terminology (von Bertalanffy, 1968) and a social systems theory framework (Buckley, 1967) for organizing a unified approach to the different kinds of practice.

Some generic and systems approaches have been criticized for aiming at practice with individuals as well as at community and organizational levels (Schwartz, 1977). The question is whether the assumptions and principles underlying direct work with individuals can effectively transfer to organizations, communities, and planning. The generic approach builds on a history of practice focusing on the individual; and individuals must change or be supported, whatever the level of intervention in the social system. To substitute principles and techniques useful with individuals for those more appropriate to organizational or community planning, goal setting, and change might render practice less effective than it could be. More important, practitioners might view individuals as the object of change when organizational, procedural, policy, or power relations are the source of difficulty. Answers to such criticism must await the further development and integration of pertinent practice theory.

In the systems approach, as presented by Pincus and Minahan (1973), practice is classified as follows: (a) *change-agent system,* consisting of the practitioner and employing agency; (b) *client system*—clients who have asked for or expect services based on an agreement or contract; (c) *target system*—people who are to undergo change to meet change-agent goals; (d) *action system*—change agent, people, and agencies activated to bring about change in the target system. Note that the client system and the target system are not necessarily one and the same. In other words, the focus of practice, of change, is not simply assumed to be the clients, their psyches, or their relationships.

This perspective liberates practice from possible "blaming the victim" approaches in which the problematic individual is assumed to be somehow defective, deficient, inadequate, or disturbed. *At times,* one or more of these things may be true. Often individual psyches and significant relationships require support or alteration to cope with defective, deficient, inadequate, or disturbed realities. Usually it is difficult or wholly artificial to separate persons or a family from their social context. *The crux of the matter is that responsibility for change may be shared by people other than the client, and they, too, are legitimate foci for change.*

That varieties of theoretical approaches exist suggests that social service practice is either disjointed or richly varied, depending on one's point of view.

The array of theoretical approaches contributed by related professionals is vast. This book focuses on *relationships* because they are at the heart of all practice, regardless of theoretical approach. All practice relationships can be enhanced by certain common skills and principles, some common techniques and knowledge. Before examining these in later chapters, however, let us first delineate the organization of social service practice in terms commonly employed by social service practitioners.

DIMENSIONS OF PRACTICE

Level of practice

In general systems theory, a system is a set of interrelated elements (von Bertalanffy, 1968, p. 38). Living systems tend to arrange themselves in hierarchical order with each part constituting a system in itself. Hence, an individual is a *whole* system (with subsystems such as the circulatory and digestive systems). Each individual is also a *part* of a larger social system, such as the family, the employing organization, or the nation. In social service practice, societies are thought of as social systems. Practice may take place at, or be focused on, small systems (*microsystems*) composed of individuals, families, or small groups, or on large systems (*macrosystems*) such as formal organizations, neighborhoods, communities, social institutions, or international organizations.

The level of system addressed (*practice or intervention level*) usually refers to where the practitioner is active on this continuum. Certainly, practice can target one level for change and activate other levels in the change process, or it may plan at a macrolevel to bring change for individuals. As we have seen, some theoretical approaches are concerned with only one level or system (individual, family, community) while others attempt to cut across all systems with generally applicable principles and techniques. The *level of practice* is not synonymous with whether practice is accomplished with clients or through other means.

Direct and indirect practice

Direct practice means that practitioners are in direct communication with clients to provide services; it can take place at any level of social systems. Direct practice relationships are also termed *helping relationships, collaborative relationships* (Pincus & Minahan, 1973, pp. 73–76), or *therapeutic relationships*, though not all direct practice relationships are therapeutic or intended to be, given the variety of fields in social services. *Indirect practice* usually denotes roles such as organizational planning, policy analysis, administration, research, and sometimes education when students or trainees are distinguished from clients as recipients of a practitioner's service.

For the direct practitioner and the administrator, practice relationships can differ greatly. The former maintains practitioner-client relationships as a central part of practice. The latter—though perhaps carrying a direct practice load—focuses on relationships with agency staff, board members, other administrators, managers of funding sources, political representatives, and others, regardless of the kind of agency being administered.

Field of practice

The *field of practice* refers to the practice specialty as derived from the population receiving services. These include, for example, medical, psychiatric, school, rehabilitation, or family planning. Sometimes a field of practice is conceived by the particular scope of practice or the particular techniques used. Social development and clinical social work might be thought of as fields or specialties in this light. Again, practice might be micro- or macrolevel, direct or indirect in most fields. At present, the term *clinical* practice denotes a direct practice, microfocus; but as practitioners become more sophisticated in the use of such techniques as prevention, outreach to potential clients, and in integrating clinical and organizational approaches in industrial practice, the term *clinical* will acquire a broader meaning.

Informal and contractual relationships

Informal relationships are not based on a contract or agreement of service; *contractual relationships* are; and both kinds of relationships exist at every level and in every field of practice. Further, both can exist in direct or indirect practice.

In direct practice, for example, a client and practitioner may have a verbal contract regarding services, but members of the client's family may have a periodic informal relationship with the practitioner. A researcher may maintain a variety of informal relationships with consultants or agency staff but have a formal contract for services with an agency administrator. Moreover, a worker may have informal relationships with members of a client population in an institution, with prospective clients in a community, or with clientele in an industrial setting for the purpose of establishing a prevention program. Some of these informal relationships are similar to contractual relations; but in reality the conceptual organization of practice is not always neatly followed.

The contractual relationship.   Although a variety of informal relationships inevitably sustain practice, for most direct service practitioner-client relationships a contract exists. The contract need not be—indeed, seldom is— a written document; it is usually a verbal agreement or understanding. Ideally, it is explicit in the minds of the practitioner and client(s), and it should incorporate five important ideas.

1. The process must be understood to involve an explicitly stated *change* on the part of the client, a third party, or a target system. However obvious this may seem, such an understanding is sometimes vague or absent.
2. Both the practitioner and the client(s) must clearly understand who are and are not *parties to the contract*. Is a client to be a spouse, a child, an employer?
3. The goals of the process must be *specific and arrived at mutually*. Research indicates that social work practice in the context of mutually negotiated and specific goals is more likely to be effective (Reid & Shyne, 1969). When the client knows what specific goals are being worked on and what outcomes to expect, there is less likelihood of mystification, exploitation, confusion, or floundering in the relationships.

4. *Confidentiality* should be a part of any worker-client contract because it provides the basis of trust in the relationship. The client should know that what is shared in the relationship is not discussed outside the relationship except in cases that the practitioner makes clear in advance, such as with an agency supervisor or consultant, when human life is in danger, or when mandated by a court of law.

5. Some idea of the *length of time* the relationship is likely to last is in order. Knowing how long the change effort will last enhances motivation and hope, resulting in better short-term and long-term results (Reid & Epstein, 1972; Reid & Shyne, 1969).

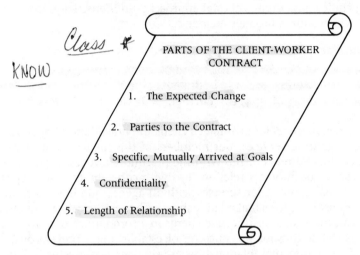

Class ✶

KNOW

PARTS OF THE CLIENT-WORKER
CONTRACT

1.   The Expected Change

2.   Parties to the Contract

3.   Specific, Mutually Arrived at Goals

4.   Confidentiality

5.   Length of Relationship

Figure 2–2.   Parts of the client-worker contract

Though in some practice approaches contracts are explicit and in others they are less so, the components enumerated here are helpful for establishing a solid practitioner-client relationship capable of generating growth and change.

Social factors

Other, less explicit, and seldom noted influences may also have a strong effect on the practitioner-client relationship. Many of these influences pertain to the contractual relationship but can be found in informal relationships as well. These may be termed *transcultural-interpersonal factors* in that they seem to derive from social mores and role expectations for helper and helped that are common to many societies. Cross-cultural observation has illuminated some of these factors (Gillis, 1974; Kiev, 1964, 1968, 1972; Torrey, 1972). The role of the social work practitioner in some ways parallels that of the medicine man, *curandero*, and other, similar roles in both preindustrial and industrial-technological societies. Once identified, they provide a clearer focus on the practitioner-client relationship in its societal and historical context.

Authority and sanction.   In many societies there are interrelated prerequisites for the role of the helping person. By virtue of his or her unique social sanction to occupy the position, the helping person acquires authority to elicit change in those seeking help. G. Devereux, a physician fighting disease in a preindustrial society, describes his successful effort to achieve the sanction of the society to pursue a modern scientific mode of medical practice.

> I simply realized that the sick Sedang, though to be given aspirin or quinine, also felt in need of ritual "support." Hence though told by me to stay indoors and keep warm, he would also call in a shaman, who would drag him out into the rainy night—turning his head cold into bronchitis—in order to perform an expensive curing rite and other ruinous sacrifices on top of it all. In order to prevent such setback for the patients, one night I simply disappeared from the village and announced next morning that I had been given shamanistic powers by the Thundergod. Thereafter I did my own shamanizing, needless to say indoors and at no expense to the patient and, even more obviously, without ceasing to hand out medicines [1969].

Implicit in Devereux's account is the fact that authority in Western industrial society derives in large part from scientific knowledge and skills acquired in educational rather than religious institutions. Nevertheless, sanction of the society to occupy a helping position is acquired through special trials or apprenticeships, and the authority of this person derives from the position occupied as well as from the possession of special knowledge, skills, and personal qualities.

Expectation of change.   One of the most powerful factors affecting the practitioner-client relationship is the expectation of change that the practitioner communicates to the client. The more confident the client is in the practitioner's authority and ability—however they may have been acquired—the more potent is the practitioner's communicated expectation in influencing the outcome of the relationship. This phenomenon involves more than a mere placebo effect (Frank, 1961, pp. 65–74). In the authors' experience, the expectation of positive change that includes more than simple reassurance and that permeates verbal and nonverbal communications has made the difference between colleagues who were highly successful and those who were less so.

The client's expectations are also significant in the relationship. John Mayer and Noel Timms (1969) have observed that working-class clients expect the practitioner to reach a conclusion based on a moral assessment of their situation and the behavior of others who "caused" it. Further, they expect the practitioner to correct their situation by helping them to implement decisions that will change the behaviors of those who caused it. The practitioner, however, is expected to engage the client in a search for causes in the client's own psychodynamics. These conflicting expectations result in client discouragement and practitioner's misapprehension of the client as being unable to engage successfully in the relationship (Mayer & Timms, 1969). Clearly, the expectation of client change must not only be positive but must include roughly similar strategies about how the relationship must lead to change.

Unique ways of relating. Unique ways of relating between the helping and helped are common in most societies, and the relationship that has behavioral change as its goal usually differs in some respects from other kinds of relationships within the society. In Western industrial society, for instance, the practitioner-client relationship includes the expression of feelings that may be considered inappropriate in social gatherings, in formal authority-subordinate relationships, or even in certain intimate relationships. Hence, a practitioner who would point out the nonverbal communications of individuals in settings not recognized as "therapeutic" or "private" would run the risk of severe social sanction. Suppose, for example, that someone at an agency board meeting should declare, "Mr. Chairman, you claim that the protesters' actions are in keeping with democratic principles, yet your red face, clenched fists, and frown say something else." Such an observation, violating the parameters of tact in a collaborative endeavor without sanction, can lead to ostracism of the outspoken individual.

In some societies, the rituals of the helping person depart radically from behaviors in everyday life. In an examination of Mexican-American folk psychiatry, Kiev recounts:

> According to this curandero, the underlying techniques of psychological healing are, in effect, verbal suggestions with physical contact, which conveys magnetism, telepathy or thought/transference, and auto-suggestion. The patient must be brought into a comfortable chair in a comfortable, partly darkened room and asked to relax. After his symptoms are inquired about, he is encouraged to stop thinking of them, to close his eyes, and to think of nothing. No one is to be treated with his eyes open, which interferes with concentration. The patient may then be told of worse cases which the healer has cured until he is completely at ease. Suggestions dealing with each symptom are repeated eight or ten times, repetition being very important. Laying on of hands is an important aspect of faith healing and derives its authority from the Bible [Kiev, 1968, pp. 5–6].

Special setting. Finally, as is implicit in Kiev's discussion, a *special setting* is a critical universal for the helping relationship. In the West, the practitioner's office is one of several typical places for a practitioner-client relationship to ensue. In other societies, the setting may be a powerful, sacred, or holy place inside or outdoors. As social workers often observe, the boundaries of the setting are important. The closing of the office door, therapy room, or boardroom not only ensures privacy but signals the beginning of the change process.

Sanctions and authority, expectation of change, unique ways of relating, and the special setting are social factors that render the practitioner-client relationship a powerful behavior changing medium. These social factors encourage and influence experimentation with new ways of perceiving, feeling, thinking, doing, and communicating on the part of the client, who, without such a relationship, might not otherwise endeavor to try new ways of coping or of being in the world. In Western society, the professional helping person has been characterized as a "permission giver" (Keen, 1974), a singularly apt description.

A helping relationship allows *temporary dependency* of the client on the practitioner, which, in clinical practice, ideally, allows the growth of social interdependence and psychological self-reliance. Like a person learning to swim, a client may cling, then try a few strokes, cling again, and try again, each time with more confidence and competence until the need for support and instruction has been extinguished. In nonclinical settings, a dependency on the practitioner's authority or expertise can also exist. That is, the client or client group expects to get something from the practitioner and depends on him or her for it—perhaps emotional support, information about how to parent or about how to gain access to powerful persons in a large-scale organization.

From a growing literature on cross-cultural counseling and counselor training (Pedersen, 1975b; Smith, 1977), Torrey (1975) isolates two prominent factors—*expectations of the clients* and *personal qualities of therapists*. His point is that the cultural differences with regard to these factors make a case for the use of indigenous, or native, practitioners in psychiatric services. The hypothetical presence of common sociocultural factors therefore does not suggest that cross-cultural practice can follow the values, skills, or even techniques of Western, middle-class social service practitioners.

Indeed, we must be careful not to become culture bound, encapsulated (Wrenn, 1975), or limited in the perspective of a dominant class (Pedersen, 1975a) as we attempt to provide services to persons of divergent class, subculture, and ethnic backgrounds. Are there ways of avoiding this trap? One answer lies in our values and objectives as they, like theory and practice, shape our practice relationships.

VALUES AND OBJECTIVES

Values, so often a source of conflict in changing times, can be a source of consensus about practice. Professionals can be distinguished from technicians in that they operate within a set of *values* and demonstrate a commitment to practice *objectives* derived from them. Hence, the wide array of theoretical approaches and varied dimensions of practice can and usually do have a common value basis. From this value basis, a set of practice relationship objectives is derived.

As a concept, values have been a part of the social sciences only since the late 19th century. Previously, discourse about what we now call *values* concerned the good, the true, the beautiful, or the ideal (Frankena, 1967). Specifically two different kinds of values concern us here. Some objects or ideas are valued for their utility; others are seen as having intrinsic worth. B.F. Skinner (1971) saw values as guides for behavior. We consider this notion of values as a powerful insight.

Professional values

We assume that social service practitioners share an unspoken, intrinsic valuing of life, from which other, more utilitarian values flow. The latter usually include, above all, a belief in the worth and dignity of the individual

(Smalley, 1971, p. 1197). Supporting values include (a) self-determination, or the right to make choices about one's life; (b) individual opportunity to meet basic needs to realize one's potential or enhance the quality of life; and (c) acceptance of individuals, which includes equality with clients and recognition and tolerance of individual differences (Hollis, 1965). Other ideals that appear frequently in the practice literature, but are usually less explicitly stated, include: healthy human relationships, humane treatment, justice, critical thinking, democratic control, the collective society, and a healthy environment.

For the most part, these values are present or implied in such documents as the 1981 *Working Statement on the Purpose of Social Work* by the National Association of Social Work (see Table 2–1). They are formulated by most helping professions into ethical codes that specify behavior in keeping with professional values. As an example, the *Code of Ethics* expressed by the National Association of Social Work is summarized in Table 2–2. In short, persons, their relationships, and the material and social environment constitute the domain of ethical practice derived from professional values. Such documents as the *Working Statement* and the *Code of Ethics* provide a common value basis for practice. This value basis in turn suggests *objectives* for practice.

TABLE 2–1. Working Statement on the Purpose of Social Work*

The purpose of social work is to promote or restore a mutually beneficial interaction between individuals and society in order to improve the quality of life for everyone. Social workers hold the following beliefs:
- The environment (social, physical, organizational) should provide the opportunity and resources for the maximum realization of the potential and aspirations of all individuals, and should provide for their common human needs and for the alleviation of distress and suffering.
- Individuals should contribute as effectively as they can to their own well-being and to the social welfare of others in their immediate environment as well as to the collective society.
- Transactions between individuals and others in their environment should enhance the dignity, individuality, and self-determination of everyone. People should be treated humanely and with justice.

Clients of social workers may be an individual, a family, a group, a community, or an organization.

Objectives

Social workers focus on person-and-environment in interaction. To carry out their purpose, they work with people to achieve the following objectives:
- Help people enlarge their competence and increase their problem-solving and coping abilities.
- Help people obtain resources.
- Make organizations responsive to people.
- Facilitate interaction between individuals and others in their environment.
- Influence interactions between organizations and institutions.
- Influence social and environmental policy.

To achieve these objectives, social workers work with other people. At different times, the target of change varies—it may be the client, others in the environment, or both.

---

*Copyright 1981, National Association of Social Workers, Inc. Reprinted by permission, from *Social Work*, Vol. 26, No. 1 (January 1981), pp. 5–6. (As summarized and clarified by Anne Minahan for participants in the second N.A.S.W. meeting on conceptual frameworks.)

TABLE 2–2. Code of Ethics[†]

Summary of Major Principles
  I. The Social Worker's Conduct and Comportment as a Social Worker
    A.   *Propriety.* The social worker should maintain high standards of personal conduct in the capacity or identity as social worker.
    B.   *Competence and Professional Development.* The social worker should strive to become and remain proficient in professional practice and the performance of professional functions.
    C.   *Service.* The social worker should regard as primary the service obligation of the social work profession.
    D.   *Integrity.* The social worker should act in accordance with the highest standards of professional integrity.
    E.   *Scholarship and Research.* The social worker engaged in study and research should be guided by the conventions of scholarly inquiry.
 II. The Social Worker's Ethical Responsibility to Clients
    F.   *Primacy of Clients' Interests.* The social worker's primary responsibility is to clients.
    G.   *Rights and Prerogatives of Clients.* The social worker should make every effort to foster maximum self-determination on the part of clients.
    H.   *Confidentiality and Privacy.* The social worker should respect the privacy of clients and hold in confidence all information obtained in the course of professional service.
    I.   *Fees.* When setting fees, the social worker should ensure that they are fair, reasonable, considerate, and commensurate with the service performed and with due regard for the clients' ability to pay.
III. The Social Worker's Ethical Responsibility to Colleagues
    J.   *Respect, Fairness, and Courtesy.* The social worker should treat colleagues with respect, courtesy, fairness, and good faith.
    K.   *Dealing with Colleagues' Clients.* The social worker has the responsibility to relate to the clients of colleagues with full professional consideration.
IV. The Social Worker's Ethical Responsibility to Employers and Employing Organizations
    L.   *Commitments to Employing Organizations.* The social worker should adhere to commitments made to the employing organizations.
  V. The Social Worker's Ethical Responsibility to the Social Work Profession
    M.   *Maintaining the Integrity of the Profession.* The social worker should uphold and advance the values, ethics, knowledge, and mission of the profession.
    N.   *Community Service.* The social worker should assist the profession in making social services available to the general public.
    O.   *Development of Knowledge.* The social worker should take responsibility for identifying, developing, and fully utilizing knowledge for professional practice.
VI. The Social Worker's Ethical Responsibility to Society
    P.   *Promoting the General Welfare.* The social worker should promote the general welfare of society.

[†]Published 1980, National Association of Social Workers, Inc. Reprinted with permission from *Code of Ethics*, 1980 Edition, published by National Association of Social Workers, Inc., Washington, D.C.

Professional objectives

The authors believe that practice will be most effective if it remains responsive to change. *Material change* (physical and economic) and *social change* (ideological, political, interpersonal, and personal) threaten values. If there are objectives that not only flow from professional values but that also incorporate the expectation of material and social change, our practice and practice relationships will remain germane to our clients' society and lives.

If we are secure in our own values, we can be tolerant of the values of others. If we value equality, then the values of others—and their right to self-determination—can be respected, though we may not wish to adopt them for ourselves. With this value stance, our relationships can be true dialogues (Bock, 1980; Freire, 1976). That is, practitioner and client are equals. The practitioner has expertise, but clients have things to teach the practitioner about their reality and how change affects them. Out of dialogue emerge mutual practice goals. Dialogue is a source of new ideas and creative solutions, a source of broader awareness of the social and economic forces that affect relationships. From such broader consciousness, people can initiate change in their lives rather than remain the passive objects of change (Freire, 1973).

If they include dialogue, practice relationships of all varieties—but especially those between practitioner and client and between colleagues—have the potential for *conscientization* (Bock, 1980; Freire, 1973) or for developing *critical consciousness*. In a stable, preindustrial society in which there is little material or social change, people's consciousness is stable; values are constant. But when sweeping material and social change hits a society, both consciousness and values begin to change, causing stress between generations, within families, and within individuals.

Paulo Freire, the Brazilian educator, calls this stage of change in consciousness *naive transitivity* (1973, p. 18). He observes that it is characterized by oversimplification of problems, nostalgia, and underestimation of the common man. The behavior of people in transitive consciousness includes gregariousness, lack of interest in investigation, and a propensity for fanciful explanations, fragile arguments, strong emotional style, magical explanations, and the practice of polemics rather than of dialogue (Freire, 1973, p. 18).

Freire saw this stage of consciousness among Brazilians undergoing economic change; but naive transitivity is characteristic of any people undergoing rapid social or economic change. The rampant inflation and economic chaos of pre–World War II Germany generated several parallels to naive transitivity in the consciousness of some Germans. Resurrection of racial superiority myths, scapegoating of certain minorities, unquestioning obedience to a charismatic leader, and other naive transitivity traits emerged. The tragedy that can befall a society experiencing rampant material and social change is a failure to progress to a more evolved social and economic system with an accompanying evolution in consciousness.

Such a progression is more likely to occur if people develop a critically transitive (or simply critical) consciousness.

> The critically transitive consciousness is characterized by depth in the interpretation of problems; by the substitution of causal principles for magical explanations; by the testing of one's findings and by openness to revision; by the attempt to avoid distortion when perceiving problems and to avoid preconceived notions when analyzing them; by refusing to transfer responsibility; by rejecting passive positions; by soundness of argumentation; by the practice of dialogue rather than polemics; by receptivity to the new for reasons beyond mere novelty and by the good sense not to reject the old just because it is old—by accepting what is valid in both the old and new [Freire, 1973, p. 18].

Critical consciousness, then, is a kind of testing of the reality and causes of change encroaching on one's life. It can arise out of dialogue in a practice relationship, and it can serve as the basis for individual, family, group, organization, or community initiative and *action*. Critically conscious persons are no longer passive objects of historical change but become the active subjects for change (Freire, 1973). Rather than adapted to their environment, they are *integrated* (Freire, 1973). Critically aware of the sources of change, they endeavor to take control of and to guide those changes toward their best interests.

Knowing that one does not suffer uniquely or alone—that there are others with similar problems with whom one can empathize—is also a practice objective expressive of professional values. Another objective that extends professional values is supporting or enabling individuals to *adapt* to their individual capacities and the changing circumstances of their lives in ways that meet their needs and are not destructive.

These various objectives that flow from professional values but are appraised to material and social change may be arranged into a continuum of practice objectives. Each objective has its parallel set of professional values (Table 2–3). There is no higher or lower objective here in terms of worth, but there is an evolution in consciousness implied for all parties to the relationships involved in each objective. Moreover, the same practitioner and clients may have different objectives on the continuum for the different problems or goals they address. But change, or the desire for change, is assumed to be the ever present social reality.

The objectives assist practice relationships in several ways.

1. The formulation of goals and the focus of skills and technique is not automatically restricted to one exclusive objective, that of adaptation.

2. Because collective empathy and integration are understood to be potential objectives, practitioners can enable clients, colleagues, and others to look beyond the client for sources of problems when appropriate.

3. All parties to the relationship—client and practitioner, practitioner and colleague—are not only preparing for change but are finding ways to become creators of change. Each is becoming critically conscious when possible.

4. The relationship is aimed at the possible rather than at the adequate. Solutions are optimal rather than merely sufficient. Prevention of similar problems becomes a goal in practice.

5. Practice is less rooted in the social and economic status quo. As such, it is less a potential tool for exploitation of those who are less powerful due to unquestioning passivity, false unchallenged beliefs, or ignorance about causes of problems.

Thus, practice values give rise to objectives for practice and also for practice relationships. Values and objectives, which provide a basis for consensus in social service practice, in effect give vision and purpose to practitioners, in that way distinguishing the professional from the technician (Federico, 1980, p. 247). They imply a commitment that reaches beyond bureaucratic proce-

TABLE 2–3. Values and Practice Relationship Objectives

Values	Objectives
1. Individual worth and potential. Opportunity to meet basic needs.	1. *Adaptation*: Coping, minimal subjective distress, basic needs are generally met, and there are few self-destructive behaviors.
2. Empathic, growth-producing, healthy relationships.	2. *Collective Empathy*: In addition to adaptation, communication and a degree of empathy with others with similar situations is elicited. For example, a depressed homemaker joins a consciousness-raising group at a women's center or a problem drinker participates in Alcoholics Anonymous.
3. Equality, critical thinking, quality of life.	3. *Integration*: In addition to collective empathy, the structural sources of problems are perceived. Contradictions in the social system giving rise to problems are critically assessed. For example, the indigent elderly are aware and sensitized to the links between their poverty and an economic system that places productivity above quality of life. Mental patients become aware of the economic benefits to entrepreneurial landlords of tenement hotels and of state deinstitutionalization policies for the mentally ill. Family workers and counselors begin to perceive the economic payoffs for the market economy in divorce, which creates new household consumption units.
4. Self-determination, democratic control of social life.	4. *Action*: Critical consciousness leads to critical action. The challenge within the structure to oneself and others in similar circumstances is seen. A possible response is perceived and an action corresponding to consciousness is taken. For example, an elderly person joins the Gray Panthers and participates in actions to affect retirement and retirement benefit legislation. Women organize to demand subsidy for socially productive labor such as homemaking and child rearing. Gay activists demand a change in the psychiatric nosology [classification of diseases]. Mental patients organize to demand adequate housing and opportunities to integrate into the community.

From "Empathy Skill and Critical Consciousness," by T. Keefe. In *Social Casework*, 1980, 61(7), 387. Reprinted by permission.

dure, agency policy, and even contemporary social policy. Together with theory and practice, they provide the shape of practice relationships.

But practice relationships have substance as well as form. That substance consists of skills, principles, and techniques supplemented by considerable knowledge of human behavior at the micro- and macrosystem levels. Later chapters will examine in detail relationship skills originally refined and researched as a part of practitioner-client relationships but which are useful in maintaining all practice relationships. Foremost among the skills important to most relationships is empathy, which is the subject of Chapter 3.

STUDY QUESTIONS

1. What level of systems do you suspect most helping professionals address in their practice? Why?
2. In addition to those mentioned in the chapter, what are some examples of direct and indirect practice?
3. What field of practice do you plan to enter or already work in?
4. Do you believe it would be possible to have a contractual relationship with an involuntary client? Give an example.
5. Do the five important parts of a helping contract accord with your own values about how a relationship should be?
6. Confidentiality helps to build trust. Under what circumstances, if any, do you believe that violating confidentiality is acceptable? If such circumstances exist, how would you handle them with your client? Is sharing information with members of one's own agency a violation of confidentiality?
7. Has your life been changed by someone's expectations of you? If so, how did the expectations create the changes?
8. Some professionals find it difficult to allow the temporary dependence of a client on themselves and their expertise. How might you react to this aspect of direct practice relationships?
9. Values are, among other things, guides for behavior. What single value do you believe to be most important in guiding your choice of a career?
10. Rank order five of your own values from most to least important. Such a values clarification exercise may help you in making decisions and dealing with crises.
11. This chapter enumerates a number of values of helping professionals. Most helping professions have codes of ethics that state or imply a set of similar values. What values are brought out in your profession's code? Do they agree with your personal values? Are you prepared to conduct your practice relationships in accord with the high standards implied in your professional code? Discuss what conduct might violate the code.
12. The professional objectives suggested in this chapter can help to orient professional practice relationships in their social and historical context. Do these objectives support your goals and hopes in your practice?
13. Discuss with your instructor or colleagues the procedures your professional association follows in reporting and sanctioning ethical misconduct or violations of its code of ethics.

REFERENCES

Alinsky, S. D. *Reveille for radicals*. Chicago: University of Chicago Press, 1946.

Alissi, A. S. (Ed.). *Perspectives on social group work practice*. New York: Free Press, 1980.

Anderson, J. *Social work methods and processes.* Belmont, Calif.: Wadsworth, 1981.

Bock, S. Conscientization: Paulo Freire and class-based practice. *Catalyst,* 1980, *6,* 5–25.

Brager, G., & Holloway, S. *Changing human service organizations: Politics and practice.* New York: Free Press, 1978.

Buckley, W. *Sociology and modern systems theory.* Englewood Cliffs, N.J.: Prentice-Hall, 1967.

Compton, B. R., & Galaway, B. *Social work processes.* Homewood, Ill.: The Dorsey Press, 1975.

Coyle, G. L. *Group work with American youth.* New York: Harper Brothers, 1948.

Devereux, G. *Reality and dream: Psychotherapy of a Plains Indian.* New York: Anchor Books, 1969.

Devore, W., & Schlesinger, E. G. *Ethnic-sensitive social work practice.* St. Louis: C. V. Mosby Co., 1981.

Dunham, A. *The new community organization.* New York: Crowell, 1970.

Epstein, L. *Helping people: The task-centered approach.* St. Louis: C. V. Mosby Co., 1980.

Federico, R. *The social welfare institution* (3rd ed.). Lexington, Mass.: D. C. Heath, 1980.

Fisher, J. *Effective casework practice: An eclectic approach.* New York: McGraw-Hill, 1978.

Frank, J. *Persuasion and healing: A comparative study of psychotherapy.* Baltimore: John Hopkins Press, 1961.

Frankena, W. K. Values and valuation. In P. Edwards (Ed.). *The encyclopedia of philosophy* (Vol. 7). New York: Macmillian Co., 1967.

Freire, P. *Pedagogy of the oppressed.* New York: Seabury Press, 1970.

Freire, P. *Education for critical consciousness.* New York: Seabury Press, 1973.

Freire, P. *Pedagogy in process.* New York: Seabury Press, 1976.

Germain, C. B. (Ed.). *Social work practice. People and environments: An ecological perspective.* New York: Columbia University Press, 1979.

Germain, C. B., & Gitterman, A. The life model of social work practice. In F. J. Turner (Ed.), *Social work treatment: Interlocking theoretical approaches* (2nd ed.). New York: Free Press, 1979.

Gillis, J. The therapist as manipulator. *Psychology Today,* 1974, *8* (7), 91–95.

Goldstein, H. *Social work practice: A unitary approach.* Columbia, S.C.: University of South Carolina Press, 1973.

Hearn, G. *The general systems approach: Contributions toward a holistic conception of social work.* New York: Council on Social Work Education, 1969.

Hollis, F. *Casework: A psychosocial therapy.* New York: Random House, 1965.

Hollister, C. D. Social work skills for social development. *Social Development Issues,* 1977, *1* (1), 9–19.

Janzen, C., & Harris, O. *Family treatment in social work practice.* Itasca, Ill.: F. E. Peacock Publishers, 1980.

Kahn, S. *How people get power: Organizing oppressed communities for action.* New York: McGraw-Hill, 1970.

Kahn, S. *Organizing: A guide for grass roots leaders.* New York: McGraw-Hill, 1981.

Keefe, T. Empathy skill and critical consciousness. *Social Casework,* 1980, *61* (7), 387–393.

Keen, S. Permission giver. Characterization suggested at a human potential workshop. Cedar Falls, Iowa: University of Northern Iowa, 1974.

Keith-Lucas, A. *Giving and taking help.* Chapel Hill, N.C.: University of North Carolina Press, 1972.

Kiev, A. (Ed.). *Magic, faith and healing.* New York: Free Press, 1964.

Kiev, A. *Curanderismo: Mexican folk psychiatry.* New York: Free Press, 1968.

Kiev, A. *Transcultural psychiatry.* New York: Free Press, 1972.

Konopka, G. *Social group work: A helping process.* Englewood Cliffs, N.J.: Prentice-Hall, 1963.

Krill, D. F. Existential social work. In F. J. Turner (Ed.), *Social work treatment: Interlocking theoretical approaches* (2nd ed.). New York: Free Press, 1979.

Mayer, J., & Timms, N. Clash in perspective between worker and client. *Social Casework,* 1969, *50* (1), 32–40.

Merton, R. K. *Social theory and social structure.* New York: Free Press, 1957.

Minahan, A. (Ed.). Working statement on the purpose of social work. *Social Work,* 1981, *26* (1), 6.

Minuchin, S. *Families and family therapy.* Cambridge, Mass.: Harvard University Press, 1974.

National Association of Social Work. *Code of ethics: summary of major principles.* Washington, D.C.: NASW, 1980, reprinted by permission.

Northern, H. *Social work with groups.* New York: Columbia University Press, 1970.

Pedersen, P. (Ed.). Cross-cultural counseling: Intercultural helping relationships. *Readings in intercultural communication* (Vol. 4). Pittsburgh: Society for Intercultural Education, Training and Research, University of Pittsburgh, 1975. (a)

Pedersen, P. (Ed.). Cross-cultural training of mental health professionals. *Readings in intercultural communication,* (Vol. 4). Pittsburgh: Society for Intercultural Education, Training and Research, University of Pittsburgh, 1975. (b)

Perlman, H. H. *Social casework: A problem-solving process.* Chicago: University of Chicago Press, 1964.

Pincus, A. and Minahan, A. *Social work practice: Model and method.* Chicago: F. E. Peacock Publishers, 1973.

Reid, W. *The task-centered system.* New York: Columbia University Press, 1978.

Reid, W., & Epstein, L. *Task-centered casework.* New York: Columbia University Press, 1972.

Reid, W., & Shyne, A. W. *Brief and extended casework.* New York: Columbia University Press, 1969.

Ross, M. G. *Community organization: Theory, principles and action* (2nd ed.). New York: Harper & Row, 1967.

Satir, V. *Conjoint family therapy.* Palo Alto, Calif.: Science & Behavior Books, 1967.

Schwartz, E. E. Macro social work: A practice in search of some theory. *Social Service Review,* 1977, *2* (57), 207–227.

Sherman, S. N. Family therapy. In F. J. Turner (Ed.), *Social work treatment: Interlocking theoretical approaches* (2nd ed.). New York: Free Press, 1979.

Siporin, M. *Introduction to social work practice: Model and method.* New York: Macmillian Co., 1975.

Skinner, B. F. *Beyond freedom and dignity.* New York: Alfred A. Knopf, 1971.

Smalley, R. E. Social casework: The functional approach. In R. Morris (Ed.), *Encyclopedia of social work* (Vol. 2). New York: National Association of Social Workers, 1971.

Smalley, R. E. *Theory for social work practice.* New York: Columbia University Press, 1967.

Smith, A. G. State of the art study. *Research and Theory in Intercultural Communication.* Austin, Tex.: Society for Intercultural Education, Training and Research, University of Texas, 1977.

Strean, H. S. *Clinical social work: Theory and practice.* New York: Free Press, 1978.

Strean, H. S. *Psychoanalytic theory and social work practice.* New York: Free Press, 1979.

Stuart, R. B. Behavior modification: A technology of social change. In F. J. Turner (Ed.), *Social work treatment: Interlocking theoretical approaches* (2nd ed.). New York: Free Press, 1979.

Taft, J. The relation of function to process in social casework. *Journal of Social Work Process,* 1937, *1* (1), 1–33.

Thomas, E. J. (Ed.) *The socio-behavioral approach and application to social work.* New York: Council on Social Work Education, 1967.

Torrey, E. F. The case for the indigenous therapist. In P. Pedersen (Ed.). *Readings in intercultural communication* (Vol. 4). Pittsburgh: Society for Intercultural Education, Training and Research, University of Pittsburgh, 1975.

Torrey, E. F. What Western psychotherapists can learn from witch doctors. *American Journal of Orthopsychiatry,* 1972, *1* (47), 69–76.

Trecker, H. B. *Social work administration: Principles and practices.* New York: Association Press, 1977.

von Bertalanffy, L. *General systems theory: Foundations, development, applications* (Rev. ed.). New York: George Braziller, 1968.

Wasserman, S. L. Ego psychology. In F. J. Turner (Ed.), *Social work treatment: Interlocking theoretical approaches* (2nd ed.). New York: Free Press, 1979.

Weissman, H. H. *Overcoming mismanagement in the human services.* San Francisco: Jossey-Bass, 1973.

Wrenn, R. The culturally encapsulated counselor. *Readings in intercultural communication* (Vol. 4). Pittsburgh: Society for Intercultural Education, Training and Research, University of Pittsburgh, 1975.

3

The Heart of Practice Relationships: Empathy

At first understanding,
I soon feel with you.
On recognizing myself in you,
I feel the you in me.
At last we are the same.[1]

Keefe, 1976

Empathy might be described as the binding substance of close, nurturing human relationships through which our common humanity is transmitted. Because of its centrality in human relationships, it has been studied increasingly over the past three decades as a major component in the helping relationship and the helping professions. Empathic skill is crucial to relationships in social work and related professional practice.

Chapter 3 attempts to determine what empathy is by reviewing its evolving definitions. Drawing on theory and research, we present a model that accounts for and helps to clarify the variety of definitions, making the skill easier to learn. We examine evidence of the importance of empathy in practice relationships, and finally, we discuss a fully developed empathic skill that incorporates the social context of practice relationships.

WHAT IS EMPATHY?

Understanding and feeling

Empathy is a behavior that includes *understanding* to some extent the roles, situation, and verbal or nonverbal communications of another person as well as *feeling with* another person. Except in rare circumstances of injury

---

[1]Copyrighted 1976, National Association of Social Workers, Inc. Reprinted by permission, from *Social Work*, Vol. 21, No. 1 (January 1976), p. 10.

or of physical or mental defect, we all have the same physiological equipment for creating and experiencing emotion. Though empathy requires us to perceive and understand another person's behaviors and communications, fundamentally we feel in the same ways. In other words, empathy is a *way* of feeling that we share with every other person at a physical level.

Since Theodore Lipps in 1897 introduced an early German word for empathy, *einfuhlung*,[2] defined as objective motor mimicry, (Buchheimer, 1963; Taquiri, 1969), students of human behavior have stressed the two parts of empathy—understanding and feeling—at different times and in different ways. For our discussion, the understanding aspect of empathy will include perceiving and thinking responses that combine to form a kind of *social understanding* (Feshback, 1975) and the ability for "imaginative transposition of oneself into the thinking, feeling and acting of another and so structuring the world as he does" (Dymond, 1963, p. 63).

The understanding aspect of empathy involves forming a mental picture of another person and what it must be like to be that person in the performance of his or her social roles. In enumerating skills required for interpersonal competence, Jesser and Richardson (1968, p. 41) suggest that one should be able to sense another person's social role well enough to be able to predict how the other person will see one's actions. Merely sensing the other person's role is what is meant by empathy without its feeling side.

Carolyn Shantz (1975), who has examined empathy in relation to social and cognitive development, believes that judgment is a component of empathic behavior. The empathic person can judge a particular situation based on how he or she might feel, how most people would feel, or how another person feels in the particular circumstance. In studying children, Shantz found that understanding and feeling dimensions are not always present together in empathy. Observing preschoolers being questioned about a child in a story that had been read to them, she found that the children usually understood the fictional child's situation but only infrequently felt the same emotion or understood the character's feelings. Shantz concluded that feeling *with* another is less frequent than simply *understanding* and that understanding does not typically include having the same feelings.

Shantz's study was limited to young children and to certain modes of assessing empathy. From her studies of children, Nora Feshback observed that as children grow older, their ability to understand social situations increases along with the ability to share the feeling states of people in these situations (p. 28). Studies of older children and adults (Iannotti, 1975; Iannotti & Meacham, 1974; Feshback, 1975; Carkhuff, 1968) likewise suggest that empathic skill can develop both the understanding component and the *feeling with* another person.

That there is more to true empathy than understanding is plainly apparent. Consider, for example, that a salesclerk, an aggressor, or even a person locked in combat with another can judge the role, predict the responses, and speculate on the other's feelings. To move beyond these and to *feel with* another

---

[2]The psychologist Edward Titchener is credited with introducing into English Lipps's concept of a kind of asthenic empathy—fusion of identity with the object being observed (Stotland, Mathews, Sherman, Hansson, and Richardson, 1978, p. 11).

person, however, is to move beyond an interaction enabling exploitation of the other person. In an empathic interaction, the most effective helping of another person is not only likely but in keeping with one's own best interests.

Consequently, while it is possible to understand another without *feeling with* him or her, a higher level of empathy would include an emotional response to the other person. There is no better evidence of this emotional component than the recording of intense physiological responses in people with high levels of empathy.

When both groups were exposed to an empathy test consisting of slides and dramatic dialogue, Gellen (1970) found significantly more vascular constriction, indicating greater physiological arousal and hence emotional response, in counselors and counselor trainees than in college science majors. Assuming that, as a group, the former are more empathic than the latter, Gellen's findings supported the theory that empathy is related to physiological responses. Vanderpool and Barrat, (1970) found evidence of greater physiological arousal on several measures during therapy interviews of psychiatric residents with higher rated levels of empathy.

To the extent that emotions are tied to physiological responses, we can deduce that empathy can have an emotional component. Such evidence comes as no surprise to effective practitioners because the feeling aspect of empathy has long been a part of their practice experience. How, then, do we blend the two sides of empathy into a useful relationship skill for practice?

Empathy, identification, and projection

Carl Rogers (1957) was one of the first to include both understanding and feeling in a definition of empathy. Rogers described *accurate empathy* as one of the conditions that is necessary to bring about client change.

> The fifth condition is that the therapist is experiencing an accurate, empathic understanding of the client's awareness of his own experience. To sense the client's private world as if it were your own, but without ever losing the "as if" quality—this is empathy, and this seems essential to therapy. To sense the client's anger, fear, or confusion as if it were your own, yet without your own anger, fear, or confusion getting bound up in it, is the condition we are endeavoring to describe [p. 99].

Rogers's definition of empathy included the feeling (affective) component but differentiated empathy from identification and projection. *Identification* means affiliating with another person's feelings to the extent that you cannot distinguish his feelings from your own. *Projection* means attributing your own feelings and thoughts to another person. According to Rogers, true empathy means understanding what it is like to be the other person and feeling with that other person but knowing which feelings you do or do not share. Rogers thus laid the groundwork for later, more systematic definitions of empathy that included both understanding and feeling as their basis.

Accurate empathy. In an important extension of Rogers's conceptualization, Truax and Mitchell (1971) suggest that the empathic practitioner must be able not only to communicate what the clients are experiencing and feeling but should be able to communicate to clients what they might say if they were more open and less defensive. Truax and Mitchell believed that "A sharp distinction should be made between a therapist's understanding and the frequency, accuracy, extent, and depth of empathic responses that are communicated to the client" (p. 318). Empathy, then, includes understanding other persons and to some extent feeling with them. But for a helping or practice relationship, an ability to communicate what is understood and felt is also important. This part of empathy skill includes providing clients with accurate *feedback,* or information about what you understand about them and feel with them.

Rogers's formulation of empathy and related skills stimulated considerable research into what were regarded as the "necessary and sufficient conditions" for positive client growth and change in a helping relationship (for an early summary, see Truax & Mitchell, 1971, pp. 299–344). More recent research and review of earlier studies (Parloff, Waskow, & Wolfe, 1978, pp. 242–253) do not support such unqualified adjectives. But empathy, together with acceptance and authenticity, are still very important skills for a practitioner to cultivate.

Empathy is a very complex skill the direct influence of which on a relationship is harder to trace than that of other skills. Indeed, it seems to be linked to the *possibility* of other skills that are found to bring more direct positive outcome from a helping relationship when a client perceives its presence in the practitioner (Orlinsky & Howard, 1978, pp. 283–329). To grasp empathy in all its complexity, a model of empathy skill is helpful.

A MODEL OF EMPATHY SKILL

Helping professionals require a model of empathy that includes not only understanding and feeling but communication or feedback as well. In short, practitioners must not only understand their clients and feel with them, they must also be able to tell them about the understanding and feeling responses they are having. In a sense, an empathic person is a mirror having both a head and a heart into which the client looks to find not only an understanding reflection of his own image but also a reflection of the texture of his deepest feelings. What behaviors bring this process about?

Practitioner behaviors

Empathy is composed of responses that are learned throughout life (Halpern & Lesser, 1960), and it can occur among several, or even many, participants simultaneously. Indeed, it has been called *emotional contagion* (Stotland et al., 1978). For purposes of simplicity, the model presented here (Figure 3–1) has but one practitioner and one client who are seeing and talking to each other.

First phase.   The empathic interpersonal encounter begins with the client's *feeling state* and *thoughts* (a). These internal conditions—which can be generated in response to purely physical as well as to interpersonal causes—stimulate in the client a variety of intentional and unintentional behaviors

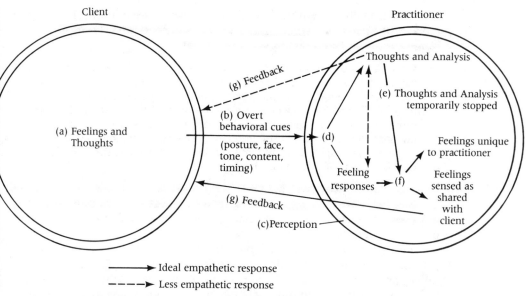

Figure 3–1. A Model of Empathy Skill

From "Empathy: The Critical Skill," by T. Keefe. Copyright 1976, National Association of Social Workers, Inc. Reprinted with permission, from *Social Work*, Vol. 21, No. 1 (January 1976), p. 12.

that serve as cues or signals to other people (b). The client talks and exhibits certain postures, facial expressions, tonal and timing *cues* which carry messages that can be both sensed and understood, though these messages may or may not be congruent. For example, a client may both cry and laugh in the course of the communication. Also, some messages may conflict with the predominant feeling of the person exhibiting them. Thus, the client might appear angry, with a rigid posture, clenched fists, and a red face while at the same time omitting anger from his verbal content, perhaps even denying anger in angry tones! As we shall discuss later, recognition of disharmonious messages and cues are routes of access to high levels of empathy and can be ideal points of intervention in practice as well as beneficial to other relationships.

The first phase of empathic behavior actually begins when the the practitioner *perceives* the client's various overt behaviors and explicit verbal message (c). These cues and verbal messages are expressions of the total picture of the client's roles, feeling states, identity concepts, and cognitive processes.

The quality of perception in high-level empathic skill differs from everyday ways of perceiving. In a summation of what he calls the *empathic cycle,* Barrett-Lennard has delineated how empathic persons would *not* perceive their clients: as objects to be studied, as subordinate partners looking for guidelines in the empathic behaviors, as sources of information about persons other than themselves, or as partners in an abstract, nonpersonal process of analysis and inquiry. Instead, an empathic practitioner must view the client as another self which feels, changes, experiences, reflects, imagines, and self-perceives. This mode of perceiving the client Barrett-Lennard calls the *empathic attentional set* (Barrett-Lennard, 1981).

The empathic attentional set is not unlike what Jourard (1966) called *transcendent perception*, which he contrasted with *need-steered perception* that is close to our way of perceiving in everyday life.

We usually observe the world under the impetus and direction of our needs, values, feelings and purposes of the moment. Such need-steered perception certainly serves a vital role in our survival and adaptation; but it also tends to blind us to all features of the world that are not immediately relevant to our present hungers, desires and values. "Desireless" or "undriven" cognition—when we simply open our eyes, ears, noses, taste buds, kinesthetic and organic receptors and let stimuli play upon them and impress them—seems to be the condition for the enriched mode of perception [p. 354].

In other words, the special quality of perception that is useful to empathic skill is relatively passive. It allows clients to speak for themselves and to affect us as equals. It precludes any hasty categorization or interaction ulterior to their own best interests.

Sometimes a practitioner may perceive and attribute meaning to only part of the client's overt behaviors, considering the remainder to be extraneous, and this may distort clear or complete reception of the client's message. Certainly, a skilled practitioner will rely in part upon nonverbal cues in addition to the verbal message and its tonal qualities. Facial expression, repetitive postural cues, and the timing of messages may cast considerable light on the client's actual state. In the course of a therapeutic encounter, for instance, a client may verbally express a positive sentiment regarding a significant event while simultaneously shifting uneasily in the chair, breathing unevenly, diverting his or her eyes from the worker, and scratching. To the practitioner, the positive verbal message is qualified by the behavioral cues supplementing its content.

In clinical or counseling settings, practitioners who place primary emphasis on immediate behaviors as opposed to client-recalled behaviors or situations, like gestaltists (Fagan & Shepard, 1970), would call disharmonious behaviors to the client's attention. Then, by means of a variety of techniques, these present-focused practitioners would help the client to achieve both awareness and more direct expression of qualifying feelings.

Perceiving the degree of harmony or discordance in another person's verbal and nonverbal messages is as important for the group therapist or community worker as it is for the individual therapist or caseworker. It is not only a guide to the behaviors and decisions of others but a measure of the level of rapport the worker has established with the group or client system.

Second phase.   In the second phase of empathic behavior, the practitioner's perception can elicit *feeling responses* (d). Evidence already discussed (Gellen, 1970; Vanderpool & Barrat, 1971) suggests that feeling responses are present in greater measure in persons of high empathic ability. In high levels of empathy, the feelings of the practitioner are most important.

In order to achieve high levels of empathy with clients, workers must allow their *initial* feeling responses to remain as free as possible from intruding thoughts. In the normal adult, self-generated thoughts, symbolic cues, or conceptual categories (Kendler, 1971, p. 963) mediate environmental stimuli and alter either the client's self-presentation or the worker's perception of it. Distorting thoughts, which may include stereotyping, value judgments, or premature analysis in accord with a theoretical schema, can interfere with both the worker's initial feeling responses and the ability to discern whether these feelings are qualitatively similar or different from the client's.

To be empathic, then, workers must allow external stimuli from clients to elicit or generate their feeling responses directly. Practitioners must momentarily allow their inner experiences to be controlled by the client's self-presentation. Briefly, emphatic practioners must hold complex thoughts in temporary abeyance and allow themselves a direct feeling response to the client(e).

Third phase.   In the third phase of empathic behavior, the worker must consciously separate personal feelings from those sensed as shared with the client (f). This behavior requires a capacity not only for psychological openness but for directing one's attention internally. (According to Miller [1969], directing internal attention while helping was originally suggested by Theodore Reik. Reik's idea is supported by research [Zanger, 1967].)

The easy shifting of attention from the client to one's own felt responses enhances empathy in several ways.

1. It makes another crucial source of information about the client available to you: your responses to the client are probably not unlike those of others who interact with him/her.

2. You become aware of personal reactions that will affect your responses to the client. Your thoughts and feelings are of course conveyed to the client nonverbally, just as his/hers are to you. If you are aware of your felt responses moment by moment, you can communicate these naturally both in nonverbal ways and intentionally in words.

3. Research shows that the degree of congruence between the practitioner's various verbal and nonverbal communications is directly related to the successful outcome of the helping process (Hill, Siegelman, Gronsky, Sturniolo, & Fretz, 1981).

4. An ability to tune in to your own felt responses and other feelings with relative ease allows you to separate those feelings you sense are shared with the client from those you experience yourself. For example, you may be momentarily startled by a client's outburst of anger though you are angry about the same thing as the client. The anger response is shared and is empathically conveyed both verbally and nonverbally. With attention to your other felt response—being startled—you may wish to convey your reaction in words. To do so is to move beyond empathy to the closely related skill of genuineness or authenticity in your relationship. This sorting out of feelings, then, is the product of directing your attention internally to learn the felt sense of the client's effect on you.

The worker who has an ability to sort the two feelings—fear and anger—can provide an angry client with important information about the effect of his or her way of expressing anger on other people. In an adversary proceeding, a practitioner who can separate feelings shared from those held alone would gain a sharp notion of an adversary's current impact upon other people involved in the encounter.

Briefly, the behaviors comprising empathy skill examined thus far include the ability (1) to perceive accurately the total picture of the client's presentation, (2) to allow a direct feeling response within oneself relatively unfettered by qualifying or distorting cognitive processes, and (3) to separate one's own feelings from those sensed as shared with the client. As already suggested, however, empathy requires another communication component if it is to be useful as a part of a helping relationship.

Fourth phase. In casework, therapy, or in practice settings where feelings and conflicts are addressed as part of the intervention contract, the practitioner must accurately mirror or feed back his or her awareness of the other person's state of being. The feedback process includes both intentional and unintentional nonverbal communication by the practitioner.

In practice, feedback has two important characteristics. First, it is tentative—that is, the practitioner's first verbalization may only approximate what the client feels at a given moment. If the client feels that the verbalization is incorrect, another is tried that may fit better, and so on, until the practitioner slowly gets a better reflection of the client's state in focus. Such phrases as "I get the sense that you feel . . ." or "maybe . . ." are qualifiers that render feedback more tentative. Each practitioner will develop a personal style. But tentativeness is important to staying with another person. Second, the character of feedback is constantly changing. Just as feelings shift rapidly at times, feedback must shift rapidly as well. In short, the self-image reflected to the client shifts as the client shifts—tentatively but as accurately as possible.

The following reproduces part of an interview with a young vocational counselor who was having difficulty with his boss. Notice the tentative nature of the feedback that the counselor provides. Also, observe how the feedback from counselor to client shifts as the client's feelings shift.

Jim: I hate the s.o.b.! He doesn't know what he is doing. I resent his power over me.

Worker: You *are* angry! He doesn't deserve his position of authority over you—I sense you feel a little helpless too.

Jim: Yeah. Just because of age. That's all, just his age. He's got nothing else going.

Worker: He is in control for no good reason.

Jim: And I can't tell the _____ off. If I do, I'm in trouble.

Worker: Your angry feelings have to smolder. I sense they cover something else—something more.

Jim: It's his haughty attitude. He thinks I'm stupid.

Worker: You feel stupid sometimes with him?

Jim: Yeah, inept.

Worker: Are you?

Jim: No, I just feel like that. I'm usually way ahead of him, but he dwells on details—nit-picker!

Worker: What else?   ✳ *Could have gone off here to involve*

Jim: Does he do?   *3ᴿᴰ party*

Worker: Do you feel?

Jim: Well, really distant. We've worked together for two years and we're still formal—"Yes sir, no sir," stand-in-front-of-the-desk stuff.

Worker: A little isolated from him—kind of alone.

Jim: That's the way he wants it.

Worker: And you? How would you want it?

Jim: (Looking down) Closer. Hell, I don't know. It seems like there should be some—realness in our relationship.

Worker: I get that you feel isolated, a little rejected or maybe unappreciated.

Jim: Yes, and I can't break through! (Tears)

Worker: Damn frustrating, damn hurtful at times. I'd feel angry myself.

Jim: (Laughter and tears at once) Yeah, I guess you know how it is.

In this dialogue, it is clear that the counselor's empathy is conveyed well verbally. There is a nonverbal component to empathy that is important as well. Research suggests several nonverbal behaviors on the practitioner's part that convey to others a sense of being understood. Simply stated, up to two-thirds of the empathic message is conveyed by the following: eye contact, forward body trunk lean, frontal body orientation—that is, worker facing client, close interpersonal space (Hasse & Tepper, 1972), nodding head, and appropriate arm gestures (LaCrosse, 1977). These nonverbal responses are portrayed in Figure 3–2—in this case a social worker talks with a young client.

Indeed, high verbal empathy is seen as unempathic when the opposite nonverbal behaviors are exhibited: no eye contact, backward trunk lean, chair rotated away from client, and speaking from far away (Hasse & Tepper, 1972), Figure 3–3.

Like verbal feedback, however, these nonverbal responses are ideally the spontaneous reflections of felt understanding with the client. Research shows that certain measures of positive outcome of helping encounters are significantly correlated, not with nonverbal or verbal behaviors thought to convey empathy, but rather with congruence or harmony of these behaviors on the practitioner's part (Hill et al., 1981).

In the author's experience, students find that assuming the behaviors that convey empathy enhances their ability to listen to, and be with, surrogate clients. The nonverbal behaviors that tell the client "I'm with you" also seem to make genuine empathy easier for the empathic person to attain. Hence, it is not inappropriate to assume the empathic nonverbal behaviors intentionally when they seem natural to an interaction and when it is desirable to convey empathy.

The presence or absence of feedback in accurate empathy depends on several factors, including the practice situation, social status differences, and the nature of the contract. For instance, a practitioner might provide more intentional, moment-to-moment feedback in a form of individual or group

Figure 3–2.   Empathic practitioner

therapy than in a community organization strategy session in which cognitive meaning would take precedence in the communication. Yet a high degree of empathy is still crucial in practice relationships with clients, colleagues, or others. It is essential for predicting behavior, building rapport, knowing the impact of some individuals on others, facing critical issues, helping clients to feel they are known, and helping them to help themselves.

IMPORTANCE OF EMPATHY

On the subject of empathy, Rogers (1975) writes, "We can say that when a person finds himself sensitively and accurately understood, he develops a set of growth-promoting or therapeutic attitudes toward himself" [p. 8]. Because of its nonevaluative quality, empathy helps clients to care about themselves. Rogers believes that an understanding person can help a client to listen to and understand himself better, and he suggests that enhanced understanding enables clients to have experiences that constitute a more accurately based sense of themselves. Because caring, understanding, and an accurate sense of self are qualities of effective therapists, Rogers believes that empathic understanding helps clients to become therapists for themselves (Rogers, 1975). Clients who see themselves more accurately as a result of an empathic relationship better

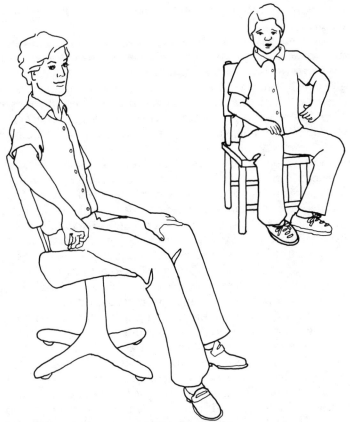

Figure 3-3. Nonempathic practitioner

anticipate their own actions and feelings in coping with problems. Hence, the client's capacity to respond to and shape the world is enhanced as a result of being empathically understood.

The importance of empathy to client growth in practice finds considerable support in studies and in empirical evidence as well. Research identifying and supporting empathy as a critical helping behavior was initiated in response to critics (Eysank, 1952; Carkhuff & Truax, 1965; Carkhuff, 1966, 1968) who questioned the effectiveness of psychotherapists and of their education. Client groups were seen to improve at rates no better than similarly troubled people who were not receiving therapy (Eysank, 1952). There was even some suggestion that counseling psychologists were less empathic after their education than when they began it (Carkhuff, 1966).

Research investigating these criticisms revealed a wide range of ability among helping persons in effecting client change and growth. The more effective practitioners seemed to have higher levels of empathy and other critical behaviors; others were actually damaging to their client's growth. When the results of effective, noneffective, and deleterious practitioners were averaged together, however, the improvement of the client groups as a whole was no better than the improvement of troubled persons receiving no formal or professional help.

Moreover, persons improving with no professional help were found on close examination to have had access to people who had listened to their problems in an understanding way. That empathy was a key ingredient in helping people to improve was true whether the helping person was a minister, a general practitioner, or a personal friend. These findings stimulated considerably more research which has helped to refine our concept of empathy and has found it to be important to the positive outcome of helping endeavors (Truax & Mitchell, 1971).

Just how empathy facilitates a practitioner-client relationship has been the subject of some investigation. Clients who can share personal information and deep feelings with a social worker or other helping person feel less alone in their suffering and dilemmas; someone else understands and cares. Clients who have a style of self-disclosure are more likely to maintain it in the helping relationship and are likely to see their counselor or clinical social worker as self-disclosing. But empathy and warmth on the part of the helping person enable the client to disclose further in the therapeutic or helping encounter (Halpern, 1977), and as personal disclosure increases, the feeling of trust—the bedrock of any positive relationship—must increase as well.

The client's experience of the practitioner as empathic is not simply the result of outward cues or of reflective comment; empathy must spring from the total experience of client and therapist alike. Social worker Pauline Lide (1966) identified this process as a *dynamic mental representation* of the client which includes, together with the client, environmental forces shaping his destiny and the worker's theoretical knowledge, practice wisdom, and experience with similar people and situations. This mental representation helps to bridge the emotional distance between worker and client and facilitates emotional understanding of the client (Lide, 1966).

Barrett-Lennard (1981) sees the empathic process as including phases of listening and resonating, communicating the resulting empathic understanding, and received empathy. *Resonation* does not mean simply acting concerned or adopting the postures and gestures associated with empathy. It means communicating one's felt experience of the other in all the verbal and nonverbal, intentional and naturally automatic ways appropriate to the relationship.

That we are dealing with more than an intellectual skill is underlined by research relating to teaching and empathy. Education of professional helping persons that places heavy or exclusive emphasis on cognitive skills and intellectual understanding can be harmful to the students' capacity for empathy (Carkhuff & Truax, 1965; Carkhuff, 1968). In contrast, education emphasizing experiential learning modes (Carkhuff, 1966; Keefe, 1975; Larson & Hepworth, 1979) has been found more effective in developing empathy.

Empirical evidence, then, not only suggests that empathy is important in practice but indicates several other important things: empathy can be taught; empathy skill can be enhanced; empathy is not an esoteric quality exclusive to professional helpers but is potentially a quality of all people; empathy is complex—a feeling and intuitive skill as well as an understanding and cognitive skill.

Extending cognitive elements

From both their education and their work, social workers know that a client's poverty is often the result of factors other than character defect or accident of birth. Poverty is a historical and structural fact of our economic system, and poor people are among the casualties of this reality. Socioeconomic contradictions are reflected in a great many individual problems—depression, insecurity, child abuse, alcoholism, hypertension, suicide, and mental illness, to name but a few (Catalano & Dooley, 1977; Gabarino, 1976; Brenner, 1976; Pierce, 1967; Brenner, 1973). For the social work practitioner, a sophisticated empathy is mediated by a cognitive grasp of the realities of the client's and also of the worker's societal context (Keefe, 1978). Characteristic of that context is its changing quality.

Social and economic change are ubiquitous in an advanced market economy. Sophistication as to the direction of these changes and the interests they serve extends empathic skill to the level of *critical consciousness* (Freire, 1973). At this level, the social and economic changes are assessed and their meaning is considered in relation to the lives of workers and clients alike.

When augmented by a critical consciousness, empathic skill is less likely to be a tool of social control or of social oppression than of liberation. That is, empathic skill is less likely to participate in bending clients to interests beyond their own. On the contrary, it is a skill that helps clients to understand, critique, and change their realities so that they can better pursue their own goals and potentialities. In Freire's terms, workers and clients are less *passive objects* of social and economic change than they are potentially the *active subjects* of change (Freire, 1973).

Though not always called by this name, critical consciousness that thus extends empathic skill has been a traditional part of the wisdom of social work practice and should be preserved regardless of the kind of practice. But if critical consciousness and wisdom are extensions of the cognitive side of empathy, the emotional, intuitive side of empathy has its extension as well.

Empathy and compassion

Practice experience, theory, logic, and empirical findings all suggest that empathy is composed of both understanding and feeling responses. If we press understanding and feeling to their limits, we move beyond a "self-other" mode of relating. We move beyond understanding and feeling to compassion.

By viewing another person as a composite of social roles, situation, history, physical body, and communications, we are viewing not a person or self but an impersonal configuration of forces in interaction. Under the intense scrutiny of the rational, analytic mind, the atoms, molecules, organs, chemical reactions, unconditioned and conditioned responses, role performances, cognitive networks, and economic behaviors that make up the other person can efface his/her personhood. In the absence of empathy, the client becomes an object, a thing. Carried to its limits, this objectification *removes* the self in other individuals. Turned inward, this same analytic eye sees one's own self as but a composite illusion. Empathy, then, helps to preserve both the humanness of others and the subjective integrity of the self.

Empathy becomes compassion when we see that the impersonal forces and social relations that compose each of us are like eddies of consciousness in a stream of life flowing of one substance. When we are able to feel with another person—a capacity that follows interpersonal understanding—we begin to sense our deep mutual similarities. With intuitive, nonverbal serenity, we feel as the client feels. Client and worker feel together the suffering, joy, anger, or poignancy of life.

Though the worker has his own separate feelings as well, the shared feelings are, in a sense, shared selves. When our feelings *for* become a feeling *with*, when we experience emotional communion with selves beyond our own selves, feeling then becomes compassion. Workers, colleagues, clients are participants in the same drama. Perhaps this practice skill is a basis for solidarity in the social and personal crises that will confront us in the years ahead.

Having identified, defined, developed, and used empathy for the betterment of people, the helping professions are now responsible for ensuring its continuing use and dispersion into relationships beyond the helping contract. In an age of thermonuclear war, racial hatred, intolerance, economic oppression, starvation, and overpopulation, empathy is a quality conducive to survival. It also serves as a basis for other qualities, behaviors, and skills in practice relationships. Among these, *acceptance* of clients is important in helping them see their suffering in its true situational context.

STUDY QUESTIONS

1. Empathy includes both understanding and feeling. Recall a time when you had empathy with a person under stress or in a crisis. Can you remember how you and this person felt? Did you understand the person's situation and response?
2. Recall a time when you were helped by, or interacted with, an empathic person. How did you feel in response to being understood? Did it change your feelings or behaviors?
3. Recalling Rogers's definition of accurate empathy, can you think of times when you felt with someone but did not tell him or her? How might you tell him or her about your empathic feelings now?
4. Empathy can occur when you are fully attentive to another person and what is being communicated. This suggests that you are entirely in the present, focused on your senses. Practice this state of mind next time you walk somewhere you walk often. Do you notice anything new?
5. Do the nonverbal behaviors suggestive of empathy remind you of people you know? Are these people effective and skilled in their relationships?
6. Empathy is not only an important relationship skill but also a quality conducive to survival. Why? How can empathy help us to survive the personal and general crises we may confront as practitioners?

REFERENCES

Barrett-Lennard, G. T. The empathy cycle: Refinement of a nuclear concept. *Journal of Counseling Psychology,* 1981, *28* (2), 91–100.

Brenner, H. M. Estimating the social cost of national economic policy: Implications for mental health and criminal aggression. Achieving the Goals of the Employment

Act of 1946—Thirtieth Anniversary Review, Joint Economic Committee of Congress, 1976, Washington, D.C.: U.S. Government Printing Office.

Brenner, H. M. *Mental illness and the economy.* Cambridge, Mass.: Harvard University Press, 1973.

Buchheimer, A. The development of ideas about empathy. *Journal of Counseling Psychology,* 1963, *10* (1), 61–70.

Carkhuff, R., & Truax, C. Training in counseling and psychotherapy: An evaluation of an integrated didoctric and experiential approach. *Journal of Counseling Psychology,* 1965, *29* (4), 335.

Carkhuff, R. Differential functioning of lay and professional helpers. *Journal of Counseling Psychology,* 1968, *15* (2), 118.

Carkhuff, R. Training in the counseling and therapeutic practices: Requiem or reveille? *Journal of Counseling Psychology,* 1966, *13* (3), 360.

Carkhuff, R., Kratochuil, D., & Friel, T. Effects of professional training: Communication and discrimination of facilitative conditions. *Journal of Counseling Psychology,* 1968, *15* (1), 68–74.

Catalano, R., & Dooley, D. Economic predictors of depressed mood and stressful life events in a metropolitan community. *Journal of Health & Social Behavior,* 1977, *18* (September), 292–307.

Dymond, R. F. As quoted in Buchheimer, A. The development of ideas about empathy. *Journal of Counseling Psychology,* 1963, *10* (1), 63.

Eysank, H. J. The effects of psychotherapy: An evaluation. *Journal of Consulting Psychology,* 1952, 16 (5), 319–324.

Fagan, J., & Shepard, I. L. (Eds.), *Gestalt therapy now.* Palo Alto, Calif.: Science & Behavior Books, 1970.

Feshback, N. Empathy in children: Some theoretical and empirical considerations. *Counseling Psychologist,* 1975, *5* (2), 25–30.

Feshback, N., & Roe, K. Empathy in six and seven year olds. *Child Development,* 1968, *39* (1), 133–145.

Freire, P. *Education for critical consciousness.* New York: Seabury Press, 1973.

Gabarino, J. A preliminary study of some ecological correlates of child abuse: The impact of socioeconomic stress in mothers. *Child Development,* 1976, 47 (1), 178–184.

Gellen, M. Finger blood volume responses of counselors, counselor trainees, and noncounselors to stimuli from an empathy test. *Counselor Education & Supervision,* 1970, *10* (1), 64–74.

Halpern, H. M., & Lesser, L. N. Empathy in infants, adults, and psychotherapists. *Psychoanalysis & Psychoanalytic Review,* 1960, 47 (3), 32–42.

Halpern, T. P. Degree of client disclosure as a function of past disclosure, counselor disclosure, and counselor facilitativeness. *Journal of Counseling Psychology,* 1977, *24* (1), 41–47.

Hasse, R. F., & Tepper, D. T. Nonverbal components of empathic communication. *Journal of Counseling Psychology,* 1972, *19* (5), 417–424.

Hill, C. E., Siegelman L., Gronsky, B. R., Sturniolo, F., Fretz, B. R. Nonverbal communication and counseling outcome. *Journal of Counseling Psychology,* 1981, *28* (3), 203–212.

Iannotti, R. The nature and measurement of empathy in children. *Counseling Psychologist,* 1975, *5* (2), 2–25.

Iannotti, R., & Meacham, J. A. The nature, measurement and development of empathy, as quoted in R. Iannotti, *Counseling Psychologist,* 1975, *5* (2), 24.

Jesser, R., & Richardson, S. Psychosocial deprivation and personality development. *Perspectives on human deprivation,* Washington, D.C., U.S. Department of Health, Education and Welfare, 1968.

Jourard, S. Psychology of transcendent perception. In Herbert A. Otto (Ed.), *Explorations in human potential.* Springfield, Ill.: Charles C Thomas, 1966.

Keefe, T. Empathy and social work education. *Journal of Education for Social Work,* 1975, *11* (3), 69–75.

Keefe, T. Empathy: The critical skill. *Social Work,* 1976, *21* (1), 10–14.

Keefe, T. The economic context of empathy. *Social Work,* 1978, *18* (6), 460–466.

Kendler, H. H. Environmental and cognitive control of behavior. *American Psychologist,* 1971, *26* (11), 963.

La Crosse, M. B. Comparative perceptions of counselor behaviors: A replication and extension. *Journal of Counseling Psychology,* 1977, *24* (6), 464–471.

Larson, J. A., & Hepworth, D. H. Skill development through competency based education. *Journal of Education for Social Work,* 1978, *14* (1), 73–81.

Lesh, T. V. The relationship between zen meditation and the development of accurate empathy. University of Oregon, 1969, Order No. 70–9450. *Dissertation Abstracts International,* 1970, *30,* 4778B–4779B.

Lide, P. D. Dynamic mental representation: An analysis of the empathic process. *Social Casework,* 1966, *47* (3), 146–151.

Miller, R. R. An experimental study of the observational process in casework. In P. Fellin, T. Tripodi, & H. J. Meyer (Eds.), *Exemplars of social research.* Itasca, Ill.: F. E. Peacock Publishers, 1969.

Orlinsky, D. E., & Howard, K. I. The relation of process to outcome in psychotherapy. In A. E. Bergin & S. L. Garfield (Eds.), *Handbook of psychotherapy and behavior change.* New York: John Wiley & Sons, 1978.

Parloff, M. B., Waskow, I. E., & Wolfe, B. E. Research on therapist variables in relation to process and outcome. In A. E. Bergen & S. L. Garfield (Eds.), *Handbook of psychotherapy and behavior change: An empirical analysis.* New York: John Wiley & Sons, 1978.

Pierce, A. The economic cycle and the suicide rate. *American Sociological Review,* 1967, *32,* 475–482.

Rogers, C. R. The necessary and sufficient conditions of therapeutic personality change. *Journal of Consulting Psychology,* 1957, *21* (2), 99.

Rogers, C. Empathic: An unappreciated way of being. *Counseling Psychologist,* 1975, *5* (2), 8–9.

Shantz, C. Empathy in relation to social cognitive development. *Counseling Psychologist,* 1975, *5* (2), 19.

Stotland, E., Mathews, K., Sherman, S. E., Hansson, R. O., & Richardson, B. Z. *Empathy, fantasy and helping.* London: Sage Publications, 1978.

Taquiri, R. Person perception. In Lindzey, Gardner & E. Aronson (Eds.), *The handbook of social psychology* (Vol. 3). Reading, Mass.: Addison-Wesley Publishing Co., 1969.

Truax, C., & Mitchell, K. M. Research on certain therapist interpersonal skills in relation to process and outcome. In A. E. Bergin & S. L. Garfield (Eds.), *Handbook of psychotherapy and behavior change.* New York: John Wiley & Sons, 1971.

Vanderpool, J. P., & Barrat, E. S. Empathy: Towards a psychophysiological definition. *Diseases of the Nervous System,* 1970, *31* (7), 464–467.

Zanger, A. Clinical empathy as a function of attentional patterns and identification tendencies. Smith College School of Social Work, 1966, Order No. 67–4156. *Dissertation Abstracts International,* 1967, *27,* 4347B–4348B.

4

The Accepting Relationship

More than just a characteristic of a relationship, acceptance is also a skill that can be learned and developed. In professional practice, acceptance (like empathy) can enrich relationships with clients, colleagues, and others. Moreover, when clients sense that they are accepted by professional practitioners, their functioning improves (Orlinsky & Howard, 1978).

Acceptance is communicated in a variety of ways. Because nonverbal and unintentional behaviors convey a large part of the message, much of this skill is related to the warmth and regard a practitioner naturally communicates. Acceptance generates an atmosphere that is conducive to client growth. Chapter 4 examines how acceptance fosters helping relationships, its ideal unconditional quality, and its important nonverbal and spontaneous nuances. The client's all-important perception of acceptance is explored and examples of acceptance, conditional acceptance, and nonacceptance are provided.

THE FALSE BURDEN

To sever human beings from their interpersonal context, even for helping purposes, is like sawing a branch from a tree in order to force the branch to grow another way. That an individual client is the focal point of his interpersonal environment is increasingly being recognized and integrated into professional practice relationships. In social work, Hollis (1964) suggested the *person-in-situation* as the entity toward which caseworkers should direct their activities. Social work, family therapy, and counseling (Laing & Esterson, 1971; Satir, 1967), radical therapy (Angel, 1971), and other perspectives assert that a client's problematic behaviors reflect problematic interpersonal situations.

"When one is in trouble, all are in trouble" (Satir, 1967) succinctly contradicts the attribution of an illness to the mental mechanisms of a single person. The simplistic, outdated idea that a client's problems arise mostly from mental malfunction not only supports the view of problematic interpersonal behavior as disease but blends conveniently with the view of the poor—and of others not safely encapsulated in middle-class lifestyles—as morally or characterologically defective.

Clients themselves often believe that their problems are strictly the result of their personal inadequacies, which naturally adds to the false burden they bear. This overload may relieve family members of the necessity of changing their own behavior; it may relieve organizations or institutions of the necessity of policy or organization change; ironically, it may excuse them of responsibility for personal growth. To label someone's problems as illness is to grant that person entry into the passivity and helplessness of the sick role so that inadequate response to temporary crises may become permanent maladjustment and dependency.

But false burden, no matter for whom the client is scapegoating, must be removed if the person is to assume true responsibility for changing either his or her behavior or circumstances to the greatest extent possible. Through the helping relationship, the practitioner with highly developed empathy and critical consciousness relieves the client of the false burden but does not relieve—at least not permanently—the client's true burden of finding the ability to respond to his or her situation, *response-ability* (Perls, 1971). Knopp (1972) describes the practitioner's task as a kind of judo.

> It is as if I stand in the doorway of my office, waiting. The patient enters and makes a lunge at me, a desperate attempt to pull me into the fantasy of taking care of him. I step aside. The patient falls to the floor, disappointed and bewildered. Now he has a chance to get up and to try something new. If I am sufficiently courageous and persistent, he may learn to become more curious about himself, to come to know me as I am, and to begin to work out his own problems. He may transform his stubbornness into purposeful determination, his bid for safety into a reaching out for adventure [p. 2].

class

Relieving clients of their false burden and making them responsible for changing their own behavior or circumstances is not easy. The first and most important job of the practitioner in this task is to accept the client as a person capable of such change. Acceptance is therefore critical in creating a helping relationship that generates trust.

Scapegoating, labeling, and other manifestations of the false burden would not be possible without some degree of agreement and cooperation from the client. Whether defiant, vitriolic, aggressive, brilliant, paranoid, passive, or severely troubled, the client usually has incorporated at least part of the family's, the school system's, or the society's low or negative opinion of him or her. Ageism, racism, sexism, and class bias contribute to these perceptions. The client sometimes collaborates in undermining his or her own self-esteem.

For the practitioner to accept the client is to convey a message that the latter is a person of worth. The anxiety-ridden client may also be a great lover, a good parent, a very clever or striving person. Groups of welfare recipients are also capable of questioning and challenging the dehumanizing aspects of their circumstances. The drug addict may also be a creative artist. In short, each client has redeeming attributes, and a practitioner must accept each as a person capable of breaking the cycle of personal difficulty.

In both words and actions the practitioner must say in effect: "I accept and value you as a person. You are a participant in the creation of your problems, but many other events and people contribute to them as well. Your problems are the result of your needs, the needs of other people, and the needs of the organizations and society of which you are an integral part. I accept you as capable of responding to and changing some of the things that brought you to me. At core, you are as good and deserving of love as anyone else." The value of this message, however it may be delivered, was most potently realized by the author in work with clients having destructive patterns of behavior.

ACCEPTANCE AND SELF-DESTRUCTIVE PATTERNS

For some people, relationships that start off well end repeatedly in rejection and anger. For others, ambitious projects create problems far greater than the projects were designed to solve. For examples: a young man engages in a succession of love affairs each of which ends in his rejection; a businesswoman finds her capital wasted again and again on spurious projects aimed at surefire wealth. Such people seem curiously blind to consequences that others perceive easily. The catchall term for these behavioral patterns is *self-destructive*.

Having adopted a negative opinion of oneself, validated by a thousand punishing reminders of inadequacy and thoughtlessness, the client may seriously question the practitioner's acceptance. Indeed, acceptance of those who see themselves as undeserving may precipitate mistrust and devaluation of the practitioner or the helping relationship. The practitioner may be challenging all the self-fulfilling prophecies, negative expectations, and confirmations of unworthiness, ugliness, stupidity, destructiveness, or mental incompetence that helped to create that negative opinion. But the contradiction between self-perception and that of the professional helping relationship becomes a catalyst for change. That these clients will test their acceptance is inevitable.

The first crisis of the relationship is the client's attempt to invalidate the practitioner's acceptance with its inherent message of self-worth. The delinquent teenager may test the limits of his probation officer's or house parent's authority by breaking windows or shoplifting with no way of avoiding being caught. Between interviews, the ineffectual mother may yield her mothering role completely to her own mother, who "knew" that the outcome of her daughter's attempts at autonomy was "inevitable." Some clients may test repeatedly until a seed of acceptance grows big enough to be seen.

Usually the practitioner points out the underlying reasons for such testing. If this is done too soon or is insufficiently understood by the practitioner, however, the testing behavior may only further validate the client's sense of unacceptability. If it is done well, confronting the reasons for the testing behavior allows the seeds of self-acceptance to grow in the client. Let us examine the dynamics of acceptance in an example from social work practice with an individual client.

The case of John

John was a brilliant young man, a child of the upper middle class. His parents were entrepreneurs, who, through the success of their own labors, had a growing small business. Owing in part to John's exceptional intelligence, his parents had feared and rejected him. With deep resentment, he had worked long hours in their business. In school, this truly gifted child became bored, rowdy, and unmanageable. He quit high school before his junior year, with the result that legitimate channels to the achievements of the mind and particularly to science, John's abiding interest, were blocked.

On leaving school and being exiled from home by his parents, John joined the nomadic host of young people traveling about the country in quest of a counterculture. Parodying his parents' entrepreneurial model, he survived by buying and selling marijuana and LSD. As he matured, he employed his talents in a variety of research assistant positions, though these seemed consistently to end in the discovery of illegitimate credentials or in disputes with employers. In addition, his intimate relationships were successive disasters as his lovers left him for one reason or another.

John was aware of his intellect. His knowledge of electronics and physics was astounding for a person having less than a high school education. As the counterculture, with which John had so firmly identified, began to pass into a new age and to co-optation by Madison Avenue, John sought direction and solace from the author on a private basis. His case was typical of many during that period of social unrest.

Over the course of a few months, John seemed to gain a sense of direction and sought formal training in electronics. But the training was boring, and his knowledge and inventiveness threatened his instructors. Abiding defensiveness about his lack of formal education, his occasional arrogance, and his sharp intellect caused people to react to him uncharitably. Adding to this chronic stress, a seemingly stable love affair blew up, and this rejection reinstated a sense of worthlessness which John would seldom articulate. He disappeared into the maze of a large city.

John's second call for help came one Sunday morning, and we talked as we walked about the empty streets. John said he had been unwittingly turned on to heroin. He said the experience was bliss; he liked the people who had introduced him to it; and he wanted to know whether the propaganda about "H" was true or more of the same "baloney" he had heard about hallucinogens during his early teens. I replied that as far as I knew, heroin was a "death trip" for heavily addicted low-income users. Aroused, John said that life had held little joy for him and that he anticipated nothing better than his experiences on heroin. The prospect that these experiences might be short-lived, that he would likely die long before his time, was not a compelling reason to avoid further involvement.

By late afternoon, I told John how I thought he was set up for his current bind. I bluntly confronted him with the self-destructive potential in this initially blissful experience. In the course of much give and take, I said that I thought both the bliss and the potential for self-destruction inherent in heroin use might be very compelling to him in particular and explained why I thought so. We talked about the "need" for things to turn out badly and about his view of himself.

At dusk we walked to the center of one of the city's larger bridges and watched the day fade. John said that he needed a reason for discontinuing heroin use. I knew that an argument based on values, chastisement, or threats of misery and death would have no effect on him. In the end I recall saying, "I can't give you any persuasive *reasons* why you should not become a user. You don't want reasons. What I know at this moment is that I truly care about you—you're a very special person—that's really all I can say." Soon we said goodbye.

Perhaps partly due to the encouragement of an accepting relationship, John avoided further involvement with heroin. Subsequent contacts over the years have indicated that he has acquired a more positive self-image despite the frustrations and pains an exceptionally gifted person with no formal education suffers in these years of credentialism. John needed information, insight, and an accepting relationship: information about heroin use, insight into his own "script" (Berne, 1961), and a relationship in which his own value as a person could be verified and shared. For the self-destructive client, an accepting relationship is the key to restoring or generating an affirmative self-image and to determining more positive consequences in long-term patterns of endeavor and interpersonal relating.

NUANCES OF THE ACCEPTING RELATIONSHIP

Unconditionality

Various helping professions have identified acceptance as a key ingredient in work with clients. In social work, Biestek (1957) defined acceptance as "a principle of action wherein the caseworker perceives and deals with the client as he really is, including his strengths and weaknesses, his congenial and uncongenial qualities, his positive and negative feelings, his constructive and destructive attitudes and behavior, maintaining all the while a sense of the client's innate dignity and personal worth" [p. 72]. Biestek differentiates between acceptance and approval, suggesting that a helper need not approve of the clients' behaviors but should accept them as they are. Rogers (1957), too, posited *unconditional positive regard* as a necessary condition in psychological counseling: "To the extent that the therapist finds himself experiencing a warm acceptance of each aspect of the client's experience as being a part of that client, he is experiencing unconditional positive regard" [p. 98].

Notice that Rogers' definition mentions acceptance of the client's experience, not behaviors. He points out the unconditional nature of this acceptance by noting that it includes acceptance of painful, bad, fearful, and abnormal, as well as positive, mature, and good social feelings. It includes accepting a client's inconsistencies, and finally it does not depend on whether the client is meeting the practitioner's needs to move along satisfactorily in the therapeutic relationship. Rogers, then, sees acceptance as allowing the client to be his or her own self. It is this self, ideally, that is accepted and thereby affirmed.

Affirmation

The acceptance of each aspect of the client's experience affirms the client's self. In this atmosphere of affirmation is nurtured the individual's identity as a subject of action, thought, feeling, and experience. The self is experienced as active, causal; moreover, it is known to and valued by another. Such an atmosphere is conducive to growth, self-acceptance, concern for the future self, goal setting, and hence problem solving. It is an atmosphere in which self-worth militates against self-punishing and self-destructive behaviors. This atmosphere was present in the helping relationship with John in the example above. Acceptance that generates this atmosphere of affirmation is rounded out in several ways.

Warmth

Various terms connote acceptance but denote slightly different kinds of behavior. *Positive regard*, for instance, is similar to positive valuing; both presuppose that the practitioner shows the client *respect*. But there is more. *Interpersonal warmth* is communicated largely nonverbally and usually only momentarily. It is a vehicle for acceptance. Respectful and valuing statements about the client are accompanied by a smile, appropriate touching, pleasant surprise, and enthusiasm for the client's rendition of personal experience. An outgoing manner, an outreaching to the person, carry the affirmation that is critical to acceptance.

These qualities of warmth, which Rogers termed *unconditional positive regard*, were widely researched along with empathy and genuineness as the necessary and sufficient conditions that a practitioner offers to bring positive growth in clients (Truax & Mitchell, 1971). More recent research does not support such enthusiastic adjectives, but the skills are nonetheless quite important (Parloff, Wascow, & Wolfe, 1978, pp. 242–253).

Client perception.   Practitioners know that warmth and acceptance give them a lift, and research reveals a similar phenomenon among clients. A review of 13 studies of client perceptions of the helping encounter showed unanimous accord that warmth is significantly associated with a positive outcome of the process (Orlinsky & Howard, 1978, p. 298). In contrast, two studies cited by the same authors (Orlinsky & Howard, 1978, p. 298) found that when clients perceived the practitioner as critical and hostile, the outcome for the client was negative. These findings raise questions. What if I do not feel accepting or warm? What if I cannot accept a client in the way recommended as beneficial?

NONACCEPTANCE

The accepting relationship should not make superhuman demands on the practitioner. There are behaviors, roles, lifestyles, and people we cannot accept when we have insufficient understanding to see them as a part of a larger interpersonal system. In fact, psychologist Charles Truax (1966a and 1966b) warned that even the positive regard of outstanding therapists is sometimes conditional on client behaviors. Furthermore, acceptance is conveyed in the helping relationship not only by means of vocal assertion but by tone, facial expression, frequency of helper communication responses, and in other ways. Acceptance is a feeling that will be communicated or not despite the best intentions of the practitioner. For the latter, the best policy is to sense his or her feelings of acceptance or nonacceptance accurately and communicate these directly to the client.

For example, unconditional acceptance does not imply that a practitioner never gets angry at a client; anger is a normal part of any relationship. To suppress it or try to put it aside is to endanger the relationship because it may well be communicated nonverbally anyway. The client senses not only the anger but the cover-up as well. Anger can be expressed in nondestructive, even nonrejecting, but effective ways. An intensely reported irritation is very different from a hostile demeaning of the other person or a withdrawal of acceptance. If, at last, even the desire and potential for change in a client do not elicit feelings of acceptance in the practitioner, referral to another practitioner is in order.

Sometimes a client, colleague, or other person may arouse in the practitioner anger, anxiety or other negative feelings disproportionate or inappropriate to the relationship due to a resemblance to something unpleasant in the past. Because such resemblances may not be sensed, the feelings they elicit may be inexplicable to conscious logic. This process Freud called *transference neurosis* or simply *transference*—that is, old feelings and conflicts are transferred to the new relationship. It is not considered to be a conscious phenomenon; when it occurs, we may not be fully aware of it.

Disproportionate, inappropriate, or inordinately intense feelings should be examined as possible products of our own transference. Such feelings and their related behaviors on the part of the practitioner—often elicited by the client's transference—are termed *countertransference*. When they occur, we should consult with colleagues to identify them and explore how they may affect the relationship with the client. If they interfere with our acceptance and warmth, they will hamper the process of helping. When they are such as to preclude a positive outcome, a client might best be referred to a colleague with clear, tactful, and judicious explanation and preparation. The client's needs come first—he or she needs an accepting relationship—and an authentic practitioner.

Examples of acceptance and nonacceptance

A few examples of accepting and nonaccepting remarks can sharpen our understanding of this skill. Because expressions of acceptance and warmth are largely nonverbal, however, it is difficult to convey them fully in writing. Keep this caveat in mind while reading the following examples of accepting, conditional accepting, and nonaccepting remarks.

Accepting
"I know you find this a bitter thing. Despite how hard it is, you're able to talk about it. It shows your strength in the situation."
"George, you know, you're right!"
"No, it's not something I would do. But right now, it's what you have to do. Your way isn't mine, but it's best for you—and that's OK by me."
"Sally, God but it's good to see you again!"
"I care about *you*."

Conditional Accepting

"You've done very well today. You've shared a lot of feelings and worked
   out some goals. I think you're doing just great."

"I wish you could be a little more responsive in those times—get more of
   your natural self involved."

"Maybe you did OK. Be careful next time."

"I want you to start to open up."

Nonacceptance—Negative Regard

"I don't care what they did. You blew it—as usual."

"All right, let's cut out the tears and get on with it."

"Goodbye, loafer."

"Before we get started with your problem, I want to mention the fees."

Bear in mind that acceptance is a thread that is embroidered through a
positive relationship. Acceptance and warmth are conveyed in a hundred
spontaneous and unintentional ways, and there will always be lapses. If the
practitioner accepts himself or herself, however, the potential is there for the
acceptance of most others.

The essence of the accepting relationship lies in the practitioner's skill in
sensing and openly communicating acceptance of the client. Only when practitioners acknowledge human limits on their ability to recognize the conditional nature of acceptance are they free to use fully the nurturing potential
of the accepting relationship.

This relationship is nurturing in the sense that it affirms the selfhood of
the one accepted. It makes honesty and trust possible, and it allows both
practitioner and client to discover themselves in an open and straightforward
encounter. Such a relationship in turn allows the client's impact on the feelings
and thoughts of another person without the mask of propriety or the deception
of fear-covering kindness which gives false images of the impact on others. In
both the practitioner and the client, acceptance nurtures authenticity and related
qualities which will be examined in Chapter 5.

STUDY QUESTIONS

1. This chapter asserts that, in a sense, a person *is* his or her situation. Give examples
   of ways we commonly think of people and their problems in isolation from their
   situation or context.
2. We maintain that a practitioner must accept clients as persons capable of changing
   their behavior and environment. Are there clients for whom this kind of acceptance
   is impossible?
3. Are there kinds of clients whose behaviors you would find so repugnant that you
   might have difficulty relating to them? If so, what might you do to see that they get
   help?
4. Have you been the victim of racism, sexism, or ageism? Did the experience(s) affect
   your self-acceptance? What other feelings were evoked in you?
5. How does acceptance militate against low self-worth and self-destructive behavior?
6. Do you know persons who are uncommonly accepting, warm, and affirming toward
   other people? How do you feel when you interact with them? Can you identify
   what they do to convey these qualities?

REFERENCES

Angel, J. (Ed.) *The radical therapist*. New York: Ballantine Books, 1971.

Berne, E. *Transactional analysis in psychotherapy*. New York: Grove Press, 1961.

Biestek, F. P. *The casework relationship*. Chicago: Loyala University Press, 1957.

Hollis, F. *Casework: A psychosocial therapy*. New York: Random House, 1964.

Knopp, S. B. *If you meet the Buddha on the road, kill him*. Ben Lomond: Calif: Science & Behavior Books, 1972.

Laing, R. D., & Esterson, A. *Sanity, madness and the family*. Baltimore: Penguin Books, 1971.

Orlinsky, D. E., & Howard, K. I. The relation of process to outcome in psychotherapy. In A. E. Bergin & S. L. Garfield (Eds.), *Handbook of psychotherapy and behavior change*. New York: John Wiley & Sons, 1978.

Parloff, M. B., Waskow, I. E., & Wolfe, B. E. Research on therapist variables in relation to process and outcome. In S. L. Garfield & A.E. Bergin (Eds.), *Handbook of psychotherapy and behavior change* (2nd ed.) New York: John Wiley & Sons, 1978.

Perls, F. S. *Gestalt therapy verbatim*. New York: Bantam Books, 1971.

Rogers, C. R. The necessary and sufficient conditions of therapeutic personality change. *Journal of Consulting Psychology*, 1957, *21* (2), 95–103.

Satir, V. *Conjoint family therapy* (Rev. ed.). Palo Alto, Calif: Science & Behavior Books, 1967.

Truax, C. Reinforcement and nonreinforcement in Rogerian psychotherapy. *Journal of Abnormal & Social Psychology*, 1966, *71*, 1–9. (a)

Truax, C. Some implications of behavior therapy for psychotherapy. *Journal of Counseling Psychology*, 1966, *13* (2), 160–170. (b)

Truax, C. B., & Mitchell, K. M. Research on certain therapist interpersonal skills in relation to process and outcome. In A. E. Bergin & S. L. Garfield (Eds.), *Handbook of psychotherapy and behavior change*. New York: John Wiley & Sons, 1971.

5

Authenticity

A choice that confronts everyone at every moment
is this: Shall we permit our fellows to know us as
we are, or shall we remain enigmas, wishing to
be seen as persons we are not?

Sidney Jourard (1971, p. vii)

Authenticity is an interpersonal skill that can be used in all varieties of
practice relationships, but it is particularly useful in collaborative relationships
with clients. Authenticity involves disclosing oneself in particular ways and
involving oneself with a particular demeanor in a relationship. Highly developed authenticity requires both warmth and empathy. Finally, authenticity is
a skill that can provide those with whom one interacts with information about
themselves that they probably cannot acquire in other relationships.

TRANSPARENCY, GENUINENESS, AND DECORUM

Transparency (Jourard, 1971) and genuineness (Rogers, 1957) are closely
allied concepts when they refer to qualities of self-presentation. Taken together
they may be termed *authenticity*. An authentic person consciously holds little
or nothing back in interactions with others. Feelings and thoughts, however
uncomfortable when shared, are deliberately, though tactfully, communicated as they occur. Authentic persons are *transparent* in the sense that they
conceal few thoughts and feelings and do not intentionally play artificial roles.
They do not present a public self at wide variance with their experience of
themselves in thought and feeling. Authentic persons are *genuine* in the sense
that their words match their feelings and thoughts to the greatest extent possible.

Sidney Jourard (1971) presented professional helpers in particular with
an invitation to authenticity.

Authentic being means being oneself, honestly, in one's relations with his fellows. It means taking the first step at dropping pretense, defenses, and duplicity. It means an end to "playing it cool," an end to using one's behavior as a gambit designed to disarm the other fellow, to get him to reveal himself *before* you disclose yourself to him. This invitation is fraught with risk; indeed, it may inspire terror in some [p. 133].

We might ask whether the authenticity that Jourard proposes is possible within all social systems, each with its own rules of social interaction, taboos, and limitations on self-expression. It would seem that authenticity would either radically change the rules of interaction or result in the offender's rejection and ostracism. Jourard's invitation is indeed "fraught with risk" if we believe that authenticity would cause an individual to violate rules of decorum and to lose face.

Goffman (1967) defined *face* as "the positive social value a person effectively claims for himself by the line others assume he has taken during a particular contact. Face is an image of self delineated in terms of approved social attributes" [p. 5]. This suggests that bringing forth information inconsistent with one's social worth or being out of touch with behaviors appropriate to one's position in a social situation can result in a *loss of face*.

Once he takes on a self-image expressed through face he will be expected to live up to it. In different ways in different societies he will be required to show self-respect, abjuring certain actions because they are above or beneath him, while forcing himself to perform others even though they cost him dearly. By entering a situation in which he is given a face to maintain a person takes on the responsibility of standing guard over the flow of events as they pass before him [p. 9].

Resolving the conflict between being authentic and maintaining face in a given social situation lies in being tactful and in empathizing to some degree with other participants. Even strongly felt opinions and strong emotional reactions can be expressed with sensitivity toward the other person's perspective. For instance, "Dr. Smith, I know you have my best interests at heart, but your treatment makes me sicker than I was before." Or "I know this is not easy to take from an employee, but your manner of relating to us comes across as haughty and inconsiderate. I feel anger toward you." The risks are still present when authenticity is tempered with tact, but they must be weighed against the risks of continued oppression, suffering, or even physical illness (Jourard, 1971) that may develop as the cost of maintaining a social mask markedly different from a hidden private self.

Practice relationships of a collaborative nature are usually deliberately designed to encourage the client to express feelings and thoughts without risk of losing face. An executive may cry more easily before an analyst than before a board of directors. Very often, however, the client brings social taboos or self-expressive limits to the helping relationship. Practitioners sometimes naively interpret the *nonexpression of feelings* as an incapacity without first considering the client's definition of the situation and the social limitations or rules he has applied. Often, a practitioner functions as a "permission giver," communicating that feelings seldom expressed in everyday life may be expressed in the helping relationship. In this way the practitioner redefines the situation as one in which the client may express feelings without risking a loss of face.

AN IDENTITY MODEL

A professional practitioner serves as a model in expressing thoughts and feelings in a spontaneous and unguarded way. The model of an unflappable, impersonal, detached, superrational demigod, a product of misconstrued psychoanalytic technique, is inappropriate in the helping professions.

Simply stated, traditional psychoanalytic technique attempts to foster a transference relationship between patient and analyst. The patient may relate to the therapist in ways determined more by unresolved conflicts and feelings toward parents and significant others than by the reality of the therapist's personality. But transference enables patients to reexperience situations and fantasies, which allows them to develop insight into personal behavior so as to work through conflicts toward a more constructive outcome than when the conflicts were first generated. The more neutral the analyst is toward the patient, the more a blank screen and the less a distinct personality, the better the opportunity for transference to take place.

Many practitioners who conduct psychotherapy or engage in related activities have regarded the now archaic image of the neutral, objective, uninvolved therapist as appropriate to such activities. Unless the practitioner is using psychoanalytic technique, however, this decorum is inappropriate. Indeed, almost the opposite self-presentation has been empirically substantiated as generally predictive of good results for practice relationships with clients (Orlinsky & Howard, 1978, p. 307). In authentic relating, the practioner's feelings and thoughts are shared with the client. An early proponent of this view was Carl Rogers, who suggested that effective helpers are simply themselves in the helping relationship, without pretense (Rogers, 1958). Like empathy, genuineness was found to produce positive outcomes for the client across many theoretical approaches and techniques (Truax & Mitchell, 1971).

More recent reviews of research do not unequivocally support the notion that authenticity is "all you need" regardless of the problem, the theoretical perspective, or other factors that affect the practice relationship (Parloff, Waskow, & Wolfe, 1978, pp. 242–252). When the process of the relationship is examined, client perception is seen to be important. Evidence suggests that when a client perceives authenticity in the practitioner, the relationship is likely to have a positive outcome (Orlinsky & Howard, 1978, p. 307). This is probably because the behavior of an active, involved, spontaneous, authentic practitioner serves as a model for clients, encouraging imitation and modeling behavior in them (Jourard, 1969).

Carl Rogers (1957) challenged the model of an impersonal or distant professional helper in a definitive statement about what a genuine therapist is: "It seems that within the relationship he is freely and deeply himself, with his actual experience accurately represented by his awareness of himself. It is the opposite of presenting a façade, whether knowingly or unknowingly" [p. 97].

Rogers' definition and the research it stimulated have helped to redefine the practice relationship with clients as a social situation in which both the client and the practitioner are expected to relinquish artificial self-presentations and to express moment-to-moment thoughts and feelings as they occur in the helping interaction. In other words, not just in clinical settings but in all areas of practice, the practitioner need not carry the norms of everyday social situations into the relationship to avoid loss of face or to preserve an artificial mask at variance with his or her sensed experience of self.

SPECIFICS OF AUTHENTICITY

Some of the unevenness in the research on authenticity (Parloff et al., 1978) is probably due to imprecise definitions of what this skill is in actual practice. Like empathy and acceptance, authenticity is a complex skill that is woven into the fabric of a relationship, and as such it must be examined together with other skills and factors that influence and are influenced by it. Such factors include, in addition to the skills already examined, specific *ways* of being authentic and nonverbal behaviors of the practitioner.

Demographic and personal disclosure

From both deduction and research we know that clients' willingness to disclose themselves is closely related to their degree of self-disclosure in the past (Jourard, 1971; Halpern, 1977). This willingness is affected by the practitioners' disclosures as well (Halpern, 1977); but the kind of disclosure that generates a similar response in a client is *not* simply baring one's past or intimate concerns. Sharing relevant demographic information about oneself at appropriate times elicits a better response than sharing more personally revealing information, especially when the disclosures are coupled with a degree of warmth expressed toward the client (Simonson, 1976). Examples of demographic and personally relevant disclosing follow.

Client: I'd like to talk about my kids. (Aside to practitioner) Do you think you can help me tame them?

Practitioner: Sure, we can talk about our kids here. I've got kids like several of the others. Three of them—a teenager, a toddler, and one in the middle. It sounds like yours must be causing you some hassles right now [demographic].

By sharing that she has children, the practitioner has presented, in addition to her authenticity, a basis of common experience with the client and other parents in the group, which probably increases their confidence in her *Class* as a potential resource. This might be seen as *moderate disclosure*. In the following example, the information relates to personal problems and conflicts and might be termed *highly disclosing*.

Client: I can't get past my anger at them. Every time I meet a new guy I start asking inside my head, "How's this _____ going to make his move?" We never have a chance.

Practitioner: Anger won't let you trust? Won't let you take a man as he is? I know that: That's what ended my own marriage. It takes time to work your way out.

Certainly this example comes closer to the private life of the practitioner. The question is whether it comes closer to the concerns of the client. At what point does very personal disclosure become a burden on a relationship that is supposed to be directed primarily at the client's needs? Let's sort out this issue.

Disclosure versus involvement

The key to optimal authenticity seems to lie in the related skill of empathy. The quality of authenticity is enhanced when a practitioner maintains a level of empathy that is focused on the client's needs, feelings, and thoughts. This focus allows the practitioner less opportunity and inclination to be scanning his or her memory for personal experiences. Instead, the practitioner is responding with unique feelings and thoughts of immediate relevance to the client's presentation.

When these immediate client-focused responses are shared, the practitioner might be seen more as *self-involving* than *self-disclosing* (McCarthy & Betz, 1978). We suggest, then, that optimal authenticity is an unguarded, spontaneous sharing or disclosing of one's reactions to the other person's communications. The more one is practicing high-level empathy skill, the more one's authenticity is one of involvement with the client. The following dialogues are hypothetical examples of self-disclosing and self-involving responses to the same client. Client statements are reconstructed from actual interviews.

Client: Is it normal? Did you ever get so mad at one of your parents that you imagined killing them—just hitting them over the head with an axe? I'd never do it, but I've imagined it.
Worker: Yes, sometimes the anger gets so intense. I remember hoping my old man would get in a car wreck when I was your age [self-disclosing].

This response may shock or burden the client, overriding any advantage of enhancing trust that it may elicit.

Worker: You better believe it. I know how angry a guy can get. You think of awful things. So awful you think you're the only one who could dream them up. It happens to a lot of us, I know! [self-involving].

This response makes the same point but does not burden the client with discomforting specifics.

Client: So I had to stop working with the kids and go on unemployment. There they are, back to lolling in front of the TV. I'm not there to help make their lives interesting—bearable. The damn politicians saved another buck for their missiles. Kids are garbage to them.
Worker: I know how that gets to you—we had our budget cut 25% [self-disclosing].
Worker: (Deep sigh) You struck a note with me there. It seems like you feel you're being told your work is not needed for this grand new society— survival of the rich and selfish, right? [self-involving].

Note that the self-disclosing responses rely on worker recall and recounting of specific facts and events. The self-involving responses rely on emotional sharing of the worker's experience.

McCarthy and Betz (1978) found that self-involving responses cause a practitioner to be seen as more expert and trustworthy than do self-disclosing responses. Self-involving counselors elicited more references in subjects to themselves, while self-disclosing counselors elicited more questions about, and reference to, the counselor. The speculations of McCarthy and Betz about the advantage of a self-involving style are instructive. They suggest that the self-involving practitioner keeps the interview focus *on the client*; the self-disclosing practitioner draws attention to himself or herself and especially to the past, thus distracting clients from self-exploration.

To repeat, optimal authenticity is related to empathy. To be empathic is to be closer to the clients' experiences of themselves in the moment. With attention present-centered, the spontaneous, unguarded sharing of our felt reactions to the client is more likely. Where relevant, demographic or moderate personal disclosure is preferred to recall and the recounting of deeply personal experiences.

Congruence

Much that is spontaneous and unguarded in human communication is nonverbal. Several nonverbal behaviors of communicating empathy are related to a positive outcome of the helping relationship when they are congruent with corresponding verbal responses—that is, when practitioners' feelings and thoughts are in harmony with their words, tone of voice, facial expression, movements, and gestures. Interestingly, the presence of nonverbal behaviors thought to convey empathy alone does not generate a significant positive outcome for clients (Hill, Siegelman, Gronsky, Sturniolo, & Fretz, 1981). What has congruence of verbal and nonverbal expression to do with authenticity?

It might be said that words and tone convey the information and the feelings of the public self, while bodily gestures and timing behaviors convey the feelings of the private self. When the two messages are harmonious, authentic, and congruent, relating is probably occurring. When the words and tone say one thing and the gestures and body say another, the communicator is not fully aware of the extent, intensity, or complexity of his or her feelings and may be dissembling or maintaining an artificial front. Such incongruence can lead to a rapid loss of authenticity.

Inauthentic relating

Clinical experience tells us that when practitioners try to hide a natural response from a client, they may be successful in saying what they want to convey, but chances are that in the course of an interaction the nonverbal messages that convey contradictory messages will become apparent to the client. When the worker's whole self is not involved, when something is held back, the message to the client is one of insincerity, sowing a seed of distrust and a sense of uneasiness. Worse, the client may decide that certain emotions are not to be shared in the relationship, in which case a collusion of "what is acceptable to talk about" can develop in the relationship. In everyday relationships such collusions are enforced by social norms and are commonplace; but such collusion hampers relationships with clients, colleagues, and others in which trust is the foundation of collaboration.

Thus, naturalness and presence are necessary to authenticity; attempts to present a self at variance with the true self is phoniness. Remember, however, that feelings and thoughts themselves are often mixed and contradictory. Spontaneously communicating contradictory emotions is often a boon to clients who believe that contradictory feelings cannot exist. Indeed, sometimes the most authentic response is simply to admit that one does not know how one feels. Admitting to confusion is better than pretending to feel what is not felt. Practitioners are people, not gurus. Pretense to the latter is a prescription for phoniness.

AUTHENTICITY, ACCEPTANCE, AND TRUST

A client who senses acceptance, begins to feel secure in the helping relationship, and trusts the helper, can follow the helper's example and begin expressing moment-to-moment feelings nondefensively. Authentic relating is one means by which a client and practitioner can use the keys of trust and acceptance to unlock the doors of self-awareness.

A case example

In a relationship in which a degree of trust had developed, the following interaction (approximated) took place between a social worker and her client. Mr. R. was a large, aggressive man who had just come from an office where he had applied for food stamps. He opened the door while knocking loudly.

Mr. R.:   (Angrily) Mrs. P____, I want to talk to you!

Worker: (Surprised) Mr. R____, what's the matter? (Scooting her chair back a bit)

Mr. R.:   Those damn people at the food stamps, they treat you like dirt! I went in with my money like you said. I waited two hours. Then they said I couldn't buy no stamps unless I had a birth certificate or driver's license. I ain't got a driver's license or no birth certificate. So I go home and get the letter the courthouse sent about my birthday. They said that would do okay.

Worker: So what happened then?

Mr. R.:   (Getting angrier) So then I get back and wait another hour and they close for to go to lunch!

Worker: They went to lunch and left you sitting! (Eyebrows raised)

Mr. R.:   Yeah, so I wait for them to come back. Then they say the letter is okay, but I need a letter from my father saying he don't send me money. My old man never sent me no money. He wouldn't send no letter neither! (Hits the desk top with a loud thump)

Worker: (Jumping) Wow! They did get to you. That makes me mad too! They could have told you about that the first time. Tell me, did you blow up at them when you went to get the court letter?

Mr. R.:   Yeah, a little. The blue-haired lady got real mad.

Worker: I'm mad at the way they treat you, and you scare me a little too!

Mr. R.:   (Somewhat incredulous) I scare you? I'm really mad. I don't want to scare you, but I'm really mad! They treat you like dirt.

Worker: If they got scared do you think they would want to help you or give you the runaround?

Mr. R.:   That lady with the blue hair, she gave me the runaround.

Worker: If you hit her desk and she got scared of you, then mad at you, she probably wouldn't make getting stamps any easier—right?

Mr. R.:   Yeah, so what am I gonna do now?

Worker: (Shrugging) I don't know. . . . Let's cool off and think what to do. (Pause, she lightly pounds the desk top with fist) They *do* treat people like dirt sometimes.

In a context of acceptance and trust, the worker provided Mr. R. with a unique opportunity to become aware of his impact on others. The worker sensed her empathic response to Mr. R. but did not conceal her fear reaction with anger or a façade of professional cool; instead, she fed both reactions back to him. Through the good fortune of having an authentic worker, Mr. R. was made more aware that the anger he elicited in others was in part born of their fear of his own frustration and anger.

A worker's feelings toward a client are sometimes very difficult to deal with, however. One question invariably arises out of a consideration of authentic relating: If I don't like my client, do I tell him so? Won't this be damaging, giving him a burden he should not have to carry? The author's position is that if you harbor anger, dislike, strong attraction, or other intense feelings toward a client, the client will discern these anyway through your nonverbal communications, and they may then have an adverse effect on the relationship. In most cases, such feelings should be directly but tactfully shared and discussed with the client. Why?

Often, a worker's feeling responses toward a client are also to be found among significant others in the client's life. With an authentic worker, the client has a chance to learn firsthand about his or her effect on those others. For example, the mannerisms of a gregarious, assertive young man may be interpreted by women as overly aggressive and sexually provocative. A female practitioner may experience the mixture of attraction, fear, and anger that he typically evokes in women. If she shares her responses authentically, tactfully, and constructively, he may gain valuable insight into his manner of relating to women.

For another example, to achieve behavioral change among staff members, an aggressive administrator may use intimidation to the long-run detriment of morale and loyalty. An authentic worker might point out the intimidation and share the feelings accompanying the grudging compliance. An authentic response to intimidation or other manipulative behavior stops it dead in its tracks. This is because manipulation requires the persons manipulated to suppress, deny, or pretend that they operate without the fear played upon in the manipulation. When the feeling is shared publicly, the leverage of the manipulative behavior is lost, and, the manipulator presumably learns a valuable lesson about his or her impact on others.

Another reason for sharing intense feelings is that, in addition to providing feedback, it helps the person addressed to learn that relationships can persist without these feelings being acted on. Hence, a young woman may discover that she is attractive to an older male therapist. This may flatter, but it will also help her to learn that relationships with men are possible without a sexual component and that sexual attraction does not always require action. If an attraction or dislike is such that it interferes with an effective and appropriate helping relationship, transfer the client to another practitioner. With thoughtful planning and explanation, the client may be helped to see that the transfer is not uncommon and is no one's fault.

Finally, in some fields of practice there are clients who, because of severe problems or limited capacities, cannot handle intense feelings in a worker. Knowing who is vulnerable is largely a matter of judgment, but a practitioner might ask, is my communication regarding these feelings serving the client's needs or my own? Will the client's needs best be served by authenticity or by transfer to another practitioner?

CONCLUSION

Authenticity is important to effective relationships with clients, with colleagues, and with others whom one encounters both in practice and everyday life. Perhaps more than other skills, however, it is most easily employed in the special social situation of the helping or collaborative relationship with clients. This is because it is so interrelated with acceptance, empathy, and attention to the immediate interaction. At times it also entails a change of the normal rules of everyday interaction. Moderate self-disclosure, spontaneous self-involvement and congruency between one's verbal and nonverbal communications are empirically refined aspects of authenticity that make it a skill most special to the helping relationship.

Authenticity, together with empathy and acceptance, is a skill that can enhance the effectiveness of practice relationships. Social workers, as well as other practitioners who rely on relationships, know well that skills are not panaceas. A solid set of skills that can be universally effective with all kinds of problems, relationships, and levels of intervention, requiring nothing else, is a myth. Practice and practice relationships are far too complex for this to be the case (Parloff et al., 1978). Nevertheless, we are persuaded that these skills are helpful in most relationships that sustain our practice. Coupled with a knowledge of communication and a command of our specialty, authenticity as well as empathy and acceptance equips us for effective and rewarding practice.

STUDY QUESTIONS

1. Are there situations or relationships in which you find it difficult to be authentic? If so, what is it that makes authentic relating difficult for you?
2. How does practitioner authenticity help a client to change?
3. Give examples of demographic disclosure and personal disclosure.

4. State in your own words the difference between self-disclosing and self-involving responses within a relationship. Give examples of each.

5. How can admitting confusion or disclosing an inability to say exactly how you feel at a particular moment potentially help a client?

6. What kinds of feelings would you have difficulty being authentic about in a relationship with a client? How can these be handled in a manner constructive to both of you?

7. How can authentic relating facilitate practice relationships with boards of directors, employers, and supervisors?

8. Why is it difficult to manipulate an authentic person?

REFERENCES

Goffman, I. *Interaction ritual*. New York: Anchor Books, 1967.

Halpern, T. P. Degree of client disclosure as a function of past disclosure, counselor disclosure, and counselor facilitativeness. *Journal of Counseling Psychology*, 1977, *24* (1), 41–47.

Hill, C. E., Siegelman, L., Gronsky, B. R., Sturniolo, F., & Fretz, B. R. Non-verbal communication and counseling outcome. *Journal of Counseling Psychology*, 1981, *28* (3), 203–212.

Jourard, S. The effects of experimenter's self-disclosure on subjects behavior. In C. Spielberger (Ed.), *Current topics in clinical and community psychology*. New York: Academic Press, 1969.

Jourard, S. *The transparent self* (Rev. ed.). New York: Van Nostrand Reinhold Co., 1971.

McCarthy, P. R., & Betz, N. E. Differential effects of self-disclosing versus self-involving counselor statements. *Journal of Counseling Psychology*, 1978, *25* (4), 251–256.

Orlinsky, D. E., & Howard, K. I. The relation of process to outcome in psychotherapy. In A. E. Bergin & S. L. Garfield (Eds.), *Handbook of psychotherapy and behavior change: An empirical analysis*. New York: John Wiley & Sons, 1978.

Parloff, M. B., Waskow, I. E., Wolfe, B. E. Research on therapist variables in relation to process and outcome. In A. E. Bergin & S. L. Garfield (Eds.), *Handbook of psychotherapy and behavior change: An empirical analysis*. New York: John Wiley & Sons, 1978.

Rogers, C. R. The characteristics of a helping relationship. *Personnel & Guidance Journal*, 1958, *37* (1), 6–16.

Rogers, C. R. The necessary and sufficient conditions of therapeutic personality change. *Journal of Consulting Psychology*, 1957, *21* (2), 95–103.

Simonson, N. R. The impact of therapist disclosure on patient disclosure. *Journal of Consulting Psychology*, 1976, *23* (1), 3–6.

Truax, C., & Mitchell, K. M. Research on certain therapist interpersonal skills in relation to process and outcome. In A. E. Bergin & S. L. Garfield (Eds.), *Handbook of psychotherapy and behavior change*. New York: John Wiley & Sons, 1971.

6

Communication Principles
and Techniques

Skills and techniques are often distinguished from each other. To paraphrase *Webster's,* a *skill* is an ability that contributes to proficiency or expertness; a *technique* is a method or procedure. As discussed earlier, a practice relationship skill such as empathy, acceptance, or authenticity may comprise several principles and techniques. Chapter 6 examines principles from communication theory that are of value in enhancing skills and facilitating practice relationships.

The principles and techniques examined here compose a useful part of a practitioner's repertoire regardless of field of practice, level of intervention—individual, family, group, community organization, or administration—or theoretical approach. Each is introduced because of its wide applicability in enhancing practice relationships. Although some of the communication principles and techniques were developed from a practitioner-client relationship model, each has been found useful in other practice relationships as well.

Of course, many techniques are of special necessity to specific fields of practice and levels of intervention. Just as relationship skills are not sufficient to all practice relationships, the principles and techniques presented here are not *all one needs* regardless of the practice situation. Still, practice relationships can be considerably enhanced by a broader awareness of communication principles and a more concise foundation in widely applicable techniques.

After defining interpersonal communication and looking at some of its parts, we develop the concepts of *meta-communication* and *meta-awareness* that are the essence of good practice relationships. Relevant examples from practice will delineate some refined human communication behaviors and patterns that facilitate our understanding of individuals and relationships. Techniques of universal applicability in practice relationships will be enumerated. Finally, the chapter presents some techniques specific to practitioner adjustment, personal effectiveness, and health.

USEFUL CONCEPTS IN COMMUNICATION THEORY

The transfer of meaning

In the context of practice relationships, *communication* can be succinctly defined as the transfer of meaning. The units of meaning that are transferred are called *messages*. Figure 6–1 is a representation of communication concepts of importance specifically to professional practitioners and is derived from both practice experience and other models of interpersonal communication (McCroskey, Larson, & Knapp, 1971, p. 8; Harrison, 1974, p. 82).

In human beings, face-to-face communication is, of course, intimately interlaced with behavior. Each participant in the communication emits behaviors; some behaviors communicate, some do not. Some students of communication contend that all behavior is communication. Because it is impossible

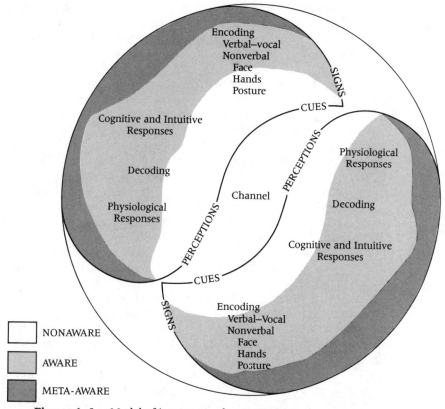

Figure 6–1.   Model of interpersonal communication

not to behave, "one cannot *not* communicate" (Watzlawick, Beavin, & Jackson, 1967, p. 49).

Practitioners typically use the terms *verbal* and *nonverbal* in everyday practice. Communication theory gives us more exact and useful terms. A verbal *sign* is a communication standing for something else. A nonverbal *cue* is a stimulus that we perceive. A communicator translates or *encodes* temporarily private meanings into signs and cues that form a composite message. Whether the communication is intentional or unintentional, the person originating a message will be termed *the sender.* The person responding to the message will be termed *the receiver.*

A person who perceives the behavior or messages of another has some sort of response, at least at a neurological and chemical level. The receiver may *decode* the sender's signs and cues, giving the communication meaning. If the response elicits further physiological, intuitive, and cognitive behaviors that hold meaning for the receiver, a communication has taken place. Although the sender may not *intend* to communicate a particular meaning, the receiver may pick up one nevertheless. A receiver might regard "Oh, my sore leg!" as an appeal for sympathy, for example, though the sender may have intended it only as an exclamation of fact.

The *channel* of communication is whatever carries the message. It may be a telephone line or the light and sound waves of a consulting room. The channel limits the perceptual apparatus the receiver can use to decode a message. We can only hear a telephone message; we can only see a typewritten message.

Having decoded the message, the receiver has both immediate and delayed physiological responses, some of which are experienced as feelings. The brain reacts with the translation of sensory information. Along with a verbal representation, the receiving person may generate visual, tactile, olfactory, or even taste images of the message's meanings, while a variety of verbally and nonverbally symbolized responses may further stimulate other internal responses. Some responses are accessible to the receiver's awareness; others are not. Some are verbally described; others are not. A portion of the message and even of the receiver's response to it may be out of the receiver's awareness. Some of the nonverbal responses, especially, may be communicated back to the sender in the form of cues below the receiver's level of awareness. For example, when George says that he has been fired, he not only sees the surprise on Bill's face but also detects a slight, momentary grin of satisfaction. Bill may be aware only of surprise.

Both the intentional and unintentional overt responses of the receiver constitute part of an encoded message returned to the sender. Facial cues, often subtle and short-lived, gestures, body postures, and nonverbal vocalizations, such as gasps or grunts, supplement and either ratify or detract from the meaning of the verbal message. Some of these parts of communication can be examined in the collaborative practice relationship. Pointing out and talking about nonverbal client communications enhances client and practitioner awareness of the feelings, conflicts, and deeper meanings suggested in their expression.

Meta-communication

When practitioners address the way they and their clients are communicating, they are *meta-communicating* (Watzlawick et al., 1967), or communicating about communication. As Figure 6–1 suggested, the two communicators are to some extent aware of their own internal responses, the nonverbal communications, and the pattern of interaction occurring between them. This *meta-awareness* is that part of us that is aware that we are aware and watches our responses. While communicating, people may be in touch with, and acknowledge the presence of, their meta-awareness to varying degrees.

Meta-communicating often entails use of the meta-awareness faculty. For example, a practitioner might say to a client, "As we've been talking, I've noticed that you wipe your eyes from time to time. I wonder whether you're aware of this too?" Such a statement may be a means of testing the accuracy of one's empathy or of addressing a suspected suppression of feeling. Other meta-communications: "You usually speak fluidly and easily. I just noticed that you began to chop your words off short and lower your voice when we brought up your relationship with Jack"; or "If I observe your face closely as I talk about school, you seem to begin to frown but quickly cover it up with a smile. Am I right?"

The meta-communication is not an interpretation but an observation. It does not suggest *why* a cue or sign is emitted or *why* a particular pattern has developed but rather points to it. This qualification is important to practitioners who believe, as the authors do, that in a pluralistic society many nonverbal communications have individual and particular meanings as opposed to universal meaning. We believe that these communications are best reexpressed in a more conscious way and interpreted by clients themselves. Enabling clients to reexpress more consciously what they communicate by other means can help to identify and resolve conflicted feelings.

Significant communications

Of first importance in enabling another to communicate more consciously is *clarification of meaning*. It has been suggested that persons with serious problems distort the *paralinguistics* (sounds and vocal qualities apart from the actual words) in the communications of others (Gill & Beier, 1973). Does a verbal or nonverbal part of a message carry meaning about which there is agreement? Does a gesture that denotes emphasis to a client connote aggression to the practitioner? Do the client's vaguely expressed thoughts of worthlessness portend suicidal intent to the practitioner? To these and the myriad other communications that constantly arise in the course of practice relationships, there is one emphatic answer: *check it out*, meta-communicate.

Harrison (1974) describes one kind of communication useful for practitioners to watch for—*adaptors*.

> Adaptors are nonverbal markers that originated in the satisfaction of self-needs, such as eating, cleansing oneself, scratching an itch, or rubbing tired eyes. Over time, however, they have become part of the individual's habit repertoire. They may be produced in adult life, in abbreviated form, quite divorced from their

original need-fulfilling context. They may suddenly emerge when an individual is feeling tense, or tired, or particularly relaxed and satisfied. The producer usually does not create the adaptor with the intent of communicating. The production may, in fact, be done with little awareness. But for the observer, the adaptor may have sign value; it may be an informative indicator of the performer's inner state [p. 101].

Gestalt therapists engage in frequent meta-communication about adaptor cues emitted by clients. Their intent is to bring to consciousness the feelings expressed by the adaptor but not verbally communicated by the client. An adaptor cue that carries meaning at variance with the verbal content of the client's message is often suggestive of a conflict within the client.

Disharmonious communication

Communication concepts can serve a diagnostic function for the helper. When nonverbal cues are not in harmony with the verbal content of a message, problems of self-awareness or conflicts are likely to be present. It might be hypothesized that what is verbally expressed, together with what is expressed nonverbally but with intent, together constitute a communicator's consciousness.

To the authors, the so-called unconscious mind is not a mysterious realm of instinctual forces but is composed of feelings and thoughts carried in the musculature and in the images of the nonverbal, intuitive mind. These thoughts and feelings are accessible, manageable, and growth-generating in the context of a helping relationship in which the practitioner is alert to the communication concepts that grant access to nonverbal domains. What is called the *unconscious* is finding expression in the whole of the client's communications. To the extent that the practitioner uses meta-awareness and meta-communication, the "unconscious" domain becomes more conscious, more manageable, and less powerful in controlling the client's behavior.

The mixed message and its underlying conflict can be directly addressed. One way to get at the underlying conflict (and its resolution) is to have the client engage in a mock dialogue between the opposing or alienated parts of the self (Levitsky & Perls, 1970, p. 145). For example, the client might be asked "Chuck, can you give a voice to the hand that has been clutching your leg?" The client might say "I'm Chuck's hand and I feel tense, tight, and I'm holding on . . . I'm afraid of letting go." To which the practitioner might respond "Can you use your imagination and put the part of you that wants to hold on into that empty chair and tell it how you feel about it?" The dialogue between the alienated parts of the person's self would continue until a creative synthesis had taken place leaving the client better integrated and aware of feelings that he could not previously verbalize.

In addition to adaptors, other kinds of nonverbal communications that practitioners can usefully address include body postures, gestures, and facial expressions. Most practitioners intuitively assign meaning to such behaviors, but in this regard a few cautious generalizations should be considered. For instance, popular books on nonverbal communication have assigned meanings to certain bodily postures, although the meaning of a given posture can vary from culture to culture, from social class to social class, and from individual to individual. Nevertheless, some practitioners assert that a *closed posture* (arms folded, legs crossed) denotes a closed attitude toward the subject at hand and that an *open posture* suggests the client is psychologically opening up.

Only when the relative comfort of the room temperature, the level of anxiety, the fear of sexual advance, the degree of affection from others, and a host of other variables are considered is it likely that the meaning a practitioner assigns to a particular open or closed stance parallels the meaning for the client. Here again, the practitioner functions best when noticing changes in posture and meta-communicating about their meaning with the client. Such an empathic approach is superior to making a covert interpretation that could be wrong or, worse, announcing a dogmatic interpretation that the client might accept without checking its meaning. The latter approach, which suggests a low level of empathy by the practitioner, might further confound a client's awareness of his or her own feelings.

More specificity is possible with gestures, in addition to their use as communicators of adaptor responses. Harrison (1974) outlines categories of hand gestures in Western society. *Illustrators* demark size, emphasize points of punctuation, follow the flow of the idea being expressed, or draw pictures in the air. *Regulators* interrupt with the palm facing another person, assert with the palm parallel to the ground, and turn the palm upward while offering an opinion or idea. *Emblems,* such as a *V* sign for victory, can denote verbal phrases (Harrison, 1974).

Facial responses exhibit qualities to be aware of in practice relationships. Facial cues are complex because they can be altered to modify the true representation of one's feeling state—sham smiles or insincere concern are obvious examples. Incompletely authentic persons might cover their true feelings with a mask of another affect, as some people mask fear with anger. Eventually, however, the covert feelings tend to find expression in posture, timing of responses, or patterns of behavior.

For the practitioner, the response of choice to nonverbal communications is meta-communication, a reality check that clarifies meaning and expands the communicator's awareness of what transpires in the relationship. The communication may take on certain patterns, which can also be observed from a perspective of meta-awareness. However, exercising judgment is critical in deciding the appropriateness, timing, and consequences of meta-communicating about them.

Communication patterns

When one person addresses another, there are four possible response patterns (Watzlawick et al., 1967).

1. *Accept.* The receiver can *accept* the communication and respond appropriately to the meaning of the message in keeping with the *line of face* (Goffman, 1967, pp. 5–46) the person must maintain in the interaction. "John, I like your new car!" "Oh thanks, I just got it today."

2. *Reject.* The receiver may *reject* the sender's message with a complete lack of direct response, ignoring the sender or turning away.

3. *Disqualify.* The receiver may *disqualify*—that is, communicate a response that invalidates the sender's or his own message as a relevant communication. He may radically change the subject, digress, or obscure his response in strange mannerisms that disqualify the other person's message and to some extent the other person's self.

Client: Why does he do such things to me?
Worker: I think we'd better talk about where you're going to live.

4. *Symptom utilization.* The receiver claims not to hear or comprehend the messages because of hearing deficit, insanity, or other defect or malady. It is suspected that symptom utilization is a part of the behaviors sometimes labeled *schizophrenic* (Watzlawick et al., 1967).

Rejection and disqualification.   Rejection and disqualification are quite common responses between marital partners, who are often entirely unaware of them. In one of my experiences, a married couple had a severe communication problem that adversely affected their entire relationship. A typical interaction will illustrate the problematic pattern.

Mr. and Mrs. Q. had sought help with a variety of marital problems and both looked miffed when they sat down in my office. Mrs. Q. looked down at her hands, fingering her dress. Mr. Q., who had slung his right arm over the back of his chair and crossed his legs, sat with his shoulder toward his wife. Sensing unpleasantness from their nonverbal messages, I began by asking an open-ended question.

Worker: What's happening?
Mr. Q.:   (Complaining tone) Our usual. We had a fight in the car on the way up.
Worker: (After a pause) I'd like to know what happened.
Mr. Q.:   We'll never get into anything now anyway.
Mrs. Q.:   We just don't get along. (Furtive glance at worker)
Worker: Kind of discouraged?
Mr. Q.:   I just asked what time the Smiths were coming over tonight, and I never really got an answer. (Gesture palm up toward Mrs. Q.)
Mrs. Q.:   You did too! (Angry, not looking up)
Mr. Q.:   I asked when the Smiths were coming over and you never really gave me an answer! (Arm extended hand up in amplified gesture to Mrs. Q.)
Mrs. Q.:   (Looking up briefly, disqualifying the implied question) Don't worry, we'll be ready!" (With this response, Mrs. Q. brings the issue into present time; they really want to show me what goes on)
Mr. Q.:   (Retreating to his first position with a tone of exasperation) I'm not *worried,* I just want to know when they're coming.
Mrs. Q.:   After dinner, do you want the precise minute? (Sarcasm and questioning expression masking anger)
Mr. Q.:   (Angry) Yes! I *know* after dinner; *when* after dinner?

Mrs. Q.: (Glances at the worker as if to say, "See what I mean?") Sal said sevenish. There, does that satisfy you? I suppose not.

Mr. Q.: I have to pick up Bo's ball for him before the league meet tomorrow night. (Gestures of explanation with both hands, softer tone, pause) Since I won't have time before or after dinner, do you think it would be possible for you to do it tomorrow?

Mrs. Q.: (Peeved, disqualifying) Where is *his* wife? Can't she pick up his little ball?

Mr. Q.: (With sarcasm and emphasis, smiling) She works. Do you think it would be possible?

Mrs. Q.: (Without looking up) I'm going to be very busy tomorrow.

Mr. Q.: (As if to score a point) Yes or no?

Mrs. Q.: I'll see.

Mr. Q.: (Rocks his head back, turns further away from Mrs. Q., and gestures with a mock suffering expression) You see, I can't *ever* get a straight answer!

The couple both knew that Mr. Q.'s last statement was true but were not clear why. Mrs. Q. frequently disqualified his communications. It emerged that she was afraid of him. As she tensed and responded to his anger, she would try to answer what she felt was the source of his questions and in that way avoid argumentative exchanges. When not to the point or when addressed to concerns that he did not actually have, her responses angered him, and the anger in his voice and gestures threatened her further. The Q.s were locked into a pattern that frequently *escalated* into serious confrontation. A hostile response from one was met with a similar response from the other. Considerable meta-communication and inquiry as to masked feelings eventually enabled a greater degree of empathy and communication to develop.

Symptom utilization. Briefly, a person might respond to others with a bizarre word-salad of scrambled or idiosyncratic speech, thereby effectively insulating himself or herself from the discomfort of having to relate to another person. The origins of this response lie in a history of relating to people who communicate double meanings. Double meanings are orders or assertions that say yes and no simultaneously. For example, "Johnny, *share your* truck with Billie!" To the child, "share" means "give up." His truck is his only as long as he controls it. In this example, the child's limited comprehension plays a part in creating the double meaning.

Later in life the double meanings may be strictly a function of the speaker. A teenager with a parent who says "Stay home and study or you will fail; you are such a poor student," or "You should play with your friends instead of fighting; no wonder they don't want to play with you!" is subject to the double meanings of his parent's invectives. When long perpetuated in a situation from which the person cannot escape, a *schizophrenogenic* ("schizophrenia-causing") pattern is learned. Instead of suffering the confusion and pain that he eventually comes to expect from *everybody,* not just significant others, the person either withdraws from human contact or keeps a distance between himself and others by means of symptom utilization.

Two patterns of communication.   In addition to ways of reacting to a message, there are two patterns of communication very useful for practitioners, especially when working with two or more people who communicate regularly. The patterns often hold clues to the nature of the relationship and are helpful in enabling people—especially marital partners—to learn new and more constructive ways of interacting.

1. *Symmetrical* (Watzlawick et al., 1967) interaction is most easily envisaged as an enlarged mirror image. Thus, in an interaction between marriage partners, one partner may raise his voice, while the other partner makes a one-up point and raises her voice, and so on until the two are shouting, each trying to top the partner's last dig. The language, volume, and seriousness of the charges leveled grow in intensity, or escalate—sometimes to physical blows.

2. A *complementary* (Watzlawick et al., 1967) pattern finds one partner usually one-up and the other usually one-down as with "My God you're sloppy!" "Yes, I guess I am." In the author's experience, this pattern accompanies a relationship in which one party is coercive and the other is obstructionistic. Frequently, the coerced partner withdraws and seeks gratification outside the marriage.

With some meta-communication and suggestion—even teaching—about how to vary the patterns of communication, destructive locking into one pattern or the other might be avoided. The escalating argument requires one partner to deescalate the encounter in some way. For instance, "Damn you, you're really unconcerned with my feelings!" "And are you at all concerned with mine?" Deescalating: "Yes, I am, and I guess I know you really are concerned for mine sometimes, too." A break in a complementary pattern is exemplified in the famous movie scenes of the 1930s wherein the henpecked husband—or sometimes the downtrodden wife—after years of mousey compliance, suddenly finds new courage and declares, "I'm in charge now!" To this, the surprised spouse responds with happy release from the top-dog role in the relationship.

Practitioners in administration and community organization and those who deal with advisory boards can benefit from being able to recognize symmetrical or complementary patterns that escalate or become rigid to the point of destructive consequences for the parties involved. Some thoughtful intervention at appropriate times can facilitate communication that has become stymied when these patterns are a source of difficulty.

In summary, certain communication principles have significant value for the practitioner in understanding and enhancing communication in practice relationships.

1. Potentially, all behavior can communicate, intentionally or unintentionally.
2. When a message is perceived by another, it is impossible *not* to communicate.
3. Many of the nonverbal cues of communication have private, idiosyncratic meaning for the client.

4. Nonverbal parts of communication, especially adaptors, are expressions of feeling states.
5. The best approach to communicating in practice relationships is to meta-communicate frequently and directly. This enhances empathic feedback to the other person, checks out and clarifies private meanings, and enhances awareness of feelings and of the relationship in both or all parties.
6. Awareness of the client's unspoken feelings can be a superordinate goal in all relationships, even the most pragmatic and tangibly task-oriented.
7. Harmony of verbal and nonverbal communications is a sign of personality integration and lack of conflict. Disharmonious communications are a sign of conflict and incongruence and an opportunity to address troubling feelings.
8. The categories of reactions to messages and communication patterns are helpful in understanding interactions and should be well integrated into a practitioner's knowledge of behavior.

Although not essential to successful practice, knowledge of communication principles can certainly enhance our practice relationships. Techniques are perhaps even more important tools. The next section presents some basic techniques of wide applicability.

TECHNIQUES

There exist a variety of classification or organizational schemes for traditional practice techniques. Our synopsis draws liberally on some contemporary and enduring schemes (CSSNY, 1958; Hollis, 1965; Reid and Epstein, 1972; Fortune, 1981). But we shall focus on techniques that are useful in collaborative practice relationships as well as in most fields of practice and at most levels of intervention. We have found, for example, that the same techniques valuable in helping a client assess a marital relationship are also valuable in helping members of a tenants' rights group assess their interpersonal situation in the context of a confrontation with landlord-owners. Both cases require the same skills and techniques in addition to specialized techniques. Most of the techniques discussed here are part of the common domain of social work and related professions.

Current classification schemes are useful for research purposes, but we believe that any classification of technique is somewhat artificial. Techniques overlap. They can be used in a variety of situations, and often one requires another to be effective. Some schemes delineate *supporting* and *sustaining* techniques from change-inducing techniques (CSSNY, 1958, pp. 15–19; Hollis, 1965, pp. 83–89). We see people as constantly in change and in constantly changing situations; so techniques can support only change. Similarly, it is impossible to separate the cognitive from the affective, personal from interpersonal situations, or emotion and behavior from their context. Though recognizing that the underlying theories of personality, behavior, and practice may differ, the realities of practice do not sustain a rigid application of these theories.

We organize the techniques presented here according to their degree of complexity. That is, some require only skillful phrasing of an empathic response; others require an elaborate teaching-learning-monitoring endeavor by the practitioner. Although we move from the simple to the most complex behaviors required for a given technique, the *value* of a given technique lies in its appropriateness to the client's problems and the relationship. This in turn rests upon the theoretical grounding and wisdom of the practitioner.

Asking questions

Class

Questions should be asked to elicit information or to sound out feelings, understanding, and perceptions. They have long been a standard technique (a standard source is Benjamin, 1969) and are the vehicle of other, more elaborate techniques.

In general, questions should be brief to be more easily understood. People under stress can usually attend to fewer ideas at a time—a short question gets better results. Good questions aim at *what* or *how* rather than *why* (Long, Paradise, & Long, 1981, pp. 24–25). That is, questions that get to behavior rather than motivation or causation avoid the trap of analyzing *why* people do what they do instead of looking for and changing problematic behaviors. A question that begins with *why* says in effect "Start thinking or remembering." Questions that begin with *what* or *how* say "Let's get to specifics." Finally, *why* questions can be implied criticisms of the person questioned. "Why did you say that?" can imply "You shouldn't have said that!" (Enright, 1970, p. 116).

Open-ended questions (unanswerable with a simple yes or no) can help other persons to share more about themselves or their situation. These are particularly useful to facilitate discussion in groups or to deepen the level of feeling in the group's interaction.

Note that the more skilled practitioners are, the fewer questions they are inclined to ask. This is because they have become comfortable with taking the risks necessary to make tentative empathic statements. Consider the following two responses:

Board Chair: I can't get these people moving. They just seem to be here to occupy a seat and take notes. They eat up time I could spend getting something done.
Worker: You think they lack motivation or don't know what they're supposed to do?
Worker: That's frustrating. I've noticed the note taking. I've seen your impatience.

The first response leads the chairperson to speculate on the board members' motivation and on their perception of their roles. Though useful, this forces feelings of frustration to take second place to a cognitive exercise. The second response asks no question; it focuses on what is observed and the chairperson's feeling. Most important, it requires no directed response to a question that overrides the feelings; it tells the chairperson that this worker is really with him; but it does not preclude an analytic approach to the situation.

Making a tentative, empathic statement instead of asking a question does not make the other person responsible for responding to you in as directed a way. In effect, you are beginning where they are. Usually, a moment's hesitation can render the felt-sense of the client as a statement rather than as a question. The effect on the interaction of minimizing questions is to elicit more—especially more feelings—from other persons. It also allows them to feel more comfortable in the relationship. They sense your empathy and do not feel continually compelled to respond to questions which can have a subtle straining effect for you both.

Seen in the worst light, asking many questions controls the interview in a way that ensures the other person always responds to you; you're never on the spot. This subtle form of dominance strikes a blow at the heart of egalitarian practice relationships and—more practically—can bring about an early termination of the relationship.

You must ask more questions at the beginning of most practice relationships. With clients, you are gathering information about the facts of the situation or problem confronting them. With colleagues, board members, and others, you are forming the factual and emotional basis of commonality. Questions are more frequent than when support of the relationship is preeminent. Nevertheless, a skillful practitioner relies on empathic statements and other techniques to a large degree, even in the information gathering periods. Questioning for information is not the only use of this technique, however. Questions are the vehicle of other techniques. One such technique useful at the start of a problem-focused relationship is partialization.

Partialization

Whether dealing with a client with an array of anxieties or a community leader confronted with a host of grievances by constituents, the people with whom we deal are usually feeling overwhelmed by their difficulties. How we begin to address these difficulties is greatly shaped by our theoretical approach to practice. But regardless of approach, partialization is a useful technique. It is a source of immediate relief and confidence, and it helps to form a contract in a collaborative relationship.

Partialization is simply breaking the situation or problem down into manageable parts. Many people feeling stressed enough to seek assistance see their hassles as a monolithic circumstance that renders them anxiety-ridden, helpless, or depressed; in short, the problem is overwhelming. Experienced practitioners are familiar with feeling momentarily overwhelmed themselves in response to a client's rendition of problems. But from this feeling of empathy with the client, genuine partialization can begin.

For example, a woman with several concerns—an incarcerated husband, a delinquent daughter, a small son, budget problems, and an obnoxious landlady for her cellar apartment—was mildly depressed. Circumstances prevented our tackling everything at once. After gaining an understanding of her array of problems, feelings, and strengths, we chose first to work on finding her a new place to live. We explicitly discussed how we could work on only one thing at a time, and Mrs. Jones found solace in this approach. "One thing at a time!" she repeated. We decided to look for a new and cheaper apartment.

We felt relatively good about the chances for success of this first goal. Moreover, we saw the dark, damp oppressive cellar in which she lived as representative of the "hole" Mrs. Jones had gotten herself into in her life. A pleasanter apartment for less money brought new motivation to Mrs. Jones. A renewed sense of mastery enabled her to approach management of her daughter, parenting of her son, and a decision about her marriage with more confidence.

A part of the problem array that is representative of the whole and that can be addressed with timely prospects of some success is where the work of most practice relationships should begin, whether they are clinical or administrative in nature. Partialization relieves anxiety, builds new confidence, and establishes trust in the relationship. Most approaches to practice incorporate partialization in the way they sort out goals and tasks, problems to be solved, or systems to be addressed. But whatever the approach, the problems, or situations addressed, practice relationships involve feelings. Encouraging their constructive expression is a technique of the utmost importance.

Encouraging expression of feelings

Often envisaged as steam in a boiling teapot or as water behind a dam, feelings can build up and, when not routinely vented, can explode in destructive ways. Some authors call encouraging the expression of feelings *ventilation* (CSSNY, 1958, p. 17; Hollis, 1965, pp. 96–97). But we might also think of feelings as physiological responses to stimuli. They can go unexpressed. They can be elicited repeatedly, by repetitive thoughts. They can be novel, uncontrived responses to situations. Or they can be the product of rumination and intent. In one way, feeling responses resemble other behaviors: they will recur when recurrence brings rewarding consequences.

Hence, expressing feelings of inadequacy that elicit support from others or expressing anger that compels cooperation are in a sense rewarded by the reactions of those to whom they are communicated. So, feelings that are initially reactions to novel situations can become emotional styles. Sometimes these may bring short-term advantages or compliance from others, but they may also cause relationships to wear thin.

When encouraging feeling expression, the worker's own notions of how human feelings operate will become important. Certain generalizations are helpful with most practitioners.

1. Feelings are of the *present*. Asking a person to recall a specific incident will usually elicit feelings in the present about that incident and others like it. This is better than asking a person how he or she feels about a situation in general.

2. A tentative empathic statement is better than a question. Focusing on what you sense the other person to be feeling makes some expression possible. A general question may elicit so many feelings at once that a client may draw a blank or be unable to sort out a response.

3. One feeling can hide another. Anger, for example, can cover fear. Often simply asking a person whether she can sense another feeling behind the anger is enough to evoke an underlying anxiety.

4. Feelings that have become part of a rigid style that blocks action or coping can also block progress in a practice relationship. A colleague who would rather complain than take cooperative action, a client who cries whenever the subject of goal setting arises, may both be expressing feelings rather than acting on the world. This may be because they are used to others acting for them and they expect you to do the same. The relationship seems to be frozen in repetitive feeling expression that does little either to release energy or to originate new approaches. In this case, direct description of what you see and how you regard it as a barrier to progress is in order.

Ms. Brown was a young woman who had had a supportive client-counselor relationship with a male counselor throughout college. She had never dated, however, or established a relationship of any length with another man, though she wished to. She sought help for a variety of seemingly minor problems, but it quickly became clear that she wanted help in working out her feelings toward relationships with men.

It developed that occasional liaisons were soon broken off. Although she would repeatedly begin to look at problematic aspects, she would soon begin to cry and bemoan her inadequacy. When she recalled the years with her college counselor, it became apparent that she had done the same with him. She had gotten support and attention but had avoided taking risks in relationships that were less one-sided. When shown that her frequent tears interfered with her looking at new ways of being, risking, and relating, she was able to move to some beneficial objectives for her relationships and begin to test them out.

Questions and empathic statements are not the only ways of helping people to express feelings; the use of dreams and "role dramatization" are examples. But there are times when feelings spill out with great intensity with seemingly little encouragement. If this occurs very early in the relationship, it is beneficial to prepare the person for feelings of guilt or shame that may naturally follow from "telling a stranger so much." A simple expression that sharing is OK in a client-practitioner relationship is usually enough to prevent a client's failure to keep appointments because of a feeling that too much has been exposed too soon.

Universalization and reassurance

Universalization (CSSNY, 1958) is a simple technique that relates to the common feeling that one is hopelessly alone in the kind of problem or the kind of feelings one has. *Universalization* is simply sharing with clients that they are not unique or strange; perhaps many others have had the same dilemmas, thoughts, or feelings. This should be based, of course, on some reality, either practice experience or knowledge of the problem.

Client: I sometimes feel like I hate my kids—just *hate* them! Then I think, what kind of mother am I? I shouldn't be a mother.

Worker: These feelings of intense frustration and anger are there, but they're not acceptable. Kind of like a parent should feel love but never hatred.

Client: You must think I'm a real witch.

Worker: I think nothing of the sort. In fact, in my experience most parents have such feelings from time to time. Most also find them discomforting when they do. It's as if the angry, even terrible, thoughts mean we're bad parents."

Universalization might be seen as a supportive technique. It provides some reassurance, so that clients feel less alone and able to move ahead as others have.

Closely related to universalization, *reassurance* (CSSNY, 1958, p. 16; Hollis, 1965, pp. 85–88; Fortune, 1981, p. 98) means reminding people or groups of their strengths and capacities to meet the probable realities that confront them. It is not a flippant "Everything will turn out all right." To be effective, reassurance must be based on the practitioner's felt response to the other person's ability and opportunity to cope. Genuine reassurance unburdens and motivates.

Client: I don't know if I can be that tough. When she starts to turn on those tears and calls me "Mama," I get easy.

Worker: Now you know the consequences of not setting limits—and you're not only a kind person but a good parent. You'll handle it.

Here a mother is reassured both about her personal qualities that have been manipulated in the past and about her ability to understand and handle her role as parent. Reassurance goes hand in hand with people trying out new behaviors and can be used in innumerable ways to support constructive change.

Providing information and advice

Providing information and advice are usually considered to be separate techniques, but we believe that they are very much the same. Providing information is simply giving people facts about reality that they can use to understand or achieve their goals.. Giving advice is essentially providing information about their prospective behavior or choices. Voluntary clients not only expect information and advice, they expect practitioners to advise more than they usually do in collaborative relationships (Reid & Shapiro, 1969). The author's practice experience suggests that persons of low socioeconomic status or with low verbal skills want advice more than others.

Giving people information that they need to cope with or change some aspect of their environment is a part of egalitarian practice. We are not in practice to mystify or pretend to esoteric knowledge that cannot be shared. Telling a client to look for ways a problematic behavior is reinforced, how best to approach a powerful bureaucrat, or where to find the local tenants' organization are all forms of information we can provide.

Advice is more complex because it usually assumes that the information includes suggestions about *how to proceed,* which are based on *values.* Practitioners should therefore clarify the values on which their advice is based and allow the person being advised to check that advice against their own values. What this basically means is allowing the other person to know where you are coming from with your advice.

Bad advising avoids revealing values. For example, some practitioners hold strong values regarding the nature of the family and the role of women in it so that women feeling stress in marriage have frequently been advised to go home and redouble their efforts as wives and mothers. In such a value framework, if there are marital problems such as occasional physical abuse, they are related to the women's inadequacy. Bad advice may well be meeting the practitioner's needs or values at the expense of the client's best interest. If values are unstated, the client has only the authority of the practitioner to support the advice.

Practitioners should therefore be up front with their values and the sources of the advice they give. For example, "As you know, I favor supporting a marriage relationship whenever possible. You'll have to consider this when I suggest trying a few things before calling it quits. It's really going to be your decision what to do." This statement is important in advising because it makes clear that responsibility rests with the person advised.

Finally, advice that does not work may be due to resistance to practitioner authority or lack of motivation. The refrain "I did what you said, and it didn't work" may be generated by a healthy need to remain autonomous of practitioner authority, or it may simply signal bad advice. In any case, advising is providing people with more options from which to choose than they had before.

Testing reality

One of the greatest services a practitioner can render is to help another person test reality. This technique is not confined to clinical practice with clients whose ability to perceive reality is hampered by inordinate, ego-shattering stress. A colleague afraid of a supervisor's assessment, an administrator concerned about staff morale, a friend uneasy about a physical health symptom—all are in circumstances in which reality testing is in order to preclude worry or groundless action.

Testing reality may be as simple as encouraging someone to go to a physician and check out his or her fear; it may entail reassuring an intoxicated drug user about the nature of the immediate environment. It might involve introducing someone to an authority or calling a staff meeting to check out feelings. People stop testing reality when they are afraid or when their mental models of their interpersonal reality supplants their checking out what is true (Lemert, 1962). Simply asking him what he thinks may be sufficient to test out reality for one person. Discussing logically the perceptions, alternatives, and consequences of actions are ways of helping individuals and groups stay in touch with reality.

Groups can become closed systems the members of which support one another's misconceptions or wishful thinking without going outside the group to check the reality of their views. The authors have observed several losing causes in political elections and union organizing that could have profited by going beyond the in-group to learn the reality of the group's situation. Parenthetically, whole societies can be caught up in a tragic failure to test reality, choosing instead to rely on charismatic leaders or designated authorities to tell the people what is real and right. In the past, such episodes have endangered and destroyed millions of lives. Today they can endanger not only human life but the prospects for continued life on the planet.

Testing reality is synonymous with empirical testing. The fundamental question is "what is real?" Individuals, groups, and societies must base their actions on reality if they are to survive. Practitioners may not have the inside scoop on what reality is, but we have an obligation to enable others to try to find out.

Clarifying feelings

The ancient Taoists were fond of pointing out the two-sided, or polar, nature of life. There is seldom good without bad or strength without weakness to define it. Night requires day and day requires night for either to exist as a concept. Feelings, too, are seldom without opposite counterparts. Even less frequently do feelings about relationships remain all positive or all negative; they are usually mixed. But romance, strict notions of various social roles—mother, son, and so forth—and sometimes religion tell us that feelings are to be one way and unchanging. Many clients believe that they are evil, less than human, or sick if they have mixed feelings, especially toward loved ones.

To help a client learn that mixed or even strongly ambivalent feelings are normal in most close human relationships (universalization) can be liberating. This is especially true for young people with more rigid notions about how people are supposed to be in a love relationship or in a parenting role. *Clarification* is simply the technique of helping individuals to sense and express the feelings they have. In this process they may learn words for sensations they harbor but could not verbally express. They may also discover anger beneath attraction or vice versa.

The process involved with clarification of feelings is primarily one of providing empathy while deliberately exploring a client's feelings about a particular relationship, a situation, or person. That feelings can be mixed or contradictory, that they can be intense, and that they can be expressed nondestructively are all potentially useful discoveries for clients in the context of a relationship that allows feelings to be labeled and clarified. In essence, clarification helps people to vent feelings and to label them. With words to describe how we feel, we have a better chance of understanding ourselves and communicating with others.

Separating desire from expectation

Social roles are made from prerogatives and expectations. The expectations others have of us shape the conduct of our social roles. Sometimes our self-concept includes deep and intense ideals, commitments, or preferences. When the expectations that others have for us in our current roles conflict with earlier acquired ideas about our self and our desires, considerable stress can result. The radical shifting of roles in response to contemporary economic and technological changes leaves many people conflicted and stressed.

For example, marital partners may discover they have radically different expectations of each other. A young women aspiring to a career outside the home may find that her spouse, parents, and in-laws expect her to devote herself to being a wife and mother exclusively. Or a young woman may discover that her peers expect her not to want to give birth and to parent. A man may question the role of money-maker or soldier because of personal desires that conflict with standard role expectations.

Such a conflict often manifests itself in the form of resistance to role tasks or in poor role performance by otherwise adequate people. A housewife who was unable to meet her spouse's and in-laws' expectations regarding the appearance of the home or the preparation of meals found herself exhausted. Repeated efforts to establish goals that would enable her to function better as a homemaker (which she claimed to aspire to) were largely unsuccessful. Finally, an application of the techniques of separation of desire from expectation went roughly as follows.

Class

Client: So I just sit. I want to be a good wife, but I don't want to clean up or fix dinner. Things just go to hell. Jim comes home expecting a decent house and a meal after working all day but finds me and everything in a mess.

Worker: It's as if what you want and what you do don't match. This seems unfair to Jim.

Client: Yep. He ought to throw me out. His parents would never approve of that—even though they don't approve of me.

Worker: Jim should reject you. His parents don't approve. You're not pleasing these important people. Do you want to?

Client: Yes, I wanted to be a decent wife.

Worker: What do you want now? We've tried several approaches. But one can only move from where one is. What do *you* want now?

Client: (Sigh) I don't want to be responsible for the house and cooking.

Worker: What *do* you want?

Client: Something interesting to do. College was stimulating. I want something interesting, exciting. The wife role isn't it—God, if they could hear me!

Worker: They would disapprove?

Client: I'm not the little doll they want.

Worker: It sounds like there is a difference here in you. You want to please Jim and his parents, yet you want to find something more interesting to do than the way they define you.

Client: That's why I'm such a slob—I'm rebelling, right?

Worker: Maybe. What do you want to do?

Client: Figure out some way to get into some things I'd like. Gads, this is going to be heavy!

Worker: Other people are going to have to get used to the idea that you are making some changes. Let's keep your wants in mind, too.

Client: (Laughing) I'll start a list. *-Worker picks up on contradiction*

-What do you really want?

Refocusing to the moment

Feelings are experienced in the present, yet much of human interaction is carried on as if feelings and most of our senses don't exist. One way feelings and senses are blocked out of awareness is by concerning oneself with the should-have-been or the might-be of life. In practice, this sad propensity manifests itself in excruciating recollection of problematic events which client and practitioner dwell on analytically as if thereby to divine present and future behavior. This approach may be yet another misappropriation of psychoanalytic techniques. Often the practitioner is made into a computer to "figure out" the client's problems, behavior, motives, and feelings.

Behavior is best changed as it occurs. Troublesome relationships are best worked out in the present. While refocusing to the moment does not preclude a look at a problematic situation, it is the practitioner's responsibility to refocus attention to the present. "What are the feelings you feel now about that as you remember it?" or "Your fight yesterday was evidently a serious one from what you've said. Can we look at where we are now and talk about it?" There are many ways to bring another person back to the present—or as the Gestalt therapist, Fritz Perls, said, to lose the mind and "come to your senses" (Perls, 1970, p. 38).

In the present, we can see our effect on others and their response more clearly. We can sense our own feelings and how we express them and, most important, we can become aware of the short-term consequences of our actions and of ways to modify them to bring about different results.

Reflecting

Reflecting is closely related to *interpretation, confrontation* (CSSNY, 1958, p. 18) and *person-situation reflection* (Hollis, 1965, pp. 100–116). As used here, reflecting is a technique of thinking aloud about other persons, their behavior or relationships. Destructive or problematic patterns of behavior can be identified. Motives not fully conscious to the client can be speculated about. Behaviors can be interpreted as the product of unmet needs or conflicts. Clients can be confronted with behaviors for which they do not consider consequences. The many uses of reflection clearly overlap with other techniques.

Generally, reflection aims at understanding clients' behavior and situations. Like empathy, it is best done in a hypothetical vein because people often resist seeing the problematic sides of themselves. To be most effective, reflection should be used together with considerable support for the client's strengths. If what one reflects on is likely to be anxiety-provoking for the client, timing and judgment are important.

Client: So I quit and went back home. I took some classes but dropped them. Mom paid the tuition, so now I owe her $800.
Worker: So your try at moving out didn't work out so well.
Client: She took me around to find an apartment and paid the deposit. But I can't get enough for rent with my part-time job. I'll have to let it go.
Worker: Where will you live?
Client: At home I guess.
Worker: John, as I think about your recent doings, I see you moving out, moving back, moving out. You seem to defeat yourself when you're on your own, and you seem to alienate your mom when at home. It's as if you want to be on your own and yet you don't. But you don't want to be on the apron string either.

Client: I guess that's true when you look at it. I can see I do it to myself.
Worker: Can we sort it out—who's in charge here—which part of you?

Of course, much needs to be done to work out John's ambivalence and dependency-autonomy needs, but recognizing the behavior pattern from reflection is a first step.

Role rehearsal

Role rehearsal is a technique useful with mildly retarded persons, young people, or clients trying out new roles with little background or experience from which to draw in performing the new role.

The practitioner may be running a group in which parents can try out new parenting techniques by assuming the role of parent for the group. The author has found that a number of marginally retarded young people profited from rehearsing an employment interview, playing themselves first and then the employment interviewer. This role rehearsal enabled them to gain a grasp of the social situation that was entirely novel for them and for which private fantasy could not have prepared them.

Role rehearsal is used in unique ways with marital pairs flexible enough to adopt each other's roles in various interchanges. Some practitioners will have a couple stop in the middle of an argument and switch seats and sides. Compelled to argue sincerely the other's point of view, they gain an empathic grasp of their partner's point of view and feelings.

Role rehearsal requires participants to be serious. Anxiety will sometimes cause a person rehearsing a role to laugh and step out of the role as if to say, This is not really me! If they can be helped to understand this response, clients, colleagues, and others may find the technique invaluable.

Direct intervention

Direct intervention (CSSNY, 1958, p. 18) consists in doing something tangible for another person or client and is a departure from the role definition of practitioner as limited to verbal interaction in the confines of the office. For a community organizer or group worker with task-oriented groups or institutional living situations, direct intervention is a matter of course. For clinical practitioners, it is a useful departure from traditional technique. The authors have taken passport pictures, given rides, helped to fill out applications, written reference letters, built furniture, refurbished homes, picketed, directed craft activities, and taken part in many other direct interventions in behalf of clinical practice relationships.

Direct intervention builds trust, liberates a practitioner from traditional role limits, breaks down class and status barriers, and provides help not structured into formal social service institutions. The two cautions here are to use one's skills within the realm of one's professional expertise and to keep one's identity separate from that of the client.

Meditation

To the helping professions meditation is a relatively new and unique technique—unique in being useful for well-being of clients and practitioners alike. Meditation is a complex behavior. Briefly, meditation is learning to focus and hold one's attention on one thing. Though simply stated, the task itself is quite challenging. The object of attention can be a design (*mandala*), a word repeated to oneself or in a group (*mantra*), an idea or mental image, a part of the body, a sunset, or breath. Body postures range from the cross-legged *lotus* posture to simply sitting upright in a chair. (Sitting upright is important to prevent one's falling asleep and to prevent body cramps from a slumped posture.)

Beginning meditators will try the task for 10–15 minutes, working up to 20–30 minutes a session. The task itself is difficult because of interruptions. Noises, bodily discomfort, daily concerns, worries, fantasies, memories—all encroach on the task of keeping one's mind on the object of meditation. Usually a meditator must continually refocus diverted attention back on the meditation object. The discovery that one is not always able to control one's attention is sufficiently disconcerting to some to cause abandonment of the technique before giving it a good try.

Gradually, periods of concentration come which eventually give rise to feelings of ease, rest, confidence, and quiet. Euphoria and oceanic feelings are also reported. Sometimes one recalls intense or seemingly insignificant events from the past. When coupled with the relaxed body, it may be that one undergoes a kind of discharging of emotional tension or desensitization to noxious memories (Keefe, 1979, p. 321). Meditators *seem* to experience a release of energy and a feeling of general well-being. But what are the goals of meditation technique for practice?

For the client—relaxation, gaining a broader perspective on the small things that make life a hassle, and increased self-awareness, especially of feelings. These hypothesized benefits appear to have some basis according to the author's clinical experience. For the practitioner, three benefits of meditation may transfer to practice. First, one's feelings are more easily sensed. Second, by allowing thoughts to enter and leave conscious attention without clinging to them, we can perceive without categorizing or labeling too quickly. This kind of perception helps us to allow clients and others to speak for themselves and affect us as they are. Third, meditation can help to clear our tension and thoughts between events so that we can give full attention to whatever is before us.

Helping practitioners can teach meditation when we have learned the technique ourselves and practiced it for some time. There are several good sources for learning to begin meditating (Kaplean, 1967; White, 1974; Costain, 1975), and various programs are available to teach meditation (see, for example, Mahesh, 1968). The best way to become proficient in this new technique, either for your own benefit or for use with clients, is to learn from a professional colleague. For an account of how meditation may enhance practice, research into its effects, and a guide to its use as an advanced practice technique, see Keefe (1979, pp. 313–331).

Rapport and termination

The various theoretical approaches to practice usually set forth consecutive phases of the practice process with each client or group or intervention. These phases are sometimes tied to perceived phases of practitioner-client relationships; others serve primarily to organize the presentation of practice technique. In some respects, phases of practice are natural realities; in others, they are artificial forms imposed on the relationships which must be used flexibly in the real world of practice. Examples include the beginnings, middle, and endings of the functional approach or the steps of the problem-solving approach. Siporin (1975) incorporates five processes: engagement, intake and contract, assessment, planning, intervention, and evaluation and termination.

Theoretical approach will determine the particular steps or phases of the practice process one follows. With our focus on practice relationships and our interest here in identifying techniques of general usefulness, two processes implied by most schemes are noteworthy.

Building rapport starts at the beginning of every relationship. When two or more people meet in relatively low-structure situations to begin to relate for an extended period of time, rapport is important. *Rapport* means agreement or relationship, especially a harmonious relationship. As a technique, it involves using each of the relationship skills we have studied toward achieving an agreement to work well together. Commonalities are emphasized over differences. Parties to the new relationship are mutually responsive. Perhaps more than any other technique, building rapport brings into play the practitioner's unique personality and creative use of relationship skills.

At the end of a relationship, *termination*—as much a process as a technique—becomes important. Termination of a relationship is classified as a technique because, despite its inevitability in all relationships, it can involve specific initiatives on the practitioner's part. Here we will mention a few that can be useful in any relationship that has lasted long enough for affectional ties or emotional investment to occur.

Compared with human relationships outside of practice, practice relationships usually come to unnatural ends. For instance, the members of a small group who have worked through difficulties together and who live in close proximity would develop natural and mutual affinities which would draw them together for socializing, support, and enjoyment. In stable communities such groups can endure throughout the members' lives. In contrast, a small therapy or support group is usually seen as terminating when involvement and interest decline and members have grown in ways that allow them to reach out to new endeavors or relationships that compete with group involvement. When growth-producing relationships end, a regression is natural.

Parties to a relationship may behave as they had during the relationship's early stages. Old problems and fears may temporarily resurface. These regressions can be seen as attempts to perpetuate the relationship or group. Practitioners should discuss the anticipated last interview, visit, or meeting well in advance to allow for feelings about termination to come out, both in themselves and in others. Practitioners, too, sometimes find termination difficult and experience feelings of loss and sadness. We may cling to a client or group that has provided a rewarding practice experience and of whom we have grown fond. Insight can be a useful guide during termination.

Again, authenticity and empathy are central to successful termination, but there are other, specific things we can do. Some practitioners like to tell clients that "the door is always open," which is appropriate for some relationships. We prefer to tell clients and colleagues that we'll be thinking of them and to drop us a note or call and let us know what they are doing. This approach conveys to clients that they are valued, but it does not suggest that they are expected to fail or to need help again. If they do, they know where you are. Of course, the expectations one leaves with a client are carried by far more than closing words. Understanding, acknowledging, and constructively sharing our own feelings is important to successful termination.

CONCLUSION

Chapter 6 has looked briefly at communication principles and techniques that can be applied in practice relationships. The particular theoretical approaches you are learning will introduce you to many other, more specialized principles and techniques. The secret to developing a good repertoire of technique to supplement practice skills is to *try them out*. Like learning any very complex behaviors, using new techniques entails a degree of risk to ourselves, but having a compendium of principles and techniques on hand to refer to and try is the best way to develop practice effectiveness. To limit ourselves to a few tools is ultimately to limit the kinds of relationships we can build. Ideally then, we should discover and generate new principles and techniques throughout our practice careers. What we have learned here can provide a basis for continued growth regardless of our approach, field, or level of practice intervention.

STUDY QUESTIONS

1. Give examples of cues we use in everyday interaction.
2. Actors must be very meta-aware of their performance and must meta-communicate about their performance with a director. In what situations in your experience have you had to meta-communicate to be more effective?
3. Have you experienced disqualification of an attempt to communicate? How did you feel? What kinds of people in our society frequently have their messages disqualified?
4. What are some advantages of asking open-ended questions with clients?
5. What is a drawback of asking a client many questions? Why is it better to make tentative empathic statements than to ask questions?
6. Some believe that the mark of a good practitioner, at any level of practice, is the capacity to structure a novel situation and to partialize the problems confronted. Why? Do you agree?
7. What do we mean when we say "Feelings are of the present"?
8. Why should a client be cautioned that advice, when given, arises from the practitioner's values?
9. How can we help persons to test reality? How is this useful to them?
10. How can meditation theoretically help us to cope with practice?
11. Why are *building rapport* and *termination* referred to as process techniques? What skills foster rapport?

12. A good way to make techniques a permanent part of your repertoire is to review them in the text and then to try them out in practice or in everyday relationships. This will help them to come to mind naturally, and it may also enhance your relationships. Take care, however, not to turn friends and family into clients unwittingly.

REFERENCES

Benjamin, A. *The helping interview.* Boston: Houghton Mifflin, 1969.

Community Service Society of New York (CSSNY). *Method and process in social casework.* New York: Family Services Association of America, 1958.

Costain, E. E. *Meditation for peace of mind.* New York: Dell, 1975.

Enright, J. B. An introduction to gestalt techniques. In J. Fagan & I. L. Shepherd (Eds.), *Gestalt therapy now: Theory, techniques, application.* Palo Alto, Calif.: Science & Behavior Books, 1970.

Fortune, A. E. Communication processes in social work practice. *Social Service Review,* 1981, *55* (1), 93–128.

Gill, D. P., & Beier, E. *Nonverbal communication* (Taped presentation). New York: Psychology Today Cassettes, 1973.

Goffman, E. *Interaction ritual.* New York: Anchor/Doubleday, 1967.

Harrison, R. *Beyond words: An introduction to nonverbal communication.* Englewood Cliffs, N.J.: Prentice-Hall, 1974.

Hollis, F. *Casework: A psychosocial therapy.* New York: Random House, 1965.

Kaplean, P. *Three pillars of Zen.* Boston: Beacon Press, 1967.

Keefe, T. Meditation and social work treatment. In F. J. Turner (Ed.), *Social work treatment: Interlocking theoretical approaches* (2nd ed.). New York: Free Press, 1979.

Lemert, E. M. Paranoia and the dynamics of exclusion. *Sociometry,* 1962, *25* (1), 2–20.

Levitsky, A., & Perls, F. The rules and games of gestalt therapy. In J. Fagan & I. L. Shepherd, *Gestalt therapy now: Theory, techniques, application.* Palo Alto, Calif.: Science & Behavior Books, 1970.

Long, L., Paradise, L. V., & Long, T. J. *Questioning: Skills for the helping person.* Monterey, Calif.: Brooks/Cole, 1981.

Mahesh, Maharishi Yogi. *Transcendental meditation.* New York: Signet, 1968.

McCroskey, J., Larson, C., & Knapp, M. *An introduction to interpersonal communication.* Englewood Cliffs, N.J.: Prentice-Hall, 1971.

Perls, F. S. Four lectures. In J. Fagan and I. L. Shepard, *Gestalt therapy now: Theory, techniques, application.* Palo Alto, Calif.: Science & Behavior Books, 1970.

Reid, W. J., & Epstein, L. *Task-centered casework.* New York: Columbia University Press, 1972.

Reid, W. J., & Shapiro, B. L. Client reactions to advice. *Social Service Review,* 1969, *43* (2), 165–173.

Siporin, M. *Introduction to social work practice: Model and method.* New York: Macmillan Co., 1975.

Watzlawick, P., Beavin, J., & Jackson, D. *Pragmatics of human communication.* New York: W. W. Norton & Co., 1967.

White, J. (Ed.). *What is meditation?* New York: Anchor/Doubleday, 1974.

7

Sexism in Social Service Relationships

Dolores H. Niles

The social service field and social work as a profession evidence sexism in a number of ways. That social work has been viewed traditionally as a woman's profession is reinforced by employment statistics over several decades. From the 1950s to a 1975 National Association of Social Workers (NASW) membership survey, occupational data show that the number of women changed only slightly, from 70% to 63%, in terms of the percentage employed in the field. This concentration of women in the delivery of social services bears a direct relation to traditional female roles in which women are viewed as nurturers, serving the needs of others for comfort, sustenance, and growth. Social work and social services are concerned with the disadvantaged and oppressed. Several writers have noted this caretaker aspect of social work.

As men have entered the field, recruitment and employment patterns have demonstrated some interesting sex-linked effects. Men have moved in disproportionate numbers into community organization and administration, areas that carry higher status and salaries within the profession. Through the late 1960s, men also dominated deanships and professional associations. One other indicator—attainment of the doctoral degree—demonstrates another advantage for men. A survey of social work doctorates from 1920 to 1968 reveals that 61% were awarded to men, 39% to women (Kravetz, 1976b).

In a 1976 NASW study, only 16% of all social service agencies had female administrators, and men still had higher salaries. National association leadership had become 50% female, and there had been a slight increase in female deans in schools of social work, but the number still represented less than 15%. These percentages reinforce a division in the performance of social service functions based on traditional sex roles. Men attain the more valued, powerful positions, and women fill the service roles.

Another evidence of sexism in the social service field is that women make up the majority of clients. Women are more devastatingly impacted by desertion, divorce, death of a spouse, lack of child care, lack of job skills, and low paying employment. Most families receiving Aid to Families with Dependent Children (AFDC) are headed by women; two-thirds of the 4–5 million aged, disabled, or blind recipients of Supplemental Security Income (SSI) are women. Most social agencies serve more women than men. Many programs in which women are clients reflect condescending and discriminatory policies and practices. Women are often described demeaningly as hysterical, manipulative, lazy, ignorant, and immoral. Agencies control and infantalize their women clients by means of primitive policies and practices which severely restrict women's personal choices and decisions.

In recent years, studies of sexism in social work have focused on the content of professional education, the attitudes of practitioners, and the context of the agencies and policies that shape the service delivery systems. Chapter 7 seeks to reveal the roots of sexism in our sociocultural and political heritage. We examine how these deeply ingrained attitudes and behaviors, if unattended, are reinforced by educational content and the attitudes and behaviors of educators, supervisors, and colleagues. We also examine how sexism affects the expectations of clients, agency personnel, and policy makers, as well as the social, economic, and political climate of the organizations and communities in which we all function. Finally, we examine a model for integrating higher levels of sensitivity into learning, practice relationships, and the work place.

HISTORICAL ROOTS OF SEXISM

Many centuries separate the enslavement of vanquished barbarians and the appropriation and rape of their women by conquering armies from the modern cultural imperatives that the female body is the female destiny and that it is unfeminine to be capable, to achieve, and to succeed. Nevertheless, this pattern can be traced throughout the history of civilization. The political, economic, and (often) religious roots of all oppression take their strength from the conquest and oppression of the defeated "inferior" group. People of different regions, skin color, religious and social practices have been subjugated for their economic and political value to the victors. Examples throughout history include the expansion of the Roman Empire and the conquests by the Vikings and the Spanish Conquistadors, to name but a few. Herein, too, lies the basis of racism.

The expression of hostility and degradation toward the vanquished males was further demonstrated in the rape and sexual objectification of their women, thereby appropriating the weakest of the vanquished and adding the dimension of sexism. Women were used for their work value, for sexual gratification, and for bearing new generations of slaves. This collective nationalistic behavior persisted through the centuries, establishing class-oriented boundaries and role behaviors for the leaders, the laborers, and the nurturers, and it has been reinforced in the history, science, literature, and social institutions of the modern world.

In her discussion of domination and subordination, Miller (1976) explores what people do to others who are different, and why. At both the individual level and at the level of humanity, she asks "When does difference stimulate development and enhancement in individuals, and when does it produce distortion, degradation, terror, and violence?" In *difference* we usually find the factor of inequality, particularly of status and power.

Miller discusses two types of inequality. *Temporary* inequality defines the lesser party as unequal socially (examples might include such relationships as parent-child and teacher-student). Although the goal is to end inequality, abundant evidence in human relationships demonstrates the difficulty of achieving this goal. The second type of inequality is *permanent*, based in part on the idea that we learn how to enforce inequality but not how to move away from it. Persons defined by race, sex, class, religion, nationality, and so on find themselves fixed into permanently unequal relationships. There is no assumption that the inequality is temporary. In fact, the opposite is often true, as seen in legislative, economic, and social restrictions. Table 7–1 illustrates the historical process.

Throughout history, dominant groups have taken severe measures against the efforts of subordinate groups to regain their dignity and autonomy, to maintain their racial and ethnic differences, deviations in personality characteristics, and sanctioned role behaviors. In the history of the Western world,

TABLE 7–1 How sexism and racism become institutionalized

Dominant group behaviors	Effect on subordinate group
Defines a group of people as inferior	Blacks are less intelligent Women are irrational
Defines acceptable roles for each group, reserving more desirable roles for own group	Service roles Nurturing roles
Defines acceptable personal characteristics: Intelligence Initiative Assertiveness	Submissiveness Passivity Dependency Immaturity Helplessness
Freedom of expression and action is reserved for dominant group	Expression and action are blocked and/or punished in subordinant group
Culture, influenced by dominant group, legitimizes values and behavior, legitimizes and obscures inequality through philosophy, morality, social theory and science/research	Racial and sexual inferiority are "proven" and reinforced
Status, power, and inequality are reinforced through legislative, economic, and social institutions	Segregation, voting rights, abortion laws, credit restriction, rape laws, marital property rights, employment barriers

the white Europeans and their descendents vanquished the native peoples of our continent, imported others in bondage, and fought wars to maintain their economic and political power. Just as Native Americans and Blacks can recount severe retaliation on the part of the white, male power structure, so, too, is feminist literature replete with both historical and current examples of the overt and covert punishment women have undergone for attempting to exercise personal autonomy and legal control of their bodies and circumstances.

For instance, women have been severely restricted from moving about freely and traveling because of fears for their safety and general attitudes concerning the suitability of women alone in restaurants and hotels. Even more blatant examples of the disabling impact of sexism on women have been the foot-binding of Chinese women; forced feeding of suffragettes; culturally required clitoridectomy in Africa (Russell & Van de Ven, 1976); denying women the choice of whether to bear children, even when carrying a fetus to full term is dangerous to physical and mental health; and the financial hardship often resulting from old age, divorce, or the death of a husband. This struggle continues today. Following is an exercise that can be done individually or with a classmate or friend. It may help you to sense how it feels to be powerless or victimized.

An exercise: Victimization and power

Purpose: To get in touch with the subtleties of victimization and power.
Directions: Choose a partner and sit facing each other. Take turns doing the following. Or do this exercise alone by writing your responses to the following.

1. Recall an experience in which you felt powerless or victimized and tell (or write) the story from that point of view.
2. Now, tell the story again, taking the view of the other person feeling powerless or victimized.

What do you experience when you take the second point of view? Does it change your attitudes or feelings in any way? Are there any advantages to the victim position? What are the disadvantages?

Aspects of this struggle for equality are of concern to social work and the social service delivery system. Yet even as we move into practice relationships, it is possible to carry a burden of false superiority or insensitivity without realizing it. If our own attitudes and behaviors have not been challenged by the time professional education begins, these will later impact on us, our colleagues, and clients. For instance, an underlying belief that female anatomy is a woman's destiny is damaging for the woman who finds herself occupying roles other than, or in addition to, roles as wife or mother. Whether a woman works by choice or out of financial necessity, she finds herself forced by society to deal with the conflict and resulting guilt. The belief that it is unfeminine to succeed, to be capable, or to achieve is devastating to women pursuing professional careers.

The cultural, racial, and religious differences among us greatly alter the values, attitudes, and behaviors we start with. Although we can gain knowledge about the roots of sexism and comprehend how these attitudes and behaviors are expressed at various levels of society, gaining knowledge is but one step. Developing personal sensitivity to the effect of sexist attitudes and behaviors on our own lives is another step and one that involves each of us differently. In the individual woman, a readily observable result of such awareness and sensitivity is anger, even rage. She will go through a period of heightened sensitivity and anger that will affect her relationships in varying degrees.

The men in relationships with women in the throes of this experience often respond with surprise, confusion, frustration, and defensiveness. When day-to-day relationships become strained over sexist issues, it is very important to keep communications open and to separate specific males from the system of white male dominance. This seems to allow individual women and men to identify and resolve personal attitudes and behaviors more readily. The anger they both feel is related to powerlessness. In order to turn this level of sensitivity into a positive force, we need to develop agendas for personal and collective action.

It has been demonstrated that there is no such thing as a "value-free" counseling or therapy; practitioners' values and attitudes impact on their clients. In a convergence phenomenon that has been cited, the clients' values shift closer to the norms and standards of the practitioner. Indeed, the practitioner's goals will probably include changing or restructuring the client's values and behavior toward social appropriateness and acceptability. What is the basis for this change effort? Rawlings and Carter (1977) believe that "one source of influence is political; values which are in the best interests of the dominant power group to alter get altered" [p. 5]. Sturdivant (1980) comments on the aspect of social control contained in traditional psychotherapy. Halleck (1971) feels that psychiatrists are largely unaware of their role in maintaining the status quo vis-à-vis the desired outcomes of therapy.

For social work practice to be nonsexist and nonracist, we must develop a code of personal and professional belief that couples personal awareness with the knowledge and skills required in professional practice. As Figure 7–1 illustrates, the base on to which we add knowledge, methodology, and skill in the use of self in practice relationships is composed of personal beliefs, attitudes, and values. Because sexism exists both in society and in ourselves, it is essential that our values and attitudes be challenged, that we develop a sensitivity to the effects of sexism on our lives, that we deal with the effects and develop personal and professional strategies to change the circumstances.

Perlmutter and Alexander (1977) found that

> Although the twin goals of eliminating racism and sexism have become more important on the liberal-humanitarian agenda within the last decade, their position still remains somewhat precarious even within the liberal mainstream, including social work [where] the attitudes and practices regarding the elimination of racism and sexism have been particularly intractable and have changed less dramatically than might appear on the surface [pp. 433–434].

Has this situation improved? What is the responsibility of social work educators? Have they and the theoreticians moved beyond their own culturally induced blind spots to a level of awareness and sensitivity that enables them to assist in your learning and subsequent practice? What impact have the

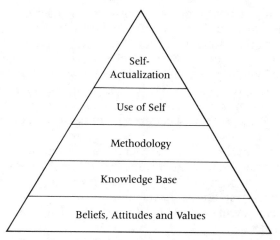

Figure 7–1. Paradigm for personal and professional development

Women's Movement and federal legislation had on social work as a profession and on the delivery of social services? Before exploring these and other questions, we shall attempt to define what we mean by sexism.

Defining sexism

Two themes run through the attempt to define or conceptualize sexism. One is based on discrimination related to the individual's gender. In the words of Kravetz (1976a), sexism is "that range of attitudes, practices, and policies discriminating against women or men on the basis of their gender" [p. 421]. Longres and Bailey (1979) claim that Kravetz missed the essence of sexism, which they see as the privilege enjoyed by males at the expense of females.

The other theme conceptualizes sexism at the societal or institutional level (Stoltenberg, 1975; Alsbrook, 1976), emphasizing the idea of male privilege and the subordination of women in a class and caste system. Institutional sexism has also been defined as a process of exclusionary procedures, rules, or actions that are sexist in their consequences, causing a greater burden to be placed on females than on males (Alvarez et al., 1979). The impact of institutionalized sexism on day-to-day male-female relationships needs examination, as does the impact on practice relationships in the social services. In short, we need to examine sexism in our society, in our own personal lives, and in our professional relationships.

In examining male privilege and female subordination, we should consider whether men consciously seek to maintain their power and privilege. On the interpersonal level, most writers who conceptualize sexism (as well as racism) as (white) male privilege attempt to demonstrate that once behavioral norms become institutionalized, those behaviors are automatic, usually not subject to conscious awareness. Thus, "in a sexist society, one should expect even normal, considerate, and sensitive men to be sexist" (Longres and Bailey, 1979, p. 27). On a broader basis, "Most institutionalized procedures and rules have been made with white males in mind. Thus conformity to the operating norms of institutions has resulted in the almost total barring of minorities and women from equal and full participation in the society in which they are nominally full citizens" (Nasatir & Fernandez, 1979, p. 272). In the broadest application—the economic and political arenas—this is not confined to power and privilege over women. Refer to Table 7-1 (p. 102) to trace the process by which values, attitudes, and behavior come together over time to legitimize and obscure inequality—in this case sexism—in a society.

Perhaps the most comprehensive definition of sexism is that which embraces both the institutional aspects that affect our movement in society and the subconscious attitudes and automatic behaviors that impact on our personal and professional relationships. Institutional aspects are observed, for instance, (a) when salaries for some jobs are kept low so that only women are hired, thereby resulting in lower program or production costs; or (b) when laws created by male-dominated legislatures fail to allow women equal financial independence or control over their reproductive decisions.

Subconscious attitudes and behaviors are observed in the camaradarie of the "good old boy" system which excludes women from the informal support network and the job advantage of mentoring; in the jokes and put-downs aimed at women; or in the tolerance of family violence and rape of females in communities everywhere. At this point you might, either individually or with a classmate or friend, ask yourselves the following questions:

About women:

Do I think men and women have different roles to fulfill?

Do I think women are the natural caretakers of children?

Do I think that certain personality characteristics are more female than male (supportive, gentle, passive)?

Do I think that some behaviors are inappropriate when expressed by women (aggression, self-assertion, independence, domination)?

About minority women:

Do I feel that minority women are less intelligent, responsible, or capable than white women?

Do I see minority women as tough, mean, or hostile?

Do I perceive minority women as sexually amoral and promiscuous?

Do I see minority women as poor risks in terms of social services and rehabilitation efforts?

Examples of sexism at both the institutional and the personal levels are countless. Ours is still a man's world. The pressure felt by individuals and the pressure brought to bear on the institutions and legal structure of our society remain as volatile today as a decade ago. Social work and social services are just beginning to show some response.

IMPACT OF THE WOMEN'S MOVEMENT

In order to develop a sense of how destructive attitudes and behaviors affect social service practice, we must first look at the attitudes and behaviors that have arisen as a result of the Women's Movement. Despite the fact that the movement began in the 1960s, not until the early 1970s could women's issues as they relate to social services be found in the professional literature. These issues included sex-role stereotyping, discrimination in employment and wages, problems in establishing financial credit, limited access to many fields of study and research, divorce and inheritance laws that place women in jeopardy, and the right of women to control their decisions regarding child-bearing.

In terms of social services and health care, additional issues emerged. The medical profession and health and social service agencies were dominated by men. Authoritative and paternalistic in practice, institutional sexism operated to maintain traditional expectations for the disproportionately female clientele. Women comprise the largest clientele of social service agencies because they are economically dependent as a result of broken families, poor wages, and disabling conditions among themselves and their families (Rauch, 1978; Johnson & Holton, 1975). They make up 60% of all office visits to physicians, 70% of prescriptions for mood-altering medications, and suffer higher rates of mental illness, particularly depression (Scarf, 1979; Chesler, 1972).

The mental health professions, including social work, were charged with "perpetuating and encouraging sexism and enforcing conformity to societal sex-role standards" (Fisher, Dulaney, Fazio, Hudak, & Zivotofshy, 1976). The ideology of mental health came under attack. Culturally accepted views of femininity and masculinity, appropriate "traditional" sex-role behaviors, stereotypic views of female psychosocial development, and an antiwoman bias in personality theories were exposed in the literature of the movement (Broverman, Broverman & Clarkson, 1970; Carlson, 1972; Norman & Mancuso, 1980; Freeman, 1975).

The methodologies of psychotherapy were decried as controlling and manipulative. Diagnostic trends that overemphasized helplessness, craziness, and depression in women, the high tendency to medicate, and the stereotypic approach to women's problems were called to task for maintaining female dependency, passivity, and servitude. Prejudgments about intelligence, educational or work goals, promiscuity, and the desire to take a "free ride on welfare" can all be cited, with a heavier burden on minority women.

A colleague's experience with the system demonstrates many of the issues. When still in her twenties, unmarried and with one child, Mary found it necessary to apply for Aid to Families with Dependent Children to supplement her salary from a domestic job. The forms included about 35 pages to cover financial assistance, medical care, and food stamps, and the initial process was both intimidating and demeaning. When two years later Mary chose to have another child, her social worker and the agency supervisor were very punitive. They implied that she was unstable and promiscuous, and only with considerable reluctance did they add the baby to the budget.

Later, when Mary began discussing with the worker her interest in going to a small private college in the city, the worker tried to talk her out of the plan, encouraging her instead to attend a technical school for secretarial skills. Finally, in the face of Mary's determination, the worker appeared to support the effort and assisted her in planning for child care, tuition, and other living expenses. Two weeks before the school term was to start, however, the social worker told her that the agency would not go along with her plan, and all hope for her financial aid seemed doomed.

Mary went to the college and explained her situation, and school officials arranged for scholarships to cover her expenses. Her family supported her efforts and cared for her children during her schooling. Mary completed her bachelor's degree four years later and obtained an interesting job—in a social service agency serving the special needs of women. Mary felt that the attitudes and policies in the AFDC agency were clearly discriminatory toward her as a woman and more particularly as a Black woman. She had received many negative messages about her role as a mother, the limitations of her intelligence and capability for education and a career, and her sexual behavior. Mary's situation occurs all too often; many women later report that they were sufficiently intimidated to abandon their goals.

The assumption that sexism does not affect the social work profession is false (Kravetz, 1976a). The fact that the worker may be a woman and interested in helping others is no guarantee that subtle sexist values and attitudes are absent. Some women have become aware of sexism in social services as they have attempted to move into positions of authority in agencies, on boards, and in academe.

In my own experience, for example, the move into program administration just six months out of graduate school carried some problems. I served as the director of a state hospital alcoholism treatment program and, as such, was the only nonmedical service chief. There was one other woman, a psychiatrist, serving as a service chief. Other service chiefs delegated to their staff social workers the task of consulting with me about referrals to our unit. I was not included in the daily meeting of service chiefs, and only after considerable assertiveness was I included in regular meetings of all department heads.

Three years later I became the administrator of a community mental health clinic with a board of directors and several county board committees to work with on budget, personnel, facilities, and ordinances. It was not uncommon to have a supervisor behave in a patronizing manner: one evening at a county board meeting, one of the supervisors all but patted me on the head as he said "I'll bet you'd really rather be at home with your family instead of sitting around listening to us men arguing about money." My own agency budget of $250,000 was being considered that evening for which I had presented supporting data and testimony. No false assumptions here.

If the literature is any indication of the state of the art, the majority of women and men in social services in the early 1970s had not yet developed a sensitivity to the subtle aspects of sexism found in the theoretical framework, the methodologies, the behaviors of superiors, our collegial relationships, and our relationships with clients. Although the literature began to reflect a developing awareness at this time, major attention to the issues did not occur until halfway through the decade. A policy statement on women in social welfare was presented to the NASW Delegate Assembly meeting in 1973. In 1976 and 1977 special editions of the journal, *Social Work*, focused on women's issues. Other articles have followed, but their frequency has diminished since 1979.

Finally, in 1980, the first National Conference on Social Work Practice with Women was held under NASW sponsorship.

Attempts to examine the issues of sexism in social work literature can be divided into several areas of interest. These include (a) defining social work as a woman's profession and the changes that have occurred as more men have entered the profession; (b) examining the position of women in the field with regard to their roles and status, wages, participation in policy decisions, and peer relationships; (c) professional preparation for the field and the curriculum; (d) women as clients in practice relationships; (e) methodologies; and most recently (f) federal legislation on equal employment opportunities and sexual harassment in the work place. Still, the issues of sexism have not been fully addressed in the literature, in the body of knowledge and concepts being taught to students, in agency policies, or in client or collegial relationships.

For examples of the latter, not at all uncommon is the male professor who refers to some female students as "Babe," suggests individual conferences in inappropriate places, or overtly offers a better grade for sexual favors. If the student dares to complain, she is considered hysterical or hostile when pitted against the self-righteous academic protected by the "good old boy" system. An example that comes to mind in the practice setting is an agency director who was known for hiring the prettiest and youngest female candidates as each position opened up. Either he soon had an affair with the new worker, or she failed in probation and left the agency.

Another example not too unusual in practice relationships involved a male social worker and a female client who sought therapy for depression resulting from a difficult marriage and impending divorce action. Over a period of a few weeks the woman romanticized her dependency on the worker. Rather than help the woman work through these feelings, he engaged in a sexual relationship with her. When confronted by the estranged husband in the presence of the agency director, the worker complained of the woman's persistent pursuit of him and blamed uncontrollable impulses for having "consented" to the affair. Utterly insensitive to his power in the relationship, he refused to see how he had exploited the woman.

An even more blatant case involved a deeply depressed client who was having an affair with a male social worker on the staff of a local agency. The worker had locked his office door mid-point through a crisis intervention intake, taken the confused and shaken women into his arms to console her, and subsequently seduced her. This relationship had continued for many months, when he announced he was leaving the city. He was totally insensitive to the exploitation of his power and hostile toward the woman's depression and suicide attempt. Only after much work was she able to come to grips with her powerlessness, shame, and anger.

Examples like these can be found in all aspects of social services, in any city or university. To explore the literature on many of these issues, read Kravetz (1976b) and Figueria-McDonough (1979), both of whom provide extensive bibliographies. The latter—a review of the literature on class, race, sex over a 15-year period—points out that social workers, though aware of the problems, have given little thought to how technologies of intervention and social service organizations impact on clients and the perpetuation of discriminatory practices. However, Figueria-McDonough suggests:

> Changes in professional ideology can be measured over time through content analysis of the documents of professional associations and the writings of leading professionals [and] since practice models are established in schools of social work and disseminated through professional journals, examination of academic curricula and articles published in social work journals is a suitable method for determining trends in the field [p. 216].

In addition to this sort of analysis, research is needed at the practice level to determine whether any change is occurring in the sensitivity and practice of individual workers. Such an evaluation of practice will not be easy. Practitioners tend to resist examination of their methods and behaviors.

In order for sexist conditions in social service practice to change, we need not only to recognize and understand institutional sexism and personal attitudes and behaviors that are sexist but to move from knowing and feeling to functioning in a nonsexist manner in our relationships. In this aspect, women are in a double bind. On the one hand, if we function as healthy women by traditional standards, this includes being submissive, dependent, and emotional. On the other hand, if we become healthy adults as defined by mental health standards, we would be assertive, independent, and rational. Further, we cannot function one way in our personal relationships and another way in our professional relationships. Such dissonance is conflicting and would result in high levels of stress and ineffective functioning. You might try the following exercise in indentifying examples of sexist thinking and relating.

An exercise: Female/male images and feelings

Purpose: To explore some of our feelings and images about women and men.
Directions: Read the following questions, write your responses. Be aware of your feelings as you do the exercise.

1. What do you think of in relation to the word *woman?* The word *man?*
2. What do you like about women? Men?
3. What do you dislike about women? Men?
4. What do you expect to get from women? Men?
5. What do you expect to give to women? Men?
6. What do you actually give to and get from women? Men?
7. What do you want from women? Men?
8. What do you fear about women? Men?
9. What other feelings do you have about women? Men?

What were your feelings? What did you learn about yourself? About your relationships with women? With men?

Within institutional sexism the very descriptors of women and women's roles are pathological in relation to concepts of mental health and maturity. According to Peak and Glankoff (1975), rehabilitation or resocialization "is often for a woman a question of reorientation to the servant role, not for open-ended self-fulfillment with all its many possibilities" [p. 510]. We will want to develop a clear personal and professional congruence of an androgynous nature so that our lives, the social services practice setting, and our relationships with our clients will reflect the full human potential of which we are capable.

FRAMEWORK FOR NONSEXIST PRACTICE

Social work was largely preoccupied in its early years with the social and environmental forces that prevented people from living full, satisfying lives. The idea was commonplace that social work is an art, based not on its own body of knowledge or theories, but on a culling and synthesis of relevant knowledge and theory from several of the social and behavioral sciences. In an effort to develop a theoretical knowledge base, the field drew heavily on psychoanalytic theory. Psychiatric social work gained a higher status as we learned methodologies that were more like psychoanalysis than like casework.

Moving away from social and environmental issues toward intrapsychic issues resulted in a historical duality in terms of social reform and direct case services. This duality is discussed extensively in the literature. Pray (1947) argues that social action lies outside the social work process and is not a function of the case services worker. Hollis (1972) warns against the worker being directly involved with the client in both case services and social reform activities. In reviewing this duality, Scurfield (1980) found:

> The conclusion most often arrived at is that the vast majority of practitioners continue to practice essentially in a manner that does not deal directly or primarily with much of the environmental cause phenomena underlying the client's problems, and that the focus is more exclusively on changing the person [p. 610].

However, the upheaval of the 1960s and the press of social programs, the human relations field of study, and the Women's Movement have all had an impact on theory and practice from outside the social service field. A focus on reality and attention to egalitarian principles in human relationships are causing us to reexamine theory and practice in light of political and economic conditions that have overridden most other aspects of U.S. life. This reexamination is still found largely outside social work, in the literature of women's studies and radical therapy. It is helpful to contemplate people's needs in this new context because it enables us to see that personal issues become, by necessity, political issues as we grow more aware of the role of power in the human condition. The early social workers were closer to this knowledge than we have been during the intervening years.

In the psychological theories of recent decades, social problems have been blamed on "sick" people rather than viewing individual problems as resulting from environmental forces. This is not surprising: it is easier to try to help or change deviant members of society than to face, and be willing to change, what is oppressive in human arrangements. Thus, social services and mental health services have been made responsible for feeding, curing, and rehabilitating the disadvantaged, the deviant, and others who don't conform to society's norms. Recall Table 7–1 and the characteristics of subordinate group members. Social service practice plays a role in maintaining the inequalities, the status quo.

Casework has remained, over the years, the major methodology in social services, although it has, along with other psychotherapeutic approaches, been mystifying both to clients and to the public. The promise that we can cure people's madness because we possess some special knowledge and skills arouses both awe and suspicion. The fact that suicide, murder, depression, irresponsibility, divorce, and diverse craziness have not been cured perhaps contributes to the search for a different analysis of the issues and more egalitarian solutions in human relations. This search may be pushing the pendulum back toward the center, between sociocultural and intrapsychic concepts. Scurfield (1980) points out that maintaining a duality in terms of the social reform function and direct case services may result in denying clients a role in actively participating in their situations. It is "inherently discriminatory to disadvantaged peoples to dichotomize arbitrarily case services from social reform activities" [p. 611].

Direct services

Let's look first at the direct services portion of social services practice. Because of the influence of psychoanalytic principles, social workers have been taught to confine themselves in practice relationships and not make themselves known as people to their clients. As a result, the worker's personality has been ignored as a factor in practice; the emphasis has been on methodology, with the worker remaining as neutral as possible. A neutral, reflective technique is evident in the following dialogue.

"I rarely feel comfortable when I visit my parents. They're always so into rapping with my brothers. I don't know how I should start—"
"You feel uncomfortable."
"Yes. It's been that way a long time. It's always been the four of them. They don't include me. I usually do the dishes or take a walk with the dog."
"And it has always been like this?"
"Yes, except when—before my little brother died. We were close and played together."
"You were close to him."

Each statement by the worker reflects the theme the client is following. Sometimes this leads to reflection and insight, but the client may also become frustrated and need a more active, probing relationship.

The belief that the therapist/worker is more aware of the clients' needs than the client, plus a tendency to keep the client in a dependent state, were both exemplified by a client who came to me from another therapist. Sarah had been seeing a female therapist for several months but felt that the relationship was not comfortable and had expressed her intention to discontinue. The therapist used most of the session to explain that Sarah was experiencing dependency and resistance. Emphatically she declared that Sarah was not ready to discontinue and would experience a return of anxiety and depression if she broke off therapy at this time. When Sarah did not make another appointment, she received three phone calls from the therapist over the next month and began to have self-doubts. Returning briefly to this therapist, she again felt uncomfortable, as if the therapist were setting her up to feel weak and powerless in the relationship. She didn't return and again got a series of phone calls.

Sarah set up a four-session contract with me, primarily to validate her perceived need to trust her own judgment. She felt that she was ready to break any dependency she had on therapy and that she had a right to "fire" the therapist just as she had "hired" her. When allowed to act on her own feelings, she did leave therapy, phoning periodically over several months to tell me she believed she had done the right thing. Traditional counselors and therapists have so preoccupied themselves with the dependence and transference aspects of the practice relationship as to neglect such reality factors as one's own attitudes, personality traits, setting and circumstances, cultural differences, and socioeconomic conditions in the client's environment.

Working with the lesbian client is very difficult for many practitioners. Shirley and Ellen were lesbian clients of mine, both of whom had encountered insensitive and humiliating experiences in their efforts to obtain help regarding lifestyle and significant others.

A professional woman who dressed attractively and looked feminine by traditional standards, Shirley explained that she had been seeing a male psychiatrist in the city but after two attempts felt that she should try a woman therapist. It was with considerable difficulty that she shared the fact that a relationship problem involved her lesbian lover. Once Shirley discovered that we could explore the issues, her options and feelings without a negative reaction, she related that the male therapist had refused for several sessions to deal with the notion that Shirley was not heterosexual. He hinted that she probably had never had a "good enough time" with a man and steadfastly focused on her anxiety and depression, stating flatly that her current lifestyle was self-destructive. She dropped out of therapy for a few months but returned when the relationship broke off. The therapist's first response was "Good, with that over, we can get down to the real problems!" She walked out of the session and never returned.

Ellen, on the other hand, was poorly groomed, hostile, and defensive. She first "came out" as a teenager while in a girls' school, although as a young adult she had been married briefly. Her only child was in a foster home. Ellen was referred to me by the local rape crisis agency because of a recent assault. She had had an earlier experience in a mental health outpatient clinic which had been humiliating and demeaning. Ellen was seeing a female social worker about assuming a greater role in her child's future, but the woman had been clearly uncomfortable with Ellen's declared sexual preference and lifestyle. Ellen became more and more defensive, feeling powerless under the circumstances.

One day when Ellen arrived for her appointment there was a man in the office who was introduced as the worker's supervisor. The session went badly, with Ellen feeling terribly uncomfortable. Near the end of the session he left. The worker turned to Ellen and said "I know you're not a lesbian. You were flirtatious and seductive with Mr. ———." Ellen was so shocked and angered by the worker's dishonesty that she never returned. Some months later, after we had dealt with the assault and her sense of safety, she accepted a referral to a court social worker to reopen the issue of serving the child.

Personality of practitioner

Only recently has the literature reflected a renewed consideration of such factors as the worker's personality, recognition of the worker as a real person in the interaction, the worker's perception of self and awareness of values that impinge on practice, and the concept of "use of self" in the relationship. In the preceding examples it may be doubted that the therapists realized how negatively their values and attitudes impinged on the relationships and blocked the client's needs.

Despite gaps in the social work literature, there is an extensive body of information indicating that counseling and psychotherapeutic efforts can both help and harm clients. Clients are not left as they were before involvement in the relationship (Carkhuff & Berensen, 1967). If counseling or therapy is successful, client values will shift toward the counselor's values. Because many practitioners may hold sexist values, they may subtly discourage their female clients from being assertive, independent, and taking responsibility (power) for their lives. Rather, clients may be encouraged to be dependent, helpless, and childlike in therapy as well as in other relationships. These practitioners will tend to attribute women's problems to intrapsychic factors and have as counseling goals the female client's acceptance of and adjustment to the very roles and behaviors that are thwarting self-growth and actualization. This is, of course, why the philosophy and values of the practitioner are so crucial.

In addition, studies show that some individuals are effective in human interactions and especially competent at helping people in distress, but there are others who are ineffective and destructive in interpersonal relationships. This research, which originated in the 1960s, has resulted in efforts in counseling psychology, for instance, to screen potential helpers and train them for optimal skills. (Chapters 3, 4, and 5 review the personality characteristics or traits, such as empathy, warmth, and so on, that have been identified and measured as common among effective, helpful practitioners.) Given this kind of information, and with the knowledge that other fields have put it to use in the preparation of practitioners, it is disappointing that as recently as 1979 the social work literature was still reflecting an effort to deal with whether the worker's role in the practice relationship should reflect the real person. Evidently the importance of the worker's personality was still not clear, at least in the literature for social work and social services.

Rhodes (1979) sees the principle as an "elusive concept," although she does define the reality relationship as the treatment vehicle and recognizes that the worker's personality is an independent factor having a major influence on the course and outcome of the interaction. "It is [the] combination of personality and professional competence that characterizes the worker's style" [p. 259]. The client's perceptions are dependent on such factors as health, stress, cultural background, and sex. The worker's personality will directly interact with the client's perception, and it is this reality aspect, based on the worker's attitudes and behaviors, that may assist the client's reality testing and ultimate adaptive functioning.

If we accept the importance of the worker's personality, attitudes, and behaviors in a counseling relationship, we see immediately how sexism can negatively impact the client. Sexism can be identified, not only in stereotypic expectations and antifemale concepts, but in sexist language, such as the continued use of terms like *girl* for *woman,* use of the pronoun *he* as an all-purpose referent, and references to clients as *hysterical females,* to name a few. Sexist interactions can also be identified in body language and terminology that express power over the client, in unsolicited touching, even in seduction. Practitioners too often assume that "symptoms" such as poor self-concept, sullenness, hostility, and guilt are the products of intrapsychic pathology, which precludes any consideration of sexist attitudes, the possible cultural differences between worker and client, and social conditions.

Finally, it is important to point out that sexism takes on a different definition for minority women. Male-female relationships and role expectations are culturally specific for Black, Hispanic, and Native American women, for instance, and may be quite different from those of the practitioner's cultural background. Thus the minority woman is at risk of being stereotyped and demeaned as a result of insensitivity arising from the practitioner's values and attitudes toward her both as a woman and as a minority woman whose culture is unfamiliar and possibly denigrated.

Feminist theory

The Women's Movement has been important in the demystification of helping relationships and therapy. Feminist therapy is based on a relationship model in which power is equalized rather than hierarchical (Williams, 1975). This liberates both parties in the relationship to be more authentic with each other. Also, the relationship is more lifelike, and there is a tendency to deemphasize pathology in a process that takes into account the client's real situation, encouraging the individual to take responsibility for herself or himself. There is no specific methodology to recommend. The following exchanges demonstrate the subtle differences between sexist and nonsexist attitudes, the egalitarianism possible in the practice relationship, and the empowering of the client to gain gradual control over her/his life.

Exchange 1

"You've been coming into the agency for what, about a month now?"

"Yes, this is my fifth time."

We've spent a lot of time talking about your ex-husband being behind in support and your son going to Juvenile Court. Even your sister's illness. Let's talk about you today."

Could sound judgmental, as if client not progressing; or not dealing with the "right" issues.

"Me?"

"Yes, for instance, your weight problem." — *Not starting where client is; coming from worker's bias.*

"Well, I—"

"You know it's not healthy to be so overweight."

"Well, I've always been plump. Maybe it has been a bit more of a problem in the last year— what with the divorce and all." — *Will worker be sensitive to stress level?*

"You have such a pretty face. If you'd lose weight you'd be really attractive. Maybe get married again someday." — *No! Also shows sexist bias, reinforcing societal stereotype of female appearance and marriage.*

"I haven't tried to diet. There's so much stress—" — *Client again expresses stress.*

"Perhaps we should refer you to a nutrition program."

"That's just one more thing to have to cope with—" — *Help!*

This worker-client exchange exemplifies poor counseling. The worker is not empathic, is directing, assuming power in the relationship by declaring the topic. Having observed that the client is overweight, the worker quickly adds that this is unhealthy and fails to hear the client's objections to the added stress that this interaction imposes. Moreover, the worker's sexist values are evident with regard to social standards of beauty and the need for the client to improve herself so that she will be acceptable to some man in the socially preferred role as wife.

Thus, instead of establishing an egalitarian relationship, the worker assumes power, deciding what ought to be important, making judgments, and treating the client in a demeaning manner. What options does the client have? If she goes along believing that the worker knows best, she remains passive, dependent, perhaps childlike. She will be "adjusted" to traditional stereotypic role expectations, possibly with increased discomfort, depression, and hostility. If she feels frustrated by the lack of understanding, loses hope, or feels anger at the worker and stops coming to the agency, she may continue in a stressful lifestyle or seek another helping relationship. The worker will probably assume that she was resistant or unmotivated, unaware that his/her own lack of sensitivity was a factor in the "failure."

Exchange 2

"We've been meeting for about a month now, haven't we?"

"Yes, This is my fifth time."

"We've been exploring several problems; the late support payments, your son's appearance in Juvenile Court, and your sister's illness. Would you like to review any actions on your part regarding these or to explore other aspects of your current situation?"

This sounds much more egalitarian; empowers client to take charge.

"Well, I think those problems are really outside of my control—I really can't do much about them. I'd like to talk about something I could work on, even if it's small."

Possibility of regaining power over small area of life as a first step.

"Do you have something in mind?"

Client is in charge.

"How about my weight? I know it's out of hand because I feel uncomfortable."

"Have you considered a diet?"

"Sort of. I've tried, but everything has been so overwhelming—"

"It is hard to diet when you have a lot of stress. It actually adds more stress, physically and emotionally."

Empathic, supportive.

"Things have settled a little. Maybe I can do this for myself."

Climate better for risk taking.

This is a much better interaction. The worker is establishing an egalitarian relationship. Through exploration, the client can proceed at her own pace, bringing up issues and deciding whether she can cope differently. She is encouraged initially to regain a sense of power over a small area of her life through this supportive, egalitarian counseling relationship.

That values and attitudes bear a direct influence on how we relate to clients and the way in which we approach counseling should be clear by now. At this point we should review the practitioner's role in the social services practice relationship and particularly in the counseling relationship. Historically, our field has moved from emphasizing the client in a problematic socioeconomic environment to placing the burden of "deviancy" on the individual's intrapsychic make-up. As a result of more recent social and political forces, we are now able to move back toward a middle ground and take into account cultural, socioeconomic, and political considerations in a more humanistic approach to our clients as they perceive themselves and the world. The use-of-self concept has gained much needed attention. For a few recent books exploring nonsexist and feminist approaches to counseling and therapy, see Rawlings and Carter (1977), Miller (1976), Williams (1975), Sturdivant (1980), and Norman and Mancuso (1980), all excellent references.

If we are learning from these events and forces, we should also be examining the theoretical framework on which we base the education and preparation of new practitioners. We should be examining methodologies and practice models. You are taking an important first step in recognizing, and perhaps changing, sexist attitudes and behaviors. A conscious and continuous effort will facilitate your professional development.

Personal and professional development

Let's return to Figure 7-1 (p. 105) and summarize the development of the practitioner. Beginning at the bottom and moving upward, we start with (a) a personal set of beliefs, attitudes, and values plus a certain level of self-awareness and understanding. To this we add (b) knowledge (ideology) and (c) methodology (the development of skills). At the fourth level is (d) the concept of use of self. This means that practitioners must be sensitive, empathic, respectful, genuine, and warm. They must be able to communicate concretely, confront discrepancies in verbal and nonverbal behaviors of clients, and be able to reveal pertinent personal feelings, attitudes, opinions, and experiences for the benefit of the client. At the fifth level we find (e) self-actualization. Self-actualizing people are more successful in using themselves in meaningful interactions with clients than are non-self-actualizers. Spontaneity, creativity, and self-discipline—all aspects of self-actualization—are vital to effective functioning in practice relationships. Self-actualization is also important in bringing together personal and professional values with the development of practice skills. To differentiate the values and beliefs we hold personally and professionally would represent a lack of congruence. They are one and the same.

Since we are evolving personally and professionally at the same time that we are functioning in practice relationships, it is possible that new concepts or experiences may cause cognitive dissonance. Hopefully, however, the necessary changes will occur to promote congruence. Otherwise our functioning in relationships would be hampered by conflicting ideas or behaviors. Congruence is not something that comes easily for those in a helping profession. Just as inconsistencies may exist in our philosophy, so might there be inconsistencies in our relationships and communications. The practitioner's use of self can be especially taxing. If congruence does not develop along with increasing levels of knowledge, skill, and self-awareness, if self-actualization is not occurring, the inconsistencies and lack of congruence between personal and professional values will result in physical and emotional exhaustion, bitterness, hostility or apathy, and dysfunctional behavior.

The latter are all aspects of the *burnout syndrome* which plagues the helping professions. Constant reexamination of values and attitudes, renewed skill development, and a balanced personal life not only prevent burnout but should also promote continual spontaneity and creativity for the practitioner. Your educational experience should help you develop this capacity. It is the role of the educator, and later of the supervisor, to guide you along this course of development. This is why it is so important that we all confront the issues of sexism in social service practice. It is crucial for our own continued growth and self-actualization, and it is vital to our ability to function in relationships with one another and with our clients.

Social change

As individuals grow more sensitive to an issue or practice, they sometimes become what has been termed a *single change agent*—that is, one person, in a given setting, believing and behaving in a way different from his or her colleagues. As we become increasingly sensitive to institutional and interpersonal sexism, our own awareness and discomfort may call attention to the sexism we encounter in people, practices, and policies. This behavior may be viewed as confusing, troublesome, and aggressive; it may be met with defensiveness, resistance, and ridicule. Indeed, we may feel reprisals.

If we confront antifemale attitudes and behavior in interpersonal relationships, we may have to resolve the communication and emotional aspects of the confrontation and the impact on the relationship. If we confront discriminatory agency policies and practices or sexual harrassment, we may anger supervisory and administrative people, perhaps even the agency board. Retaliation may include a demand for conformity or dismissal. If course content is challenged in an educational setting, reprisal might mean isolation from fellow students or poor course grades. Individual efforts to sensitize or change a perceived injustice can result in painful, stressful situations.

Since the mid-1960s, federal and state legislation has been enacted that enables women to combat discrimination in hiring and other work conditions. Title IX of the 1964 Civil Rights Act prohibits sex discrimination in education; Title VII, in places of employment with more than 15 employees. Title VII has broad application to employment and has been interpreted to include sexual harassment. The success or failure of suits brought against employers may greatly influence the change that occurs in social services as well as in other work places.

Within social service practice, client advocacy and social activism have also been arenas for controversy in which practitioners have often found themselves engaged, contrary to agency policy or broad community expectations. When personal and professional values are involved, we are severely tested, and at this point knowledge of the dynamics of power is valuable. Sensitivity puts us in touch with powerlessness; understanding the dynamics of individual, collective, economic, and political power helps us to identify appropriate levels for activity and change efforts in our practice. It is to be hoped that the educational process you are undergoing is one in which faculty and curriculum are changing also. Other areas of exploration include the agencies and communities in which you may have field placements. Field supervisors should examine the placement agencies for sexist behaviors and policies and attempt to provide students with experiences that are free of institutional and inter-personal sexism. Perhaps you and your supervisor can do one of the following field projects together.

1. Interview the director of a local agency, and ask about its administrative structure. What is the male/female ratio of the staff? Do males or females provide direct service, supervise, or administer the agency? What kind of comments do these questions elicit?

2. Examine the agency's policy manuals for personnel policies, especially sick leave and leave of absence policies. What are the admission policies for clients? Look at annual reports and/or agency goal statements, too. Do you see groups of people unserved, such as women with child-care barriers? Age barriers?

There are many other ways to determine the effects of sexism in agencies and the community. As you become aware of these and the problems that might arise over any attempt to change the status quo, you'll sense the presence of power. People with vested interests claim that such interests serve the "benefit of all" as a rationale for maintaining the status quo.

Finally, the charge has been made that social services theory and practice lack adequate practice models. In reply, Johnson (1976) pointed out that there is no one theory of human behavior that is accepted by all, no one theory adequate for all situations. Models on which we base our practice include clinical, systems theory, social functioning, ego psychology, psychoanalytic, casework, group work, and community organization. Anderson (1976) charges that we have never really come to terms with the need to develop a practice theory, that we are "approaching the uncommitted anarchy of eclecticism" [p. 2]—a conceptual anarchy that encourages the practitioner to abandon theory.

Scurfield (1980) proposes an integrated practice approach to come to grips with societal problems that impact on individuals and the problems clients bring to practitioners. "The integrated practice approach asserts that the locus of change is always within the individual and that other factors outside of the individual can impinge to such a degree as to constrict severely the range and viability of the options open or accessible" [p. 612].

To conclude our exploration of sexism in social service practice relationships, (a) our individual and collective sensitivity to sexism and (b) practice models that respond both to individual clients and to environment issues represent the areas for change. Striving to overcome personal and professional sexism, we need to test methods and models for congruence with personal values, professional values, and the cultural and socioeconomic environment of our clients. Recognizing the dynamics of the worker's use of self in practice relationships, we need also to understand the dynamics of power. Against the historical roots that have exercised strong sociocultural influences on us and the institutional nature of oppressive power over women there are counter-balancing influences in society today, and these influences can favorably impact on our personal and professional attitudes and behaviors. Growing sensitivity in the development of value-congruent models can be utilized for social service practice. It is true that to break down institutional patterns and deeply ingrained personal attitudes and values does not occur easily or readily; we believe that change is possible. The result of ridding ourselves and our work place of oppression and moving toward achieving the full human potential of all of us is well worth our personal and collective efforts.

STUDY QUESTIONS

1. What is meant by "institutionalized" sexism?
2. How is the social services field affected by the female/male ratio in employment?
3. Can the social work curriculum reflect sexist/nonsexist values? How?
4. Give examples of sexist language, behavior, policies.
5. Have you identified any of your own sexist attitudes, biases? What are they? How might you go about being more sensitive?
6. Do you think women might prefer female counselors? Why might this be a good/ bad practice consideration?
7. What implications might arise out of egalitarian counseling relationships for practitioners? for agencies?
8. Do you think opression can be reversed in personal relationships? In the practice setting? In society?

REFERENCES

Alsbrook, L. Marital communication and sexism. *Social Casework,* 1976.

Alvarez, R., Lutterman, K. G., and Associates. Institutional discrimination in organizations and their environments. *Discrimination in Organizations.* San Francisco: Jossey-Bass Publishers, 1979.

Anderson, J. D. Games social work educators play in teaching practice theories, in *Teaching for competence in the delivery of direct services.* New York: Council on Social Work Education, 1976.

Babcock, M. C., & Connor, B. Sexism and treatment of the female alcoholic: A review. *Social Work,* 1981.

Brager, G., & Michael, J. A. The sex distribution in social work: Causes and consequences. *Social Casework,* 1969.

Broverman, I. K., Broverman, D. M., & Clarkson, F. E. Sex-role stereotypes and clinical judgments of mental health. *Journal of Consulting & Clinical Psychology,* 1970.

Carkhuff, R. R., & Berenson, B. G. *Beyond counseling and therapy.* New York: Holt, Rinehart & Winston, 1967.

Carlson, R. Understanding women: Implications for personality theory and research. *Journal of Social Issues,* 1972.

Chesler, P. *Women and madness.* New York: Doubleday Publishing Co., 1972.

Freeman, J. (Ed.). *Women: A feminist perspective.* Palo Alto, Calif.: Mayfield Publishing Co., 1975.

Figueria-McDonough, J. Discrimination in social work: Evidence, myth, and ignorance. *Social Work,* 1979.

Fisher, J., Dulaney, D. D., Fazio, R. T., Hudak, M. T. & Zivotofshy, E. Are social workers sexists? *Social Work,* 1976.

Halleck, S. *The politics of therapy.* New York: Science House, 1971.

Hollis, F. *Carework: A psychosocial therapy.* New York: Random House, 1972.

Halleck, S. *The politics of therapy.* New York: Science House, 1971.

Johnson, B. S., & Holton, C. *Social work and the women's movement.* Paper presented at the National Association of Social Work Professional Symposium, Hollywood-by-the-sea, Fla., October 1975.

Johnson, L. C. Social work practice models: Teaching the differential aspects of practice. In *Teaching for competence in the delivery of direct services.* New York: Council on Social Work Education, 1976.

Kadushin, A. Men in a women's profession. *Social Work,* 1976.

Kravetz, D. Sexism in a women's profession. *Social Work,* 1976. (a)

Kravetz, D. F. Women social workers and clients: Common victims of sexism. In J. I. Roberts (Ed.), *Beyond intellectual sexism: A new woman, a new reality,* NY: David McKay Co., 1976. (b)

Longres, J. F., & Bailey R. H. Men's issues and sexism: A journal review. *Social Work,* 1979.

Miller, J. B. *Toward a new psychology of woman.* Boston: Beacon Press, 1976.

Morales, A., & Sheafor B. W. *Social work: A profession of many faces* (2nd ed.). Boston: Allyn & Bacon, 1980.

Nasatir, D., & Fernandez, J. P. Use of log-linear and hierarchical models to study ethnic composition in a university. In *Discrimination in organizations,* Rodolfo Alvarez, Kenneth G. Lutterman and Assoc., San Francisco: Jossey-Bass Publishers, 1979.

Norman, E., & Mancuso, A. *Women's issues and social work practice.* Itasca, Ill.: F. E. Peacock Publishers, 1980.

Peak, J. L., & Glankoff, P. The female patient as booty. In *Developments in the field of drug abuse,* E. Senay, V. Shorty, & H. Alksne (Eds.). Schenkman Publishing Co., Cambridge, Mass., 1975.

Perlmutter, F. D., & Alexander, L. B. Racism and sexism in social work practice: An empirical view. *Administration in Social Work,* Winter 1977, pp. 433–443.

Pray, K. *When is community organization social work practice?* Proceedings of the National Conference on Social Work. Chicago: University of Chicago Press, 1947.

Rauch, J. B. Gender as a factor in practice. *Social Work,* 1978.

Rawlings, E. I., & Carter D. K. *Psychotherapy for women: Treatment toward equality.* Charles C Thomas, Springfield, Ill., 1977.

Rhodes, S. L. The personality of the worker: An unexplored dimension in treatment. *Social Casework,* May 1979.

Russell, D. E. H., & VandeVen N. (Eds.). *Crimes against women: Proceedings of the international tribunal.* Millbrae, Calif: Les Femmes, 1976.

Scarf, M. The more sorrowful sex. *Psychology Today,* May 1979, pp. 45, 47–48, 51–52, and 89–90.

Schwartz, M. C. Sexism in the social work curriculum. In *Social work: A profession of many faces.* A. Morales & B. W. Sheafor (Eds.). Boston: Allyn and Bacon, 1977.

Scurfield, R. M. An integrated approach to case services and social reform. *Social Casework,* 1980.

Stoltenberg, J. Towards gender justice. *Social Policy,* May-June 1975, pp. 35–39.

Sturdivant, S. *Therapy with women: A feminist philosophy of treatment.* N.Y.: Springer Publishing Co., 1980.

Williams, E. F. *Notes of a feminist therapist.* N.Y.: Praeger Publishers, 1975.

8

Racism and Practice Relationships[1]

Paul Keys

A variety of factors affect social service workers in their day-to-day practice relationships. In general, these include the historical context of human relationships, the social and economic structure of society, and the practitioner's own values, theories, and skills. In terms of racism, specific factors are important in determining the outcome of intervention efforts: the historical context of racism in the society, professional ideals, individual practitioner-client relationships, group and community practice relationships, and effects unique to particular fields of practice. On a macrolevel, there are factors that impede the individual practitioner's best efforts. These are the effects of institutional and organizational racism on practice relationships, social policy, administrative relationships, research (process and priorities), and finally the effects of education on the practitioner.

To understand the influence of these factors on the typical practice relationship, it is first necessary to define and explore the history of prejudice and racism in the United States.

BASIC IDEAS

Prejudice is the term previously used to describe what is now called *racism*. Viewed as an individual prejudgment on some matter, prejudice does not carry a negative meaning; it is merely a preconceived way of looking at something. In one of the more comprehensive analyses of prejudice, Allport (1958) stated

[1] The author wishes to thank Dr. Ernest Spaights, Leon H. Sullivan Professor in Social Welfare and Educational Psychology, the University of Wisconsin, Milwaukee; and Dr. Jack Williams, Cultural Foundations of Education Department, the University of Wisconsin, Milwaukee, for their kind assistance in the preparation and review of materials for this chapter.

that it can mean a "judgment formed before due examination and consideration of the facts—a premature or hasty judgement" [p. 6]. Although this has been the historical meaning of the word in English, only in recent times has it acquired the negative meaning associated with it today. Allport also indicates that "finally the term [*prejudice*] acquired its present emotional flavor of favorableness or unfavorableness that accompanies such a prior and unsupported judgement" [p. 6].

In psychological theory, prejudice has been described as a problem that may be "understood as a manifestation of the needs of individual personalities"—that is, independent of the group to which it is directed (Simpson & Yinger, 1953, p. 49.) To understand it in this sense, attention must be given primarily to the prejudiced person rather than to the recipient of the prejudice.

In sociological theory, prejudice has been described as a social problem that is rooted deeply in American society itself. In contrast to the psychological and individual descriptions, the sociological view of prejudice looks to the power structure of society for an explanation (Simpson & Yinger, 1953). For this reason, power relations in society, as well as key economic, political, educational, and religious decisions, are examined for their sometimes hidden contributions to prejudice and racism.

Although racism and prejudice may be viewed as the same concept, *racism* gradually became the preferred term in the early to mid-1960s.

> Racism is both overt and covert. It takes two, closely related forms: individual Whites acting against individual minorities, and acts by the total White community against the minority communities. We call these two forms *individual racism* and *institutional racism*. The first consists of overt acts by individuals, which cause death, injury or the violent destruction of property . . . the second type is less overt, far more subtle, less identifiable in terms of specific individuals committing the acts. But institutional racism is no less destructive of human life. Institutional racism "originates in the operation of established and respected forces in the society, and thus receives far less public condemnation than the first type" (Knowles & Prewitt, 1969, p. 1).

Racism is seen as a broad concept that includes both attitudes and behaviors. It is the cognitive, affective, or behavioral processes of an individual or institution which lead to negative outcomes for less favored groups (Barbarin, Good, Pharr, & Siskind, in press). As such, it extends to almost all areas of society and becomes fixed in society's institutions.

In the struggles of the 1940s and 1950s, prejudice and racism were referred to as *discrimination*. Prior to this, the term *Jim Crow* and later *segregation* were used extensively in referring to the various laws that prevented Blacks from equal accommodations in public transportation, schooling, and public accommodations such as lunch counters, water fountains, hotels, rest rooms, and other public places. Jim Crow, as a term, was in effect from approximately the 19th century until the middle-late 1930s. After this time, the terms discrimination, prejudice, and racism came into greater prominence. Figure 8–1 diagrams the various periods of racism.

In the United States, the handicapped, the young, the elderly, women, homosexuals, various racial, ethnic, and religious groups are categorized by

PERIODS OF RACISM

1640	1865	1877	1890	1900	1917	1930	1954	1960s	1970s	1980s
Slavery										
	Reconstruction									
										Cuban immigrants
		Jim Crow begins			"discrimination"					
								"racism" -institutional	Vietnamese immigrants	
				Progressive era	"prejudice"					
							-individual			
	14th Amendment									
							"sit-ins"			
								protest marches		
			Separate but equal myth begins							
								urban "riots"		
				NAACP Urban League						
							Civil rights awakening	Black power		
								Hispanic protests (La Raza)		
			Plessy vs. Ferguson (separate but equal decision)							
							Brown vs. Board of Education (school desegregation decision)			

Figure 8–1. Approximate development of descriptive terms and related events for what is now called *racism*

the term *minority*. The terms *minority* and *majority* historically have denoted people who interact, intermarry, and procreate among themselves as a means of passing on norms, values, and traditions. Minorities have been defined as "subordinated groups whose right to self-determination in community life . . . is at any time jeopardized" (Longres, 1982). Minority status is measured further by socioeconomic well-being and by cultural and social acceptance. Minority status may not be permanent as minority groups may cease to be minorities when they achieve equal dignity or opportunity with the majority or reach their goals. Color alone may be a major reason for labeling a given group as a minority, and, for some groups, color is a major barrier to achieving equality of opportunity and dignity.

As used here, *minority, minorities, minority group,* and *minority status* refer to Blacks, Hispanics, Native Americans, and Asian-Pacific Americans. The term *Hispanic* includes Mexican Americans, primarily concentrated in the southwestern United States; Puerto Ricans, who predominate in the northeast; Cubans, who have migrated or been relocated to many states but predominate in South Florida; Chileans, Nicaraguans, Salvadoreans, and others. Native Americans belong to many Indian nations and are located throughout the United States. Asian-Pacific Americans include American Chinese, Japanese, Vietnamese, Laotians, Cambodians, Filipinos, and other groups.

It should be noted that many minority groups reflect all shades of the racial spectrum, from blonde and blue-eyed to olive-skinned and deep black (Ghali, 1982) so that some prefer to define minority status as "communities of families who are subordinated by other communities of families" (Longres, 1982, p. 7). Color, however, appears to be a major criterion, at least in the United States, for assigning minority status. U.S. society appears to be racist primarily on the basis of skin color.

HISTORICAL CONTEXT

Before the Emancipation Proclamation legally freed slaves, racism was not seen as a problem. Slavery was the "law of the land," and, except for a few dissidents in the Abolitionist movement, there was no widespread disagreement about subjugation of the Negro. "Thus the Negro himself was not seriously considered by the majority of men, North or South" (DuBois, 1935, pp. 37, 671). The post–Civil War Southern society condoned almost all types of debasement of the newly freed slave, or *freedman*. Records and testimony to Congress after 1866 show that "a veritable reign of terror prevailed in many parts of the South" (DuBois, 1935). Ample documentation of the atrocities committed during this period and of societal unconcern about them suggest that little if any attention was given to the effects of racism from roughly 1866 to the late 1890s. (See Bontemps, 1948, DuBois, 1975, 1899/1967, and other classical treatments of the subject.)

Progressive era

A particular form of political and social enlightenment began to take place at the juncture of the 19th and 20th centuries as organized reform was promoted in governmental, social, educational, and political spheres of American society. The form of today's labor movement became solidified in these times; the contemporary business organization had its beginnings during this period; there was a concerted effort at reform politics and public regulation of many previously unregulated activities. Many of these changes came about through the efforts of a coalition of academics, "good government" reformers, ordinary citizens, and many of the economic and political elites. This movement was known as the Progressive movement, or simply as progressivism. In most areas of American life, the Progressive era was an age of reform reacting against corruption at all levels and with a strong thrust toward giving power to the "people" rather than back to the system. But what of Jim Crow, prejudice, and racism during these heady times? The progressive commitment evidently did not extend to eliminating racism. Review of the major writings of the

Progressive reformers indicates little concern with the "Negro problem" (as it was then called).

Apart from the writings and studies of the Black intelligentsia of the day (W. E. B. DuBois of Atlanta University; Booker T. Washington of Tuskegee Institute; Carter G. Woodson of the Negro Society for Historical Research, and the Association for the Study of Negro Life and History, among others), few Progressives recognized the pervasiveness of racism at the time. There were, however, as there have alway been, Whites who for varying reasons aligned themselves with the era's Negro leadership and helped to create institutions to deal with the effects of racism. In 1910, for instance, the National Urban League was created in reaction to urban problems caused by the large migration of Blacks from the rural South to urban areas of the North. Again, there is ample evidence of racism and racist theories during these times, most often to be found in the pseudoscientific "conclusions" of a certain brand of anatomy, psychology, anthropology, and history.

DuBois led in the formation of the National Association for the Advancement of Colored People (NAACP) in 1910, and its house organ, *The Crisis* (DuBois, 1975). DuBois also illustrates the difficulty during the Progressive period of focusing attention on "the race problem." In his correspondence with *Colliers Weekly,* he asked: "Have you ever thought of this: the color line is belting the world today: about it world interests are centering. Would it not be an interesting experiment to start in *Colliers* a column—or half column—called 'Along the Color Line' or the 'Voice of the Darker Millions' and put therein from week to week, or month to month, note and comment on the darker races in America." To realize this ambition, DuBois was forced to create his own publications.

During the Progressive era, it should also be noted, Negroes were still being tortured and killed without the protection of the law, while more and more Jim Crow laws were being passed in various cities and states. For example, some of the ordinances by which Southern cities required separation of Negroes from Whites in streetcars were passed as late as 1909 (Bontemps, 1948).

Depression era

With the stock market crash of 1929 and the subsequent Great Depression, Blacks had to develop yet another response to racism. Depression-era New Deal programs were mainly responses to an economic crisis, not an attempt to usher in a new age of racial equality.

> In the field of racial equality, where there was no crisis as in economics . . . there was no "new deal." The special encumbrances of the depression were lifted for Negroes . . . but the permanent caste structure remained unaltered. . . . The Fourteenth Amendment waited as fruitlessly for executive enforcement as it had in all earlier administrations since Grant (Zinn, 1966).

Guy Johnson, a University of North Carolina sociologist (cited in Zinn, 1966), recounts the social and economic plight of the Negro in the South during the depression. "Differentials in wages and hours kept the Negro from getting ahead. Federal relief programs such as the Civil Works Administration

(CWA), etc., perpetuated existing inequalities, employment offices ignored the Negro, and wages were not equal to those of whites in too many instances" [p. 313].

Examples abound of the racial inequality of New Deal programs. For example, Negro streets were deliberately not paved (Zinn, 1966); wages were unequal (Schlesinger, 1960); and Negroes were displaced from the work programs and onto relief (Schlesinger, 1960). In the North and West, however, more Negroes were involved in the programs, especially in New Deal educational programs when the prominent Negro educator, Mary McLeod Bethune, was appointed director of the National Youth Administration's Office of Minority Affairs. Other Blacks involved in high-level advisory positions included Dr. Robert C. Weaver, a Harvard economist and later secretary of the U.S. Department of Housing and Urban Development (HUD). The first Black to head a major federal agency, Weaver was an adviser to President Franklin D. Roosevelt, and to Secretary of the Interior Harold Ickes. E. K. Jones of the National Urban League with the Commerce Department was another high level advisor.

The Forties, Fifties, and Sixties

The post–World War II years and especially the 1960s focused far greater attention on the so-called race problem, now called *civil rights* and *racism* in the fifties and sixties respectively. The racist legacy of World War II and the new racial awareness fostered among Black soldiers had now to be reckoned with. In 1941, a threatened march on Washington by A. Phillip Randolph of the Brotherhood of Sleeping Car Porters forced President Roosevelt to issue an order forbidding employment discrimination in military industries.

Meanwhile, the greatest migration in the history of Negro Americans continued. Court rulings, the President's Commission on Civil Rights, and President Harry S. Truman himself accelerated attacks on "the two worlds of race" in the United States. Also, civic and religious groups, some labor organizations, and many Whites individually joined the battle to destroy discrimination and segregation (Franklin, 1965). Another factor (Emerson & Kilson, 1965) was the increasing militancy of Blacks in response to the rise of the Third World nations in Africa, Latin America, and Asia. Racism was also increasingly being confronted because of dissatisfaction with the status quo of race relations among minorities in the United States.

Racial awareness among racial minorities peaked in the 1960s. A 1968 special issue *Fortune*, entitled "The Negro and the City," highlighted a new mood of hope admixed with anger. Though the majority still believed in nonviolence, many others believed in the "tactics of Detroit" along with Watts, California, one of the earlier symbols of the unleashing of Black rage and frustration. Interestingly, the new mood probably illustrated the "revolution of rising expectations." At the beginning of America's worst period of urban violence, a majority of Blacks felt that the Negro condition was better than it had ever been. Many believe that activism increases during periods of hope and that apathy characterizes periods of hopelessness. The sixties began with renewed hope.

New leaders emerged. The Reverend Martin Luther King, Jr., gained recognition by helping to organize a successful resistance to the "separate but equal" policy of the city bus system in Birmingham, Alabama, where Blacks were assigned seats at the back of the bus only. Roy Wilkins of the NAACP led the assault on segregated schools that ended in the Brown v. Board of Education decision outlawing them in 1954. Thurgood Marshall, later the first Black on the U.S. Supreme Court, headed the NAACP's Legal Defense Fund, which developed the legal strategy that would topple segregation in many areas of U.S. life. The National Urban League's Whitney Young (a social worker by training) led in the improvement of employment, housing, and other services to urban Blacks and other minorities.

The Congress of Racial Equality (CORE) advocated activism, sit-ins against discriminatory public accommodations, and later Black Power; its leaders were, among others, Roy Innis and James Farmer. The Student Non-Violent Coordinating Committee (SNCC) publicized racism in public accommodations through sit-ins. The Reverend Adam Clayton Powell of New York, one of the most respected Black political leaders and chairman of the U.S. House of Representatives' Education and Labor Committee, presided over the creation of the War on Poverty and major national education acts. Malcolm X and the Black Muslims gained a large following through articulate espousal of Black unity and a self-help philosophy.

There were many leaders in the forefront of various other movements (for example the Mississippi Freedom Democratic party). Many current leaders, such as Jesse Jackson, Vernon Jordan, Andrew Young, Julian Bond, and others began their leadership roles during this period under Dr. King and his mass civil rights movement, the Southern Christian Leadership Conference (SCLC).

But hope turned to bitterness with the riots in Watts, Detroit, Newark, Tampa, Cincinnati, and many other cities during the 1960s. Detailed analyses of these urban civil disorders by the Kerner Commission on Civil Disorders show a complex causation that included unemployment, social disorganization, ghetto conditions, police harassment, lack of communication, and general frustration (Kerner, 1968). Many regard *Black Power: The Politics of Liberation in America* by Stokely Carmichael and Charles V. Hamilton (1967) as the major philosophical and political treatment of racism in the 1960s. James Baldwin was one of the major literary figures whose writings influenced many in the movement of the sixties.

Other ethnic movements adopted the strategy and tactics of the Black Power movement, as it was then called—Chicano Power and the American Indian and Women's movements most notably and successfully. Ernest Galarza, César Chávez and the National Farmworkers of America Union (NFWA) are prominent in the Hispanic movement that primarily began with the organizing of farmworkers but later extended to political organization and ethnic identity. There have been many instances of cooperation between Hispanic and Black organizations to further common agendas and to attack common problems (see Rosaldo, Seligmann, & Calvert, 1974).

With the prominent role of the U.S. in world leadership, racism became increasingly difficult for the U.S. to explain in its foreign relations, especially to the newly emerging Third World countries. On the domestic front, New Deal social welfare programs had matured into the now familiar Social Security Act programs: Aid to Families with Dependent Children (AFDC); Unemployment Insurance (UI); Old Age, Survivors, and Disability Insurance (OASDI); Assistance to the Permanently and Totally Disabled (APTD). In addition, child welfare services had come into being.

By 1962, a "services strategy"—an accepted belief that social service programs could cure all of society's ills—was the prevailing social and political philosophy, with funding levels to match. In 1965, the Economic Opportunity Act (EOA) created the Office of Economic Opportunity (OEO); the Manpower Development and Training Act (MDTA) funded innovative programs designed to reduce expected postwar unemployment; and Model Cities, Urban Renewal, and a multitude of other programs were available in terms of local governmental planning and services. Private social service agencies participated in these programs through contracts and grants to provide services. It was politically fashionable to be against poverty in the early sixties, truly another "golden age" for social service programs and practitioners.

However, what was called "The Revolt against Welfare Colonialism" (Silberman, 1964) began to set in among Blacks and some other minorities who, together with social scientists and government officials, were beginning to wonder whether welfare tended to cause dependency. Did the welfare system, in addition to being self-perpetuating, not only fail to relieve dependency but actually *encourage* it? Many practitioners asked themselves whether dependency and the failure to solve many social ills was due to their preoccupation with psychoanalytic theory, individual symptoms, casework, and adjustment of the individual to society as it is rather than to reform activities engaged in by social work pioneers in the 19th and early 20th centuries. Had the professionals "made Freud their God when they should have been worshipping at the shrine of Emile Durkheim?" (Silberman, 1964, p. 312).

Minorities were concerned with the effects of practitioners and social welfare programs doing *for* people rather than *with* them: "Policy makers had a tendency, in the case of [minorities], to plan, design, and implement programs without talking to those who are going to be uplifted" (Silberman, 1964, p. 317). Many practitioners favored the type of self-help and advocacy that was planned into the Ford Foundation's Grey Areas programs and those of the President's Committee on Juvenile Delinquency (both being models and forerunners for the OEO's War on Poverty). In any event, it appeared that the social welfare programs of the fifties, and especially of the sixties, also provided specific services to minorities. Unlike many New Deal programs, there was increased hiring of minorities and vastly increased minority-oriented public and social services available.

The Seventies and Eighties

Owing in part to the progress made in the 1960s through increased Black power, racial awareness, and Black activism, other minority groups adopted more activist strategies in the 1970s and 1980s. Hispanics, Native Americans, and Asian-Pacific refugees (mainly Vietnamese) grew in number and were also increasingly represented as social service clients. About 25 million Blacks;

4 million Asian-Americans, American Indians, and other non-Whites; and 12 million Hispanics were part of the U.S. population in 1978 (McAdoo, 1982). Hispanic issues—preservation of traditional cultural values, language, and racial identity—became increasingly of interest to the services practitioner. How U.S. society views differences in Hispanic skin tones became an issue as a cause of identity problems among the affected minorities and in practice relationships as well.

Among Native Americans, questions arose concerning the scope of authority that Indians on reservations have in tribal courts. These are not mere legalistic issues though their resolution bears directly on the jurisdiction over and handling of dependent children in foster care, adoptions, and social services. Jurisdiction over Indian children and services to adult tribal members living off the reservation are also at issue in jurisdictional questions, especially in urban areas at a distance from the reservation. Should services be received (and financed) from tribal sources or from local public and private agencies? Should services to Indians on and off reservations be financed by federal, state, or local government, or in what combination by all three?

The 1978 Indian Child Welfare Act returned tribal rights of jurisdiction over dependent children to the tribes and provided some (mostly small) sources of additional funding, but this still left major questions of jurisdiction and continuing funding to the states. If services formerly provided by the state or by counties are to be given through tribal sources, should existing funds be transferred from county and state programs to tribal authorities? If so, in what percentages, and how should services be delivered to off-reservation Indians? Services by Indian practitioners with a more acute sense of tribal traditions and customs is desirable, but some very complex practical and political issues have prevented implementation of this ideal.

Asian-Pacific Americans, most notably Vietnamese after the Vietnam War, were uprooted from their homeland and resettled into various areas of the United States where they faced serious language and cultural barriers. Generally, one of their major problems was that they had no indigenous ethnic community to offer them support (Montero & Dieppa, 1982).

PROFESSIONAL IDEALS IN A RACIST SOCIETY

There are many viewpoints about the proper role of the practitioner in any type of intervention activity. The definitions of social work and of practice give some clues to expected roles; also, a review of the history and founders of the social work profession gives an indication of the expected practitioner role. Historically, practitioner and practice tended to favor reform, social action, advocacy, and political involvement in behalf of a cause or specific client group. Early social workers led efforts to change social institutions and laws and to set up new institutions to remedy certain social ills. Individual practitioners lobbied officials, exposed the horrid conditions of the poor, publicized problems, organized societies to deal with the identified problems, inspired newspaper features, and the like.

In the early 20th century, however, practitioners became immersed in Freudianism, and the role of individual practice relationships began to turn from reform toward individual psychotherapy that focused on helping the individual to adjust better to society. Social practice began to be based on a psychiatric or medical model of intervention, which persists to the present in various practice areas (for examples, review biographical sketches of Gordon Hamilton, Margaret Rich, and Mary Richmond in the *Encyclopedia of Social Work*).

Though there is no precise cutoff date, a "synthesis" movement developed after the initial Freudian peak was over. Group work, variations on psychoanalytic theory, increased work in child welfare, family, and children's areas, youth work, community organization and planning, and other forms of practice became more prominent. Until the Economic Opportunity Act brought major increases in funding for community organization practice during the early sixties, the practitioner's role as a facilitator in the individual's adjustment to society predominated.

The ideals of any profession can perhaps best be determined by reviewing its writings and professed official standards. In social work, for example, the highest and most general form of standard is the *Social Work Code of Ethics* adopted by the Delegate Assembly of the National Association of Social Workers in 1960. As amended in 1967, the code mentions racism directly for the first time: "I will not discriminate because of race, color, religion, age, sex, or national ancestry, and in my job capacity will work to prevent and eliminate such discrimination in rendering services, in work assignments, and in employment practices" (Lucas, 1977).

Discrimination arises again in connection with Section VI of the 1977 Ethics revision: "[Ethics] are unique reflections of our values, our heritage and our obligations as a profession" (NASW News, 1980, p. 10). Robert Cohen, the national office staff member assigned to the 1977 Task Force on Ethics, quoting from the revised statement, writes:

> The duties to "act to prevent and eliminate discrimination" . . . "to insure that all persons have access to the resources, services, and opportunities which they require" . . . to expand choice and opportunity for all persons, [especially] disadvantaged or oppressed groups and persons . . . to promote conditions that encourage respect for . . . diversity of cultures . . . are the essence of our social conscience and the most direct expression of the underlying values upon which our ethical code is grounded (Cohen, 1980, p. 10).

Given these statements, it is reasonable to assume that the elimination of racism (*discrimination* is the milder term used in the Ethics) in practice relationships and elsewhere is at least a high priority of organized social work and an ideal or standard for the individual practitioner. To what extent ideals and actuality coincide forms the subject of the following sections.

SOCIAL WORK PRACTICE IN A RACIST SOCIETY

Minority clients exhibit important cultural and lifestyle differences, and the ability to work sensitively with these differences is the crux of the matter of racism in practice relationships. Among the major racism issues in individual practice are the following:

1. access to services;

2. provision of culturally relevant services or a sensitivity to cultural differences in any treatment or intervention by a social worker;

3. availability of minority practitioners who will presumably have the cultural sensitivities required to work with given minorities;

4. ability of the practitioner to speak the client's language;

5. adequacy or relevance of the treatment of the minority client (a practice relationship that is not culturally sensitive may not be an effective treatment; the type of treatment given to a majority client may not work with a minority client);

6. awareness of the place of religion, beliefs, history, lifestyles, or tradition that may affect the choice of treatment (for example, folk medicine with the Indian or Hispanic client);

7. awareness of special social or health needs that may be more prevalent with a given minority group client (such as unemployment among Black youth);

8. specialized treatment modalities (services or methods) that may be more effective with a given minority client;

9. understanding the client's unique values;

10. newly emerging special problems of the client of a particular minority group (such as alienation and delinquency among some Asian-American youth);

11. specialized staffing or organizational structures that may be needed for more effective treatment of a particular minority client;

12. special needs for particular kinds of services among some minority groups (delinquency prevention, alcoholism and drug services, special health needs, special educational problems, advocacy, and so forth);

13. awareness of special ways of coping that a given minority group has developed and with which the practitioner must work (for example, the availability and role of the church or family as a support mechanism among Black and Hispanic clients, especially in areas of child welfare and aging); the role of the godparent in Hispanic culture and of the *bodega* (small grocery store) and associations as social and help centers among Puerto Ricans;

14. special attitudes prevalent among some minority groups with which the practitioner must be familiar (for example, the role of the male in Hispanic society, or the stigma associated with receiving certain types of assistance, such as AFDC or mental health services, among many minority groups).

Effects on individual practice relationships

Individual practice and racism interactions received a great deal of attention and analysis in the 1960s. Much of this early attention focused on the relationship between the minority client and the White therapist. Questions were continually raised concerning whether the nonminority practitioner was sufficiently aware of the differing culture, special problems, special needs, ways of coping, and attitudes.

For example, racial discrimination has been defined as "allocation on the basis of *irrelevant* status characteristics such as skin color and diagnostic differentiation (the allocation of . . . social commodities on the basis of relevant social and psychological characteristics in conformity with each person's individual . . . attributes), and there is a danger of confusing legitimate differentiation with irrelevant discrimination" (Eaton & Gilbert, 1969). The practical effect of this confusion of terms would be segregated services rather than services built on necessary individual characteristics.

A sterilization law in North Carolina that was directed at Blacks, ostensibly to curb illegitimacy, is viewed as discriminatory (it was a pseudodiagnosis because it was really aimed at curbing a growing Black population). Another example of discrimination rather than diagnostic differentiation is the disproportionate institutionalization of delinquent Black youth in Los Angeles or longer sentences for Black adult offenders. A special educational-medical service for minority school-age pregnant girls built on cultural differences and specialized ways of coping would be a program based on appropriate and relevant diagnosis rather than on discrimination.

Another illustration of race influencing the practice relationship is when White examiner bias influences diagnostic test results (Cohen, 1969). As early as 1938, studies of Black clients in the practice relationship noted considerable submissive behavior by the client that interfered with the development of an effective relationship (Miller, 1967). This behavior was based on fear and distrust of the White practitioner. Later studies have confirmed these findings.

The effects of racism in clinical work in fact pervade areas of clinical practice by causing the White social worker to have feelings during the social work relationship that prevent effective treatment. "Clinicians must examine their own thinking with special care, since their efforts to acknowledge and deal with racial and ethnic factors are affected by highly emotional release attitudes" (Cooper, 1973, p. 127). Color-blindness, Cooper concludes, is not totally possible or realistic, but an attitude on the part of the White worker of awareness of lifestyle, ethnic origins, and so forth, are perfectly feasible. Focus should be on individual problems and solutions, with awareness of ethnic and other issues that may influence the course of the treatment.

Yet another example of racism in individual practice occurs when diagnostic issues are obscured by ethnic ones in a mental health setting (Cooper, 1973, p. 136). Clinical effects may cause "guilt on the part of the worker leading to overcompensation, denial, reaction formation, an intense drive to identify with the oppressed, and a need to offer to the victim special privileges and relaxed standards of behavior no more acceptable to minorities than to the general population" [p. 127]. Incidentally, minorities are familiar with the permissive White worker who indulges or oversympathizes with the client to the detriment of effective treatment and change.

Let us look at an example of this process in an actual practitioner-client relationship.

A 24-year-old Black man recently released from a mental hospital attends an outing arranged by his day treatment center. He only occasionally joins in the group's activities, but he does engage in a conversation initiated by one of the counselors, a young, bright, White woman deeply conscious of injustice to Blacks. She has read about such experiences and is eager to even the score.

As the conversation proceeds, the Black patient talks of his visions, filled with aggression and violence. He is certain he can predict the future. As the group returns to the center the patient elects to sit beside the counselor commenting, as they pass through an affluent neighborhood, that the people who live there "sure have it good," and adding, "what would be so bad about blowing it up? Everybody would sure call me a bad boy then." It is White guilt (about racism) that keeps the counselor from a helpful response. Instead she reports that neither she nor any White has the right or the capacity to intervene; only a Black therapist can be of help. Yet this Black man's controls are tenuous, his impulses overwhelming. He is not just putting the counselor on, although there may be some of that; he desperately needs the strength to control impulses as he takes his first faltering steps back into the community. White guilt denied him the help he needed (Cooper).[2]

Overcompensation, guilt, and permissiveness are subtle forms of racism in clinical practice relationships which the nonminority practitioner must avoid in the interests of effective treatment.

Transference has also been the subject of much clinical discussion. Race is seen as an issue but not necessarily as one that would preclude effective transference in the case of a Black therapist and White patient. In the Black-White encounter, the therapeutic practice relationship may be strained and frustrating due to class, educational, and power differences. Anger and defensiveness by both parties may be avoided in part if the practitioner realizes that "the Black client has the right and capacities to determine what he wants to do and the strength to move himself in that direction" (Gitterman & Schaeffer, n.d., p. 152). This is consistent with the practitioner's role as enabler and helper rather than as controller.

Black adolescent parents have unique needs and values, and there are ways in which the practitioner might best intervene (Gilbert, 1974). It is suggested, for example, that for effective treatment the practitioner must understand the concepts of "neocolonialism," "survival," and "liberation." *Neocolonialism* connotes the distrust that Black youth may have for the traditional institutions designed to serve their needs, institutions created and staffed by Whites primarily to serve Whites, which may perpetuate negative views about Blacks. Self-hatred among youth is cited as an example of this phenomenon, although such self-hatred is not supported by the research of prominent Black psychiatrists.

Survival in this context is a struggle for continued existence given the repression of the past. An understanding of the specialized coping mechanisms of minorities will help practitioners to understand the means of survival utilized and help them to select appropriate strategies (kinship bonds and strong religious affiliations have traditionally helped many minorities through various types of crises).

Liberation is the goal of attaining freedom from oppression—that is, the freedom to make critical choices regarding their social needs irrespective of societal attitudes or institutional policies and practice. Trader (1977) echoes the feeling that the theory underlying practice must "take into account the cultural group to which the client belongs" and presents a theoretical framework for the nonminority practitioner.

Hispanics.   Among Hispanics, a history of agency racism helps to explain low utilization rates of social services, especially in the Southwest. A residue of suspicion from social welfare agency complicity of the 1930s to the 1950s in identifying Mexican American aliens for deportation back to Mexico (Watkins & Gonzales, 1982) still interferes with the development of an individual practice relationship. Many Mexican Americans view service practitioners as representative of the government and of possible repression. But the presence or absence of bilingual staff remains the major factor in Mexican American utilization of mental health services. It has been shown that a worker's unfamiliarity with a client's language may cause clients to focus more on trying to communicate than on the problem at hand, and the same is true in psychotherapy.

Traditional Mexican families, like other Hispanic groups, tend to retain the concept of masculine superiority and emphasis on submission to the authority of the father—the "macho" concept (Watkins & Gonzales, 1982). This, too, may cause problems in practice relationships, especially with female practitioners who have a background in U.S. feminist culture.

Hispanic needs and responses to services are unique, and there are cultural differences among the three major Hispanic groups—Mexican American, Puerto Rican, and Cuban—that the practitioner should note.

Direct services practitioners should be aware of the assistance that the natural community may offer in working with Hispanics. Delgado and Delgado (1982) present a concise description and summary of the importance of the folk healer, religious institutions, and merchant's and social clubs in treatment. Essentially, the direct services practitioner must use these natural supports as a resource where appropriate. For example, many Hispanic churches provide emergency financial assistance and care for the ill and disturbed. The *bodega*, in addition to selling groceries, is an important source of information and referral. Social clubs may perform an orientation function for newcomers. Other supports assist with credit, day care, and respite care. Relatives, "adopted relatives," neighbors, and friends may be a resource for the parent or serve as parental substitutes for children's services.

Traditional Puerto Rican culture places great importance on family, godparents, and special friends. *Machismo* or "maleness" holds a prominence that may present special relationship problems to the practitioner only familiar with contemporary U.S. culture. The practitioner should also be aware of the cultural clashes for the Puerto Rican family coming into contact with prevailing U.S. patterns. For example, traditional parental controls are made more difficult by urban American lifestyles; traditional discipline is also more difficult. Children who know English better than their parents may cause parental "loss of face" if the practitioner attempts to interpret through the child. Practitioners should especially respect the father's role and make sure that the practice relationship is one of mutual respect. For the client, respect is a deeply held cultural value and as such requires certain ceremonial rituals, (such as formal handshaking at the beginning and end of an encounter). Ghali (1982) details many of these traditions in her article "Understanding Puerto Rican Traditions."

Asian-Americans.   Practitioners should be keenly aware of the differing cultural backgrounds and other difficulties faced by the Asian-American being assimilated into American culture. Some were totally unaccustomed to Western culture and psychologically unprepared to start a new life in the United States. Language barriers were formidable. There was no indigenous ethnic community in any given area to offer support; families were separated, further inhibiting adjustment; government policy did not facilitate developing a community. Economic self-sufficiency, depression, and language were major problems (Montero & Dieppa, 1982). Further, in Vietnamese culture the elderly were revered and considered important, whereas too often in U.S. culture the opposite is true.

The practitioner may need to devote considerable attention to language classes, cash-assistance job training programs, and development of a community identity among Vietnamese refugees. Traditional psychiatric methods may be inapplicable due to language and cultural barriers. Health and education are important considerations as well. The 1975 Indochina Migration and Refugee Assistance Act (P. L. 94—23) was at one time of great assistance to state and local service efforts but with federal cuts became much less effective as a source of aid.

These few examples by no means constitute an exhaustive listing of the major issues of racism and individual practice relationships. Some of the issues (for example, White practitioner–minority client) have been intensely debated since the 1960s; others such as the unique values of the minority client, minority group attitudes, and specialized ways of coping, still need further discussion and research. Moreover, most of the literature and research has been on the Black client–White practitioner relationship. With the increasing numbers of Spanish-speaking persons and Vietnamese immigrants in the United States, and with the heightened consciousness of Native American and Asian-Pacific groups, a great deal more analysis, discussion, and research on these groups will be required to avoid perpetuating the same types of racist approaches that were previously visited on Blacks. Practitioners should examine the literature and talk with minority practitioners to increase their understanding of how to work with minorities.

Effects on group practice relationships.

The practitioner utilizing a group practice method must be aware of the same basic issues of racism in treatment as is the individual practitioner. For example, special problems of transference arise when the co-therapists are racially different (Brayboy & Marks, n.d.). A noneffective group dynamic may occur if latent but unconscious prejudices are aroused; anxiety, fear, anger, and flight may become singly or collectively apparent in the group.

The group practitioner must be aware of the effects of racism on group dynamics and become sensitive to cultural differences in order to practice this method effectively. Group intervention theory must develop not only a much greater awareness of the unique qualities of newly emerging minority groups but also a theory of practice that will enable the group worker to deal effectively with these new groups of clients. Many of the conventions and practices important in individual practice are also important in group practice relationships.

Effects on community practice relationships

Community practice or community organization has as a goal the promotion of effective and humane operations of systems. Its objectives are (a) to develop mechanisms for interorganizational exchange; (b) to negotiate between people and resource systems to assure optimum benefits; (c) to make opportunities accessible to persons in order to promote social growth; and (d) to create conditions that result in the development of new resources, opportunities, and services. Organizing, mobilizing, and exchanging are functions of community practice (NASW, 1980).

Community organization as an approach has been viewed as community action, locality development, community development, as well as resource development. Locality development is "a process designed to create conditions of economic and social progress for the whole community with its active participation and fullest possible reliance on the community's initiative" (Rothman, 1970). This was also the United Nations definition of community development. Neighborhood work programs in settlement houses, adult education community work, and overseas village-level work are all examples of community development (Rothman, 1970).

The social action approach perhaps typifies community organization in the United States as practiced in the various War on Poverty programs. It aims at "basic changes in major institutions or community practices" (Rothman, 1970, p. 21); "redistribution of power, resources, or decision making or changing basic policies of formal organizations" are its aims. One of the better known examples of this form of community organization was The Woodlawn Organization (TWO) in Chicago, though OEO and Model Cities community action programs sponsored a great variety of other community programs that used this method.

Community organizers are a diverse lot, but the major concerns about the effects of racism on practice relationships in this method seem to be along the following lines:

1. The role of the community organizer is an issue. . . . There have been examples of White practitioners who assumed a role of benevolent protector of the client group, thus impeding any real indigenous leadership development.

2. In other instances, practitioners have prevented real community change in minority communities by substituting their own viewpoints for those of the client group. In still other instances, practitioners have subverted major radical changes.

3. Basic disagreement over the goals and strategies of a conflict model has been known to divide the practitioner and urban ghetto residents.

4. Practitioner knowledge and utilization of differing minority group community resources are issues. . . . There are substantial natural support systems in Black, Hispanic, and Native American communities of which the community organization practitioner should be aware.

The following account illustrates a practitioner (community organizer) serving personal rather than client ends, almost to the detriment of the client group.

A White volunteer, who had worked with Black residents of a dilapidated, low-income, semirural slum area near a major eastern city, lived on a farm in a more affluent, nearby area. She was able to help the residents, most of whom were either elderly or welfare recipients, with day-to-day problems in an informal sort of way. When the county housing authority developed a plan to provide each resident with the opportunity to own his or her own new home and hired a Black professional as manager and community developer, she felt instant hostility toward the new professional, told the residents not to trust him, and generally attempted to subvert his efforts and maintain her former benevolent role. After much work by the new person, residents were finally convinced that there were in fact opportunities for home ownership and participation in the job and other programs being offered by the housing authority. Many residents later bought their own homes through the program and became self-sufficient through newly found job opportunities. Eventually the services of the Black practitioner were no longer needed, but the old, informal dependent practice relationship was no longer needed either.

Except for very few instances, there has been little funding or priority for community organization strategies since their heyday in the 1960s War on Poverty programs. Meeting future needs in community organization seems to lie with practitioners of this method becoming more familiar with the needs and aspirations of new groups of minorities such as Haitians, Vietnamese, Spanish-speaking, Native American, and Asian-American peoples. Particular community organization and community development needs of these groups have not been met (language classes, self-help efforts, policy changes). In addition, the organizational needs of American Blacks have changed but have yet to be met and are now crucial. Future community organizers may have to teach political awareness as a tool by which minorities can reassert themselves and promote political solutions to their own needs.

These political solutions are not necessarily limited to actions that influence governmental decision making. As demonstrated by the late War on Poverty and Model Cities programs, political participation (voting favorable candidates into office) can also cause favorable decisions by funding sources and change the way in which community decisions are made. The following case study of a community practice relationship shows the potential power that can be generated to change racism in local decision making.

In a semirural midwestern university town of 50,000, there were 2,500 minority residents and approximately 30,000 students. Minorities were generally not in positions of influence, though there was a Black city alderman, a Black school board member, and a Black city youth and recreation supervisor. A local practitioner, who was a public agency social planning director, began a series of weekly lunch meetings in a local restaurant with the alderman, minority ministers, and a few other interested persons to discuss how to resolve local issues. The meetings, in time, became so well attended that they had to be moved to the basement of a minority church (brown-bag lunch).

Discussions finally led to formation of an underground citizens' group with officers and bylaws. Unpublicized but well attended minority community workshops developed a complete list of community issues on such topics as housing rehabilitation, minority youth career development, and human services needs. The citizens' group, without publicity, decided to place its members on city and county boards and private agency (including United Way) boards in areas that reflected their issues. Letter writing and informal contacts by individual citizens, rather than in the name of the organization (but orchestrated in the citizen committee meetings), led to the appointment of citizen committee candidates to 29 of 30 committees and boards targeted.

Infiltration of such influential groups as the Community Development Block Grant committee, for example, enabled minorities (through letter-writing campaigns, letters to the editor, and informal contact with the city aldermen, supported within by the minority alderman) to defeat a proposal by the city manager to build a downtown parking lot with block grant funds. Instead, funds were voted for elderly housing rehabilitation and a minority business development start-up fund. Similar input was directed to United Way board and committee members to influence decisions on funding and the acceptance of new agencies for funding.

A new minority-oriented radio show was aired; efforts were successful to get local television stations to bring in minority programs; and a weekly minority page in the daily newspaper suddenly "appeared" when the group discussed starting a minority weekly newspaper. The group was successful for a number of years until internal bickering and a public dispute with a new and conservative mayor finally diluted its effectiveness.

Effects on particular fields of practice

Racism in particular fields of practice exhibits both old and new problem areas. Traditionally, for example, there have been the issues of transracial adoptions, adoptions in general, and foster care for children with special needs (children with special needs have included minority children in addition to those with handicaps). In the case of child welfare, minority children in need of adoptive or foster placement have often had a much longer average institutional stay than nonminorities. This might have been due to a shortage of homes, but placement programs, such as Detroit's Homes for Black Children, have shown that innovative efforts which recognize differing cultural values of minority families have had a quicker and more successful placement rate than have traditional White agency programs (Madison & Schapiro, 1973).

Cultural values.   Misunderstanding of cultural values was a prominent feature in an institutional case of the denial of grease (for example, Vaseline) to a Black child in a residential treatment center. The majority institutional staff had not understood that preventing skin "ashiness" was a major factor in the child's self-esteem (Sommer, 1964). As early as 1972, the National Association of Black Social Workers (NABSW) adopted a position against transracial adoption. Here the issue centers on the ability of the White adoptive parent to understand the culture and values of the Black child (see Jones, 1972), though many (including prominent minority professionals) argue that any permanent home placement, even with a White family, is better than continued institutionalization.

Mental health.   Mental health is another major area of practice for a great many practitioners, and the differences in minorities seeking services have been amply documented (see Davis & Swartz, 1972). Minorities tend to be more reluctant to seek services in the first place and to place a greater stigma on being classified as mentally ill ("being crazy") than do Whites.

Puerto Ricans have a higher tolerance for mental illness than most American families and may try spiritualism and other healers, trips to Puerto Rico, and other natural supports before going to a professional, by which time their problems may have become more acute (Ghali, 1982). Many groups may not understand or accept psychotherapy, which for that reason may not be an effective means of treatment (depending, of course, on the individual in the practice relationship).

Minorities also tend to have different types of mental illneses. The very prevalent community mental health center is not a total answer, though it can help to reduce stress among those who are culturally different, economically disadvantaged, and generally powerless (Mayfield, 1972). It may also be more difficult for a White practitioner to predict behavioral differences in minority clients (Krebs, 1971). In general, however, minorities "share the task of preserving the unique aspects of their respective cultural backgrounds in the midst of the American mainstream" (Siskind et al., in press).

In view of minority differences, several experts in mental health have advocated creating a more informal intake structure in mental health facilities; also a different type of interview training that emphasizes a personal relationship over the more formal "professional distance" concepts formerly used (Barbarin et al., in press). Still others have suggested that White practitioners must live in, or spend some time in, minority communities to experience the conditions that lead to minority mental illness. Again, more use of personal support networks or "natural helping networks" (Collins & Pancoast, 1967; Delgado & Delgado, 1982) has also been proposed.

Family services.   For the area of family services, more innovative services have been proposed (Creighen, 1971) that would build on the strengths of Black families identified by Billingsley (1968) and others. In general, more informal and interactional family therapy approaches have been suggested. Still, there are specific barriers in counseling minority parents that the family service practitioner must understand (Gilbert, 1974), and some of these are based on racism issues identified earlier, such as differences in extended family and kinship relations (Hays & Mindel, 1973). Limited understanding of Hispanic families (Temple-Trujillo, 1974) and other minority families by family practitioners is general. Special family therapy programs emphasizing trust have been shown to be effective for specific minority family problems (Tuck, 1971). For the White practitioner working in this area, better understanding of minority family dynamics is indicated.

Public welfare.   Racism in public welfare has been extensively publicized due to the efforts of War on Poverty programs and advocacy efforts by the National Welfare Rights Organization (NWRO). By Whites as well as by minorities (Silberman, 1964), public welfare has historically been viewed as a "colonialist" institution: "Designed to save money instead of people [it] tragically ends up doing neither" (Glasgow, 1969). In terms of equity, there is an inverse relationship between welfare payments to, and size of, a non-White population (Schneiderman, 1972, p. 44). For studies of racism and inequality in the delivery of health services, see Yerby (1966); and in housing, see Myer (1973) and Glazer (1967).

Though not all these effects are directly attributable to practice relationships, the practitioner's role in many instances has been to counsel adjustment to existing conditions rather than to encourage an active posture of social change, thus assisting in the perpetuation of racism and inequality. In the future, practitioners will be required to have still greater awareness of racist effects. There must also be a great deal more publicity, dissemination of research findings, and national promotion of efforts to change programs in the education and training of practitioners who direct social services programs or participate in direct services efforts. The need for program change is especially urgent in the case of the larger public and private institutions. Hiring more minorities in direct services and in supervisory and administrative positions in direct services has also been shown to be effective in changing racist practices.

INSTITUTIONAL AND ORGANIZATIONAL RELATIONSHIPS

Individual practitioners cannot operate in isolation from the environment in which they practice. In most cases, they are directed by policies, procedures, laws, and regulations set by the organization in which practice takes place. In addition, local, state, and national policies and laws determine how services must be given. Because these policies are sometimes based on research findings, the research efforts themselves must be examined in order to understand how racism in the human services actually begins. Educational practices exert a great influence on how human services practitioners approach their role.

The context in which these systems of policies, procedures, laws, ordinances, and regulations operate in the institutions of society is the second type of racism, *institutional racism*.

Institutional racism has been called "less overt, far more subtle, and less identifiable in terms of specific individuals committing the acts. But it is no less destructive of human life . . . [it] originates in the operation of established and respected forces in the society, and thus receives far less public condemnation than the first type" (Knowles & Prewitt, 1969, p. 40). Institutional racism is embedded in the fabric of society itself and operates in ways that may only be noticeable to its victims. It is systematic and has also been described "in terms of organizational processes, behaviors, policies or procedures which produce negative outcomes for minorities while maintaining the status or economic advantages of non-minorities. . . . [It] exists when major community systems fail to provide equitably for the diverse needs of minority groups."

Intent is not necessarily a prerequisite. Federal courts have ruled in the past that differential outcomes, though unintended, provide sufficient evidence of discrimination (Barbarin et al., in press, pp. 11–12), though more recent, conservative Supreme Court rulings have begun to change this interpretation. Examples might be systematic nonattention to minority group problems by a private agency in a city with a large concentration of minorities, a systematically higher rate of institutionalization of minority youth in residential treatment centers, or the ignoring of minorities in a needs assessment to determine the planning of mental health services. Funding issues vividly illustrate this issue, as in the case of public or private funding efforts that many think have tended to allocate dollars on the basis of traditional middle-class services and to ignore minority needs.

Social policy

Issues in institutional racism are also prevalent in practice relationships in the areas of social policy, administration, research, and education.

Racism issues in social policy have traditionally concerned the amount of minority *participation* in policy formulation and the *number* and *influence* of minorities who hold policy-making positions in human services. These factors affect relationships in general and practice relationships in particular. Historically, there were few minorities in policy-making positions in the voluntary and other sectors of social welfare (Flaming, Palen, Ringlien, & Taylor, 1972). Papers presented at NABSW conferences (Creighen, 1971) illustrate that this is still true for Blacks and document a need for a Black United Fund to support meaningful programs and more community control of institutions. Control of, and participation in, policy making for social welfare programs by affected minorities is an especially pertinent policy issue—perhaps the major source of inequality and dissatisfaction—though it has been discussed much less since the citizen participation programs of the 1960s.

Some have seen as a corrective measure a need for a "politics of control" by minorities against White-controlled institutions (Street, 1977). Minority groups are "grossly underrepresented" in the health and welfare planning structures; in addition to Blacks, Puerto Ricans and Hispanics are also generally shut out of the "powerful prestigious positions in the welfare hierarchy" (Mizio, 1972). Studies that decry the underrepresentation of minorities in health and welfare planning structures (Perlmutter & Alexander, 1978) confirm that the agency board is dominated by the power structure of the community "and excludes Blacks and other minorities."

A 1967 survey of five national agency boards showed that minority representation was about 1 in 38. A 1965 survey in Boston showed that 60% of agencies had no non-Whites on their boards, and 7% had only two or more. Similar results were reported in Pittsburgh and in Gary, Indiana (1970); only community action agency (War on Poverty) boards tended to be well integrated, and their composition is set by law.

In the private sector, even neighborhood-based settlement houses that claim to be aware of cultural differences did not tend to base board policy making on race and ethnic issues (Kogut, 1972). The 1968 Report of the National Advisory Commission on Civil Rights suggested that although public agencies have the most contact with minority and poor people, they have not been particularly innovative in bringing in minority participation (Gibbs, 1971). According to 1971 Child Welfare League of America studies, private child welfare agencies were regarded by community persons as providing services primarily for the White child.

In addition, in the sixties and early seventies, federal regulations in health planning, mental health, welfare, child welfare, and many other areas tended either to mandate or strongly to encourage minority inclusion on various state and local boards and advisory committees, sometimes specifically listing the number of minorities needed. There were also federally funded programs of outreach and training to secure and train minorities who may have been newly elected or selected to various state and local social welfare–type boards. Since that time, however, interest in this issue has declined in favor of states' rights and "local" control, though consumers themselves have brought strong pressures to bear in many instances.

A case in policy development.   The following example shows a very subtle form of racism in a state having a very small percentage of minorities mainly concentrated in major urban areas.

> A minority staff person was appointed to develop a statewide minority mental health plan as a part of the overall state mental health plan. The planner formed a representative, statewide committee composed of Native Americans, Spanish speakers, Blacks, and Asian-Americans to secure input and develop needs.
>
> The plan, among numerous other specifics, disclosed few minority mental-health workers and a larger than expected number of minorities who were not using the traditional agency-based services. One recommendation was increased public information efforts by the state to publicize the need for minority mental health services. Provision of specific types of minority mental health services was the top priority in the minority-developed plan.

A one-day statewide conference on mental health needs was held to discuss findings of the President's Commission on Mental Health (PCMH). The majority of those in attendance were direct services workers and administrators. Analysis of a survey questionnaire asking participants to rate statewide mental health needs revealed that minority mental health was rated near the bottom of the list.

A similar survey of members of the official state mental health advisory body (mostly interested private citizens not directly in mental health) rated minority mental health as top priority in the same year. The advisory body had heard staff presentations of the minority plan and had the chair of the statewide Minority Mental Health Committee as an ad hoc member. The differences in priorities were all the more striking when compared to those of the full-time direct service and administrative professionals polled at the PCMH Conference who presumably would be expected to know the most about direct service needs.

What seems most needed now and for the future is an intensification of efforts to place more minorities onto policy-making boards, committees, and advisory bodies and into responsible administrative positions in both the public and private sectors. Most often (though not readily admitted), administrators and executives are the primary initiators of policy and program proposals that may eventually be ratified by voluntary boards, city and county councils, state legislatures, and the U.S. Congress.

Intensified federal efforts to turn more programs over to state governments must have some mechanism to assure that the states (and cities and counties) devote attention to minority participation in policy making for block-granted social programs. Additionally, local and state citizens' groups and minorities themselves must be prepared for opportunities to participate in the policy-making process and exert strong political pressure to do so.

Minority pressure, perhaps coupled with legal challenges, direct action, and publicity, will be especially needed with expanded block-grant legislation at the federal level. Strong advocacy efforts such as those described by Chan, Brophy, and Fisher (in press) seem indicated. Minorities must seek and demand representation on block-grant planning and advisory committees, for example. Many planning and advisory body policies eventually determine the recipients of program funds.

Administrative relationships

In human services administration, the issues continue to be agency recruitment of minority workers (service workers, supervisors, and administrators themselves), equality in hiring and promotional processes, agency sensitivity to client needs, additional minorities above the entry-levels of supervisors, and greater attention to cultural differences among staff members.

A 1972 study of agencies in the four major U.S. cities that served the largest number of minority children showed some minority administrative and supervisory personnel but relatively few at the operating level at which actual services decisions are presumably made (Perlmutter & Alexander, 1978).

In a review of staffing patterns of these agencies, data on racial composition were either entirely absent or showed minuscule minority representation in high staff positions (Perlmutter & Alexander, 1978). For example, a 1968 study of 1088 decision-making positions in Chicago at all levels of government showed that only 5% of the positions were filled by Blacks, notwithstanding that Blacks made up 20% of the population at that time; only 5 of 135 directors of medium and large welfare agencies were Black in that same study (Perlmutter & Alexander, 1978). Similar trends were reported at the national level in juvenile corrections and juvenile courts. The same is true of other minorities.

That these issues are primarily administrative may not be immediately apparent, but bear in mind that administrators and chief executives of both public and private social agencies set the examples and determine the recruitment, hiring, and promotional policies, not to mention the "tone," of their agencies. In terms of setting the "tone," the administrator who communicates formally or informally that the agency should hire more minorities will cause subordinates to devote more attention to this matter. Further, the agency executive normally exerts *the* major influence on the direction of the agency's program. If the agency head truly desires that the program be sensitive to minority hiring and community needs, staff members will usually find a way to accomplish this. The following case illustrates how a number of these problem were resolved by an administrator of a large public agency.

In a large, county human services agency a major problem developed in the community development block-grant program that built neighborhood parks, rehabilitated rundown houses, built new county multipurpose facilities, and so forth. Distrust of the program staff became evident to the agency administrator through numerous phone calls and letters. It appeared that community leaders, many of whom were on the official advisory committees required by federal regulations, thought that the basically all-White technical staff did not understand community and minority needs. Though highly competent technically, most were physical planners or housing experts. The controversy became so heated that some advisory committees would not allow the technical staff director to attend their meetings, the purpose of which was, by regulation, to help plan the agency's program.

The agency administrator devised a plan to create an additional citizen participation position and staff it with a minority social worker. It was planned that some major program functions and almost 100 Comprehensive Employment and Training Act (CETA) staff, who mainly worked directly in community programs, would be transferred under the new position. This was to assure that the new minority person would have major program or operational decision-making capability and not be just a figurehead without real power.

As expected, there was strong resistance from the technical staff. The administrator, himself a minority person, however, had the solid backing of elected officials, the community, and his supervisor (the county manager), and the staffing plan was implemented as planned after many discussions with the technical staff to smooth the way. In operation, the community's distrust of the agency was greatly reduced, citizens' groups no longer complained; social planning and physical planning efforts meshed much more smoothly with strong citizen input. The new person quickly understood the minority expectations because he was from a similar cultural background. Though the technical staff never fully accepted the plan, they eventually became more comfortable with it as it made their work easier, too.

For the future, consumers, minority persons who are members of boards, advisory committees, advocacy groups, and citizens themselves should insist through appropriate channels that minority staff be hired at all levels but especially in practice, supervisory, and administrative areas that directly affect minority interests and programs.

Research

Research has increasingly become a major instrument in the shaping of social programs, a trend likely to accelerate with the new emphasis on accountability in human services programs. To develop broad social policies requires a wealth of knowledge about social conditions and especially the regular collection of statistical information (Turner, 1977). Research focuses on achieving a better fit between human needs and welfare goals and on increasing the likelihood of attaining these goals. It also focuses on programs, policies, interventions, consequences, and organizational context (Maas, 1977).

Racism problems in research include the following:

1. the need for training more minority researchers to focus on and advance the literature on minority problems, differences, and needs;
2. the question of protections and benefits for the subjects of research, especially since many minority communities feel they have been "studied to death" with few tangible results or benefits;
3. the stigmas that many White researchers have imposed on minorities in conducting research; and
4. the general lack of research in many areas that are relevant to minorities.

Increasingly, minority persons and communities have come to view themselves as being "overresearched" by those who would "add to the knowledge base" by asking "basic research questions" or by finding cues for basic research within the minority community. (See Williams [1974] for a vigorous account of many of these abuses.) Viewed in this light, social research can be a tool of oppression that studies minorities and reports to dominant race or class interests in order that they may use the findings to help consolidate their positions. Or it may continue to promote stereotypes and, if not actually harmful, be of little benefit to minorities or minority practice relationships.

Minority persons have increasingly begun to question the practical value of research for them. This minority notion of applied or practical research is often at variance with some researchers' belief that the major purpose of research is to "search for truth" or to "find relationships among variables." It may be that qualitative research (such as participant observation), which directly studies the real world of minority concerns and issues, might prove more useful to some minority communities than research that manipulates large amounts of statistical data to test the researcher's hypotheses. Many researchers are quite rigid in their choice of methodologies and research techniques, and much resistance could be expected to the notion of qualitative or other changes in research methodology.

Minorities often feel that they have been exploited by a researcher whose true purpose is to advance an academic career, to write the definitive book on minorities, or just to gain prominence in the field by casting minorities in a bad light. Daniel P. Moynihan's work on the pathology of the Black family (Moynihan, 1965, Rainwater & Yancy, 1967) is a classic case of a study that many minorities view as having racist tendencies. The original report suggested that there were a number of nonadaptive features of the Black family, such as female heads of families, instability, illegitimate children.

These studies have prompted a generation of researchers, including many minorities, to go over the same areas, and they in turn have found significant, overlooked strengths in the Black family. A major work is that by Billingsley (1968). Newbrough (1978) relates the history of such studies of the Black family and suggests that federal family research policies should, in the future, focus on the strengths of Black families.

Protection of the subjects of research and sensitivity in researcher-subject relationships has assumed major importance since a study of syphilis was conducted among Black males in the 1930s. Many subjects of the research project suffered the untreated effects of that disease as they were in most cases neither told of their illness nor offered treatment. Instead, they were studied in order to determine the effects of the disease. Many became old men without ever receiving treatment. Based partly on this episode, strong sentiment has developed in favor of many more trained minority researchers as well as stronger human subjects' protection laws and regulations in order to rectify or prevent future research abuses.

The theory is that minority researchers will be more sensitive to the needs of minority communities and will be in a better position to offer benefits to the subjects of their research. In selecting a topic of investigation, for example, researchers normally have a fairly wide latitude in their choice of scientific questions and problems. While maintaining scientific objectivity and methodology, they can still choose a topic that deals with pressing issues among minorities or utilize basic research findings to supply answers to urgent contemporary problems.

In addition to basic research, many federal agencies had (until the Reagan administration's federal domestic budget reductions) begun to emphasize the use of existing research findings in programs, practice, and in program and policy evaluation. Minority researchers might well guide policy makers in research areas by disseminating relevant research findings when such advice can best be used (when programs are to be reviewed, expanded, or cut back, for example, research that demonstrates the effectiveness of one approach versus another may be especially useful).

Finally, minority researchers appear to be better accepted in minority communities, perhaps because of their sensitivity to cultural issues and differences. They may be able to conduct research that is free of the inadvertant error or bias that results from poorer response rates and a less thorough understanding of factors. The result, in addition to better practical help to minorities, might be more valid findings.

Federal agencies such as the National Institute of Mental Health (NIMH), its Center for Minority Group Mental Health, and others have had a history of funding programs and funding research fellowships for minority research student support at the doctoral level (though these efforts, too, have been recently reduced at the federal level). NIMH has in the past given funds to organizations such as the Council on Social Work Education (CSWE) and the American Sociological Association to sponsor specific minority researchers while in their doctoral programs.

For the future, it appears that such support must continue if valid research in minority communities is to be realized. This support must come from federal, state, local, or private foundation sources. State-level funding would seem especially necessary if the states are to assume greater responsibilities for dealing with social issues. Unfortunately, most states have had little expertise and interest in research in general and, without appropriate pressure, may give priority to operational issues over any for research in a block-grant approach. The result might be less than adequate policies to meet minority needs (in the absence of state-level minority pressure groups) and a perpetuation of ineffective programs.

Research practitioners must begin to make maximum use of relationships with potential funding sources at the state and local levels to ensure the continuation of meaningful research given the changed directions in federally supported research after the 1980 elections. Again, membership on various committees and advisory groups is one of the better ways to monitor the funding bodies.

Education

Education in the human services is rife with analyses and self-examination in relation to minority needs and charges of institutional racism. The student revolts of the sixties forced many colleges and universities both to examine racism and to propose programs for its eradication. Major issues in education for practice are: practitioner stereotyping of minority clients, possibly due to education and training (Weiner, 1970); the difficulty of establishing courses that deal effectively with racism and whether they should be for Black or White students (Arnold, 1970); school policies, such as admission, academic employment policies, student recruitment and support, and the curriculum in terms of educating students for practice with racial and ethnic groups (Turner, 1972). These issues are important to practice relationships because the atmosphere of the professional socializing institutions helps to generate the attitudes and behaviors of future practitioners.

John Longres (1972) gives a general overview of the impact of racism and touches on several problems in education indicating not only that education has not succeeded in breaking down racist beliefs, but that it has been affected by, and has contributed to, racism in practice relationships in the past. Longres affirms that there have been problems in the past in admitting non-

White students and in hiring non-White faculty, which he attributes to a failure of educators to seek out and attract non-Whites. He cites efforts in physical education departments to show that with a commitment such recruitment can in fact be done but not when it is done "hesitantly and reluctantly."

Longres concludes that there is a cautious policy to avoid admitting "too many" minorities, an enormous consideration of grade-point averages (of entering minority students), and a reluctance to accept "nonqualified" students though admissions standards are routinely altered for other purposes (for example, to ensure a large number of applicants in any given year).

Finally, Longres points to difficulties in altering curricula to fit minority occupational goals; myths (among faculty) about the value of education for Blacks, Native Americans, Puerto Ricans, and Hispanics; myths about proper treatment strategies for non-Whites; and paternalism among faculty members (leading to the giving away of grades). Longres believes that these effects are due to institutional rather than to overt racism.

Educational elitism and racism are almost inseparable. Elitist beliefs in educational institutions and among educators may maintain that very rigorous academic standards must be upheld and that minorities are not able to compete successfully with Whites in these "demanding" intellectual endeavors. The following case illustrates this feeling.

At a mostly White benefit dinner honoring local political figures, a White professor emeritus from a very prestigious university with few minority students shares a table with a Black couple and some local and state activists. Before dinner there is casual table talk, and the professor, in an effort to discuss common subjects, asks the Black couple about Black leaders and Black schools, and they begin to discuss various Black issues in general. When the discussion turns to advanced education, the professor states that more Black Ph.D.s are needed but cannot understand why there are not more Black doctoral students. He theorizes that minorities have a difficult time getting through graduate school and must be helped; after all, graduate work is rigorous, takes much initiative, and requires a self-starting type of person.

Liberal White friends of the couple at the table are horrified by the discussion but wait for comments from the couple before joining in. The Black male of the group passes off the remarks lightly and does not mention that he is a Ph.D. candidate with an "A" average who has never required remedial assistance, or that he is attending the benefit as a reward for local political and organizing activities, at which he spends much of his free time in addition to maintaining a family, working, and completing the required doctoral coursework.

Many changes are needed in the professional schools. For example, Mirelowitz and Grossman (1975) examined social work curriculum issues and called for a commitment by practitioners to confront social systems that practice overt or covert racism. The detection and analysis of these systems is seen as a function of the schools. A model is needed for teaching ethnicity and race to students.

The non-White instructor is essential in changing many of these educational difficulties (Carter, 1978). Additional minority instructors can counter the stereotypes, give expert input into curriculum design, detect and give advice for changes in both student and faculty recruitment practices, and generally serve as role models and "magnets" to attract additional minority faculty and students. Minority students are quite reluctant to apply for or enter programs in which there are few or no minority faculty. This is not because of fear of racism and failure but may represent an insight into the fact that White faculty may not have the interest or the knowledge to supervise them and their projects if their career interests relate to direct work with minority clients. Students, for example, have been discouraged from selecting study problems or projects dealing specifically with minority treatment and community problems because the faculty felt that there was no one to give the proper supervision.

There are, however, difficulties and resistances in setting up ethnic course content (see Schlesinger & Devore, 1979). In terms of hiring patterns, most of the problems illustrated in the late 1960s and early 1970s were still present in the late 1970s (Gould, 1979) and early 1980s. There were still major problems in connection with minorities and women progressing to higher levels in schools of social work. There was evidence that practitioners were introducing innovations into racial social work practice before they had been conceptualized by academicians. Minority social workers were addressing themselves to the need to incorporate the racial variable into practice before the schools began to teach it.

In education for the human services, what is needed is not radical new directions but continuing attention to the resolution of long-standing ethnic educational issues. For example, school recruitment practices are still a problem in many areas; minority students are perhaps being recruited less effectively in the 1980s than in the 1960s when substantial community and national pressures were being brought to bear on the issue. Declining funding at all levels is leading to more competition among students; the reduction and elimination of educational funds and stipends formerly earmarked for minority students raises the question of whether the human services professions will be populated in the next few decades only by those who are affluent enough to complete their schooling without outside support. This will exclude many minorities and has enormous implications for practice in years to come. Minority faculty advancement will also continue to be an issue when it appears that the most practical method for advancement to tenured positions by many minorities is through the courts.

The Council on Social Work Education (CSWE), the accrediting agency for social work schools and education programs, will need to maintain a constant vigil over its standards in racist practices (CSWE has increasingly resorted to placing schools on "probation," which in some instances has greatly improved their recruiting practices both for students and for minority faculty members). Minorities, however, must monitor CSWE and other national accrediting bodies to assure continued progress. For other human services programs not accredited by CSWE, there should be much greater attention to affirmative action committees and political pressure on school and college board members, in addition to publicity and sanctions by the practice bodies.

SUMMARY

Racism has had a long and varied history in American society. Generally, in its overt form, it is a judgment about an individual that is not supported by facts. Explanations of why this judgment occurs range from individual and psychological views to views about the structure of society. In its covert form, institutional racism seems to derive from the (sometimes hidden) operation of societal forces.

Racism has been an unfortunate but persistent part of social programs, practice, and practice relationships since the Civil War. The effects of racism changed with the society but persisted throughout the post–Civil War era, Progressive era, Great Depression, World War II, and postwar periods. Increased militancy and opposition to racist human services practices and relationships became evident in the 1940s and merged into the Black militancy movements of the 1960s. These movements irrevocably changed human services programs through such new concepts as citizen participation, neighborhood control, and client rights. There were revolts against the most extreme excesses of human services programs, such as the colonialist thinking that led to programs attempting to do *for* people rather than *with* them. The effects of racism on practice relationships must be guarded against in both individual and group services programs and in institutional relationships as well.

In general, problems arise in individual practice and organizational relationships due to lack of understanding of minority cultural patterns and ways of coping with events. The majority practitioner may not fully understand the dynamics of a minority individual or family in an individual practice setting, and this same lack of understanding in organizational practice settings leads to racist hiring and promotional practices and the faulty design and implementation of programs and services to minorities.

Research and education in the human services have been afflicted by different manifestations of these same problems. Little concern has been manifested for protecting and assisting the subjects of research, and there has been inappropriate selection of research topics in terms of minority issues. The focusing by some researchers on what they mistakenly perceive to be minority failures has been a very serious problem. The minority student has been both intentionally and unintentionally excluded from various areas of education, and there has been a failure to address minority practice issues in the educational process. This has led to inappropriately prepared practitioners who are ineffective in serving or relating to minorities in the field.

Concern for the disadvantaged and poor appears to be cyclical. Major concern and attempts to solve the problems of poverty, discrimination, and inequality of opportunity in the 1960s finally yielded to apathy, fiscal restraint (in all but military spending), and feelings that "enough" had been done in the 1970s. At the time of this writing, the early 1980s, concern for domestic and social problems is at perhaps its lowest ebb since the economic depression of 1929. Traditionalists concerned with social issues and racism will probably use this time to regroup, to hold the line on past gains, to rebuild old coalitions and form new ones so that when the appropriate moment to expand work on these pressing issues again arises, the necessary groundwork will already be in place. Racism, however, is far from being solved; newer practice approaches will need to be researched and implemented. It will be a major and difficult effort.

SELF-EVALUATION QUESTIONS

1. *Jim Crow, discrimination, prejudice,* and *racism* differ from one another in what way?
   A. They do not differ.
   B. They are the same terms used in different periods.
   C. They are terms that mean the same but are used by different groups.
   D. Each term relates to a different type of prejudice.

2. You are in a one-on-one counseling relationship with a Spanish-speaking client. How do you refer to the client?
   A. Hispanic
   B. Spanish-speaking
   C. Chicano
   D. Spanish
   E. Mexican American

3. You are in a one-on-one counseling situation with a client who has recently moved to a large city from an Indian reservation. How do you refer to the client?
   A. Indian
   B. Native American
   C. Urban Indian
   D. Reservation Indian
   E. Native American Indian

4. Black persons generally prefer to be called
   A. Negro
   B. Black
   C. Colored
   D. Afro-American
   E. African-American

5. The Progressive era was a period of many basic reforms in American society. In what way did Progressivism relate to racism?
   A. There were various White movements that campaigned against Jim Crow and prejudice.
   B. New governmental policies were instituted against Jim Crow and racial segregation.
   C. There was little concern about problems of race or the "Negro problem."
   D. Black leaders sought to form organizations that would deal with racial issues.

6. The depression-era New Deal policies had a number of programs dealing with Black-White inequality. True or false? On what do you base your answer?

7. To give effective treatment, a services worker should understand the place of religion, any special beliefs, history, lifestyles, and cultural tradition of a given minority group. Why?

8. In general, minority clients with emotional or mental problems should be treated with sympathy and deference and allowed opportunities to act out their anger in a therapeutic relationship. True or false? Discuss why or why not.

9. Minority clients generally have a tendency toward self-hatred and blame themselves for their "victimization." True or false?

10. Community organizers, in order to be effective, should:
    A. Bring a strong sense of professionally accepted goals to the client group situation for most effective action.
    B. Assume a "protective" role in the community against bureaucratic agencies and institutions that seek to dehumanize clients.
    C. Seek out the goals and strategies of client groups and try to assist.
    D. All the above.
11. Minorities generally are more afraid than Whites of being classified as mentally ill and for this reason may not utilize mental health services. True or false? What strategies are indicated if you answer true? false?

KEY

1. B.
2. A. Terms change continually, but *Hispanic* is generally recognized as including Mexican Americans, Puerto Ricans, and Cuban-Americans.
3. B or E. Again, terms change. Moreover, various tribal leaders do not agree among themselves on one common terminology; usage may vary.
4. B, though some Black elderly may still not prefer the term.
5. D.
6. F. Assistance was a side effect or was in fact pushed by Blacks themselves.
7. No one answer. Any or all may be important in the treatment of a given minority group member depending on the individual.
8. F. There is no one way to treat minority clients. Each should be treated individually, as the case example on individual practice.
9. F. Research has not supported this assumption.
10. C.
11. T. Working through natural or community support groups is sometimes best.

STUDY QUESTIONS

1. Reread and discuss the case study on page 134 in this chapter.
    A. In your opinion, is the counselor racist or not?
    B. What seems to be the counselor's intent?
    C. Are the counselor's actions therapeutic? Why or why not?
    D. What principles are illustrated here?
2. Look again at the case on page 139.
    A. In your opinion, did the organizer mean well or not?
    B. Why would the volunteer, White community organizer be hostile to the new Black professional?
    C. Speculate on the personal needs that may have caused the White organizer to assume a benevolent protector role.
    D. Speculate on the effect that the continuation of this protector role might have had on Black residents.
3. Reread and discuss the case study on page 144.
    A. In your opinion, are the mental health professionals racist or not? Why or why not?
    B. Why do you think that the professionals would answer the questionnaire as they did? What does this illustrate?
    C. If you were conducting a staff development workshop, what specific actions would you recommend to the direct services professionals in order to be better

informed on state minority needs? What steps would you recommend to the administrators?

4. For educational issues, review the case on page 150.
  A. Do you feel that the professor was racist or not? Was this stereotyping? What might account for his beliefs?
  B. How might this professor be expected to act on a graduate school of social work admissions committee? In a classroom with minority students, might he be overly lenient or overly strict?
  C. Is this example consistent with the statements by John Longres in the chapter?

REFERENCES

Allport, G. W. *The nature of prejudice.* Garden City, N.Y.: Doubleday & Co., 1958.

Arnold, H. D. American racism: Implications for social work. *Journal of Education for Social Work,* 1970, 6 (2), 7–12.

Barbarin, O. A., Good, P. R., Pharr, M. O., & Siskind, J. A. *Institutional racism and community competence.* Rockville, Md.: National Institute of Mental Health, Center for Minority Group Mental Health Programs, in press.

Billingsley, A. *Black families in White America.* Englewood Cliffs, N.J.: Prentice-Hall, 1968.

Bontemps, A. *Story of the Negro.* New York: Alfred A. Knopf, 1948.

Brayboy, T., & Marks, M. J. Transference variation evoked by racial differences in cotherapists. In J. Goodman (Ed.), *Dynamics of racism in social work practice.* Washington, D.C.: National Association of Social Workers, n.d.

Carmichael, S., & Hamilton, C. V. Black power: The politics of liberation in America. New York: Vintage Books, 1967.

Carter, J. H., & Haizlip, T. M. Race and its relevance to transference. In J. Goodman (Ed.), *Dynamics of racism in social work practice.* Washington, D.C.: National Association of Social Workers, N.d.

Carter, L. H. The Black instructor: An essential dimension to the content and structure of the social work curriculum. *Journal of Education for Social Work,* 1978, *14* (1), 16–22.

Chan, A., Brophy, M. C., & Fisher, J. C. Advocate counseling and institutional racism. In Barbarin, Good, Pharr, & Siskind (Eds.), *Institutional racism and community competence,* in press.

Cohen, J. Race as a factor in social work practice. In R. R. Miller (Ed.), *Race, research, and reason.* New York: National Association of Social Workers, 1969.

Cohen, R. 1977 Code of ethics revisions. *National Association of Social Workers News,* 1980, *25* (6), 10.

Collins, A. H., & Pancoast, D. L. *National helping networks: A strategy for prevention.* Washington, D. C.: National Association of Social Workers, 1976.

Cooper, S. A look at the effect of racism on clinical work. In J. Goodman (Ed.), *Dynamics of racism in social work practice.* Washington, D.C.: National Association of Social Workers, 1973.

Creighen, J. E. (Ed.). *Blueprints for Black unity.* Proceedings of the Third Annual Conference, National Association of Black Social Workers, April 1–4, 1971. Chicago: Malcolm X Community College, 1971.

Davis, K., & Swartz, J. Increasing Black students' utilization of mental health services. *American Journal of Orthopsychiatry,* 1972, *42* (5), 771–776.

Delgado, M., & Delgado, H. D. Natural support systems: Source of strengths in Hispanic communities. *Social Work,* 1982, *27* (1), 83–89.

DuBois, W. E. B. *Black reconstruction.* New York: Harcourt, Brace & Co., 1935.

DuBois, W. E. B. *The Negro*. Millwood, N.Y.: Kraus-Thomson Organization Limits, 1975.

DuBois, W. E. B. *The Philadelphia Negro*. New York: Benjamin Blum, 1967. (Originally published, 1899.)

Eaton, J. M., & Gilbert, N. Racial discrimination and diagnostic differentiation. In R. R. Miller (Ed.), *Race, research and reason*. New York: National Association of Social Workers, 1967.

Emerson, R., & Kilson, M. The American dilemma in a changing world: The rise of Africa and the Negro American. *Daedalus*, 1965, *94* (4), 1055–1084.

Flaming, K. H., Palen, J. J., Ringlien, G., & Taylor, C. Black powerlessness in policy-making positions. *Sociological Quarterly*, 1972, *13* (1), 126–133.

Franklin, J. H. The two worlds of race: A historical view. *Daedalus, Journal of the American Academy of Arts and Sciences*, 1965, *94* (4), 899–920.

Garvin, C. D., & Glasser, P. H. Social group work: The preventive and rehabilitative approach. In R. Morris (Ed.), *Encyclopedia of social work* (Vol. 2). New York: National Association of Social Workers, 1971.

Ghali, S. B. Understanding Puerto Rican traditions. *Social Work*, 1982, *27* (1), 98–102.

Gibbs, I. L. Institutional racism in social welfare. *Child Welfare*, 1971, *L* (10), 582–587.

Gilbert, G. C. Counseling Black adolescent parents. *Social Work*, 1974, *19* (1), 88–95.

Gitterman, A., & Schaeffer, A. The White professional and the Black client. In J. Goodman (Ed.), *Dynamics of racism in social work practice*. Washington, D. C.: National Association of Social Workers, N.d.

Glasgow, D. The emerging Black community: A challenge to social work. In W. C. Richan (Ed.), *Human services and social work responsibility*. New York: National Association of Social Workers, 1969.

Glazer, N. Housing problems and housing policies. In Hadden, Masotti, and Larson (Eds.), *Metropolis in crisis*. Itasca, Ill.: F. E. Peacock Publishers, 1967.

Gould, K. H. Ethnic and sex-based differentials in background and status variables among faculties of schools of social work. *Journal of Education for Social Work*, 1979, *15* (3), 36–43.

Hays, W. C., & Mindel, C. H. Extended kinship relations in Black and White families. *Journal of Marriage & the Family*, 1973, *35* (1), 51–57.

Jones, E. D. On transracial adoption of Black children. *Child Welfare*, 1972, *51* (3), 156–164.

Kerner, O. Report of the National Advisory Commission on Civil Disorders. Washington, D. C.: National Advisors Commission on Civil Disorders, 1968.

Kogut, A. The settlements and ethnicity: 1890–1914. *Social Work*, 1972, *17* (3), 22–31.

Knowles, L. L., & Prewitt, K. *Institutional racism in America*. Englewood Cliffs, N.J.: Prentice-Hall, 1969.

Krebs, R. L. Some effects of a White institution on Black psychiatric outpatients. *American Journal of Orthopsychiatry*, 1971, *41* (4), 589–596.

Loewenstein, S. F. Integrating content on feminism and racism into the social work curriculum. *Journal of Education for Social Work*, 1976, *12* (1), 91–95.

Longres, J. The impact of racism on social work education. *Journal of Education for Social Work*, 1972, *8* (1), 31–41.

Longres, J. F. Minority groups: An interest group perspective. *Social Work*, 1982, *27* (1), 7–14.

Lucas, A. K. Ethics in social work. In J. Turner (Ed.), *Encyclopedia of social work*. Washington, D. C.: National Association of Social Workers, 1977.

Maas, H. Research in social work. In J. B. Torner (Ed.), *The Encyclopedia of social work* (Vol. 2), Washington, D.C.: National Association of Social Workers, 1977, p. 1183.

Madison, B. A., & Schapiro, M. Black adoption issues and policies: Review of the literature. *Social Services Review*, 1973, *47* (4), 531–560.

Mayfield, W. G. Mental health in the Black community. *Social Work*, 1972, *17* (3), 106–110.

McAdoo, H. P. Demographic trends for people of color. *Social Work*, 1982, *27* (1), 15–23.

R. R. Miller (Ed.), Race, research, and reason, New York: National Association of Social Workers, 1967, p. 108.

Mirelowitz, S., & Grossman, L. Ethnicity: An intervening variable in social work education. *Journal of Education for Social Work*, 1975, *11* (3), 28–35.

Mizio, E. P. R. Social workers and racism. *Social Casework*, 1972, *53* (5), 267–272.

Montero, D., & Dieppa, I. Resettling Vietnamese refugees: The service agency's role. *Social Work*, 1982, *27* (1), 74–81.

Moynihan, D. P. *The Negro family: The case for national action*. Washington, D.C.: U. S. Department of Labor, Office of Planning and Research, March, 1965.

Myer, D. R. Blacks in slum housing: A distorted theme. *Journal of Black Studies*, 1973, *4* (2), 139–152.

National Association of Social Workers (NASW). *First draft report of the task force on labor force classification*, 1980.

Newbrough, J. R. *Families and family institution transactions in child development: an analysis of the family research program of HEW's Administration for Children, Youth, and Families* (Contract #103–77–1043. Final Report). Nashville, Tennessee: Center for Community Studies, George Peabody College for Teachers and Center for the Study of Families and Children, Institute for Public Policy Studies, Vanderbilt University, April 1, 1978.

The Negro and the city. Adapted from a special issue of *Fortune* on business and the urban crisis. New York: Time-Life Books, 1968.

Northwood, L. K., & Reed, R. L. An agenda for research about race and social work. In R. R. Miller (Ed.), *Race, research, and reason*. New York: National Association of Social Workers, 1969.

Perlmutter, F. D., & Alexander, L. B. Exposing the coercive consensus: Racism and sexism in social work. In R. C. Sarri & Y. Hasenfeld (Eds.), *The management of human services*. New York: Columbia University Press, 1978.

Rainwater, L., & Yancey, W. L. *The Moynihan report and the politics of controversy*. Cambridge, Mass.: M.I.T. Press, 1967.

Robins, E., & Richardson, M. Psychiatric symptoms in White and in Black patients. *Comprehensive Psychiatry*, 1973, *14* (6), 475–481.

Rosaldo, R., Seligmann, G. L., & Calvert, R. A. *Chicano: The beginnings of bronze power* (Abr. ed.). New York: William Morrow and Co., 1974.

Rothman, J. Three models of community organization practice. In Cox, Erlich, Rothman, & Tropman (Eds.), *Strategies of community organization practice: A book of readings*. Itasca, Ill.: F. E. Peacock Publishers, 1970.

Schlesinger, A. M., Jr. *The coming of the New Deal*. Boston: Houghton Mifflin Co., 1959.

Schlesinger, A. M., Jr. *The politics of upheaval*. Boston: Houghton Mifflin Co., 1969.

Schlesinger, E. G., & Devore, W. Social workers view ethnic minority teaching. *Journal of Education for Social Work*, 1979, *51* (3), 20–27.

Schneiderman, L. Racism and revenue sharing. *Social Work*, 1973, *17* (3), 44–49.

Silberman, E. C. *Crisis in Black and White*. New York: Random House, 1964.

Simpson, E. G., & Yinger, M. J. *Racial and cultural minorities*. New York: Harper & Row, 1953.

Smalley, R. Social casework: The functional approach. In R. Morris (Ed.), *The encyclopedia of social work* (Vol. 2). New York: National Association of Social Workers, 1971.

Sommer, M. L. The significance of "grease" in an adolescent residential treatment center. *Journal of Nervous & Mental Disease*, 1964, *139* (2), 143–146.

Street, L. Minorities. In J. B. Turner (Ed.), *The encyclopedia of social work* (Vol. 1). Washington, D.C.: National Association of Social Workers, 1977.

Temple-Trujillo, R. E. Conceptions of the Chicano family. *Smith College Studies in Social Work,* 1974, *45* (1), 1–20.

Trader, H. P. Survival strategies for oppressed minorities. *Social Work,* 1977, *22* (1), 10–13.

Tropp, E. Social group work: The developmental approach. In R. Morris (Ed.), *Encyclopedia of social work* (Vol. 2). New York: National Association of Social Workers, 1971.

Tuck, S., Jr. Working with Black adolescent fathers. *Journal of Orthopsychiatry,* 1971, *41* (3), 564–572.

Turner, J. B. Education for practice with minorities. *Social Work,* 1972, *17* (3), 112–118.

Turner, J. B. (Ed.) *Encyclopedia of social work* (Vols. 1 and 2). Washington, D.C.: National Association of Social Workers, 1977.

Watkins, T. R., & Gonzales, R. Outreach to Mexican-Americans. *Social Work,* 1982, *27* (1), 68–73.

Weiner, M. Gentleman's agreement revisited. *Social Casework,* 1970, *51* (7), 395–398.

Williams, R. L. The death of White research in the Black community. *Journal of Non-White Concerns in Personnel & Guidance,* April 1974, pp. 117–132.

Yerby, A. S. The disadvantaged youth and health care. *American Journal of Public Health,* 1966, *56* (1), 5–9.

Zinn, H. (Ed.) *New Deal thought.* Indianapolis: Bobbs-Merrill Co., 1966.

9

Practitioner-Organization Relationships

Although the numbers of social workers in private practice and industry are increasing, the vast majority are employed in public or voluntary agencies. Whether a county social service department, a sectarian social agency, or a general hospital, invariably these agencies are formal organizations. Chapter 9 describes both their bureaucratic characteristics and their impact on the social workers in them. Formal organizations are examined from the perspective of systems and exchange theories that illustrate the effects on the practitioner of agency structure, a major part of the social context of practice.

Max Weber, the seminal writer on bureaucracy, described a bureaucratic organization as one exhibiting the following characteristics:

1. a continuous set of functions set up by rules,
2. a specific assignment of duties, responsibilities, and authority for each position,
3. a clear organizational hierarchy,
4. formal, written policies and procedures,
5. employees own no part of the means of administration,
6. free selection of staff, based on technical qualifications,
7. promotion based on seniority or merit,
8. remuneration by salaries accompanied by pensions
9. the individual is subject to strict control in doing his job (Weber, 1947, pp. 330–334).

Weber's description, however, should be regarded as an ideal. Some organizations have more written rules than others; some emphasize hierarchical authority more than others. Accordingly, some organizations are more bureaucratic than others.

KINDS OF FORMAL ORGANIZATIONS

A variety of organizational models can generally be grouped into three types. The *autocratic* structure is based on the power of the administrator and the compliance of the staff, coupled with performance sufficient to meet organizational goals. The staff person is dependent on the administrator or the organization for his or her lower order emotional/social and financial needs. (See Figure 9–1.)

In *democratic or supportive* structure, the main expectation on the individual is a high level of self-motivated performance. The individual identifies with organizational goals but does not become overly dependent on the organization. Higher levels of psychosocial needs—such as group belonging, self-esteem, and self-actualization—are met in accomplishing the work itself. (See Figure 9–2.)

A third category can be labeled *collegial.* Instead of direction from above, there is group resolution of problems. The individual depends on the group, and the group, rather than the organization, receives primary loyalty. Again, the higher order of psychosocial needs are met. (See Figure 9–3.) An agency unit, such as a mental health team with members of equal status, would approximate the collegial type.

Bureaucratic characteristics, such as division of labor and hiring practices, apply in varying degrees to all three types of organizations. The collegial model seems to violate one of the main tenets of bureaucratic theory—that there must be a hierarchical distribution of authority and control. Hierarchical distribution is not sacrosanct, however, and a group interactional model can be emphasized instead. Residential program teams, small voluntary social service agencies, or special project staff exemplify this model.

The democratic model produces a perceived sharing of authority and responsibility. The agency's table of organization would still show an administrator for structural and accountability purposes. If an administrator's organizational goals are not being met, however, the administrator's voluntary sharing of power and staff participation in the decision-making process could

(Director)

Figure 9–1.   Autocratic Structure

Figure 9–2.   Democratic or Supportive Structure

become an ideological casualty, since the first law of organizations (or any system) is survival. The vertical table of organization continues to exist, along with its upward flowing accountability requirements. Table 9–1 depicts differing locations of control.

It is possible, of course, that formally autocratic or democratic models could function informally on a collegial basis because of malfunctioning in the organization—for example, an administrator may not be competent, or the position is compromised by staff opposition. It is possible, too, that an autocratic organization could have particular programs, especially ones in which there are highly paid professionals, that could function as democratic or collegial structures. Typically, in the social service field, the bureaucratic model is used to set up autocratic agency structures. Whether the democratic or collegial models evolve depends on the ideologies and interactions of the founders, administrator, staff, and the size of the organization.

Practitioner reactions to structures

Rigid hierarchical structures have a stultifying effect on individuals; disillusionment, frustration, and alienation may be characteristic. The general public's stereotype of a bureaucrat is one who performs at a minimal level

Figure 9–3.   Collegial Structure

TABLE 9–1. Bureaucratic characteristics and management styles.

Type of Organization	Degree of Bureaucracy	Management Style
Autocratic: *Administrator Staff	Most	Authoritarian
Democratic: *Administrator *Staff	Moderate	Participative/Supportive
Collegial: Administrator *Staff	Little	Group/Supportive

*Location of control.

with a maximal amount of paper shuffling. Applying the *frustration-aggression hypothesis* to the rigid autocratic organization reveals that staff frustration arising when goals are not met can generate two possible modes of behavior—fight or flight. The fight mode involves making a commitment to change the organization to make it less dehumanizing. The flight mode involves leaving the agency or reducing one's aspirations within it.

Merton (1957) designed a five-part typology that characterizes individuals seeking cultural goals, such as success, through institutionalized means—conformity, innovation, ritualism, retreatism, and rebellion. The practitioner resigned to staying in the dehumanizing environment may justify it by ritualizing and reducing performance to the bare minimum, by valuing job security, and by wanting never to do anything new.

Social service practitioners who remain true to their values and skills may opt for fight or flight rather than fall into the role of the resigned bureaucrat. The values of individual worth, dignity, and empathic relating cannot coexist with conformity to shoddy treatment of clients and cool objectification of both collegial and helping relationships. Nowhere do social work values and skills conflict more with bureaucratic conditions than in the autocratic organization in which the principles of business management are misapplied to the organization's administration. Rebellions arise in informal staff opposition to administrator incompetency and to unjust policies and procedures. Such opposition can lead to the firing of administrators (Weinstein, 1979).

In the business sector of our economy, an organization's efficiency and accountability are conditioned by the necessity of producing a product that has enough quality to ensure demand for it over the competition's product. Management principles developed in the business sector, when applied to social service organizations, as well as other governmental, public, and educational organizations, are less directly conditioned by the quality of the product. When a new model of car is a lemon, the results for management are immediate. When the quality of casework or group therapy deteriorates due to an overload on workers, both clients and workers suffer, but management may reap the benefits of "holding the line" on the personnel budget. Under misapplied management principles, client-contact hours per worker is a measure of expediency. A measure of real efficiency would tap the conditions of practice in an agency as a means of creating the kind of climate in which workers can do their best. The autocratic organization, in which quality of service is not easily measured, can create several noxious conditions which send negative messages to practitioners.

The rigid, hierarchical structure of an autocratic organization conveys a number of messages to the individual worker. First, the needs, attitudes, values, and aspirations of the staff are basically ignored; they are treated as *units of production* by the administrators or boards of directors. Often, this economic perspective is mated to that of viewing clients as *units of consumption*. The two groups are then "lumped" together and jointly "dumped" into the category of being potential sources of saving of taxpayers' money, by reducing client benefits/services and by giving inadequate salaries and raises to the staff. This has demoralizing and dehumanizing effects on both groups, which may tend toward hostile-dependent reactions to such treatment. Such reactions compound the difficulties in providing effective services and in maintaining positive practitioner-client relationships.

Theory X and Theory Y

The second message conveyed to a worker in an autocratic design is that he/she is not trustworthy. McGregor (1960) described the conventional autocratic view of management's task and the workers in an organization and labeled it *Theory X*. In his formulation, management is responsible for marshaling the organization's resources to meet economic ends or to mold the worker to meet the organization's needs. Because the average person dislikes work, lacks ambition, resists change, is self-centered and gullible, management must reward, punish, and control the individual to do his job. McGregor pointed out that this view completely disregards our current state of knowledge. Using Maslow's "hierarchy of needs" (described later), he stated that workers have intrinsic drives to perform well and to actualize themselves.

Positing a new theory of management, which he called *Theory Y,* McGregor said that management was still responsible for organizing the elements of production, including the workers, to meet economic ends but that people are not by nature passive or resistant to change. It is the responsibility of management to nourish their motivation, their capacity for assuming responsibility, and their willingness to work toward organizational goals. It is management's responsibility to set up the conditions in which the people can meet their physiological, social, and psychological needs in their work and thereby attain organizational ends.

McGregor specifically recommended a decentralization of control procedures to give workers more freedom, an enlargement of jobs to meet more worker social and psychological needs, participative management and performance appraisal based on results. These kinds of principles could be usefully applied in social agencies as a means of developing a more ideal context for practice. Certainly, Theory Y better facilitates the attitudes and values that build a constructive organization/practitioner relationship.

Transactional analysis

The third message conveyed to a worker in a rigid, formal organization is that he/she is not mature enough to decide his/her own actions in the organization (see Figure 9−4). Rigid, hierarchical authority and reliance on written directives place the worker in a childlike role. The transactional analysis formulations of Eric Berne (1964) help to place this relationship pattern into perspective. Berne has theorized that there are three ego states—parent, adult, and child. Each state is associated with roles and communication patterns in the interactional communication processes between two individuals. The optimum communication transaction occurs between two people who are both operating in their adult ego states.

Of the three, the adult is the most rational ego state, and the adult-to-adult dyadic communication pattern is the most mature. Of the three main types of formal organizational structures—autocratic, democratic, and collegial—the last best approximates this communication pattern. The democratic structure, in which practitioners participate in the decision-making process, would approximate the collegial, but the autocratic would not even be on the same plane. In the autocratic structure, the administrator and the organization assume the role(s) of parent, which may be nurturing or disapproving, and treat the worker like an irresponsible child. Such treatment engenders frustration and hostility.

The very buildings in which social service programs are quartered frequently assault the worker's psyche. Although voluntary social and health agencies usually have acceptable quarters, public agencies frequently do not (Seabury, 1971). Offices may be too small and as crowded as rabbit hutches. Accoustical control may be nonexistent, and intercoms may interfere with interviews in which clients are discussing highly emotionally charged topics (as shown in Figure 9−5). Privacy is further invaded by incoming telephone calls.

In social service departments, clients frequently must await their turn for service in a large waiting room full of noisy children, conversations, typewriters, and intercom announcements. Practitioners may have to interview the clients in cubicles off the main room. Since local boards of directors and administrators are apt to judge their subordinates' efficiency and effectiveness

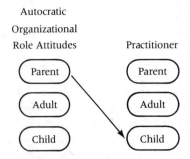

Figure 9−4.   Autocratic organizational role attitudes and ego states in interaction

Mrs. Palmer, Mr. Jones, Miss Edwards . . .

Figure 9–5. Are clients and practitioners treated with dignity and respect in this type of interviewing-room arrangement?

by the money they *do not* spend, the programs' quarters are usually dull and drab, uncarpeted, and expressive of a vague, depressed tone. No U.S. businessmen would permit clients to enter such company quarters. Of course, the message to workers is that they and their clients do not deserve better.

ORGANIZATIONAL THEORIES

Von Bertalanffy (1968) is credited with formulating much of general systems theory. Extrapolating from the biological sciences, he developed what he called the *transport equation,* which has been applied to social service agencies as shown in Figure 9–6. In essence, the transport equation shows that resources are used up in the process of serving clients, which should result in changed clients. Since the agency system exists in an environment, it must have continuous information feedback on how well it is doing internally and on potential environmental influencing factors. Internally, for example, administrators are very concerned that staff should work toward agency goals. Externally, coalitions of other agencies or client groups may interfere with acquiring agency funding.

As described by Katz and Kahn (1978), *open systems* have permeable boundaries across which resources and information flow in two directions (see Figure 9–7). Without resource inputs, the system is in a state of entropy, of wasting away. Consequently, the open system attempts to import more

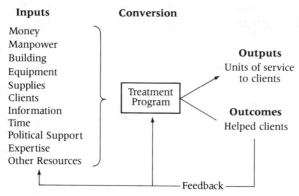

Figure 9–6. Transport equation

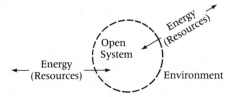

Figure 9–7.   Open system

energy than it exports. The input/output exchange of resources has a circular nature. Information feedback is needed to keep the organization on course. Successful organizations are in a dynamic state of energy exchange with other environmental elements. Factors that threaten to disrupt the system are countered by forces of restoration. Growth and expansion help the organization to maintain a dynamic and viable balance. The growth produces differentiation and elaboration of functions. As the degree of complexity increases, there is a counterforce of integration and coordination. Last, *open systems* can meet desired ends by more than one path.

In the *closed* (or rational) *system,* no attention is paid to the environment; all the focus is on internal matters, as shown in Figure 9–8.

In this system, the priorities for management are on:

1. structuring the organization to achieve goals
2. modifying the employees' behavior
3. resolving goal constraints (for example, communication or decision-making problems).

Workers are apt to be viewed as mechanical units of production who must be manipulated to achieve organizational goals. Clearly, this system most closely approaches the autocratic model of formal organization with its focus on production and "things" rather than on the workers' human-relations needs.

The last applicable systems theory is that of *social systems.* According to Behling and Schriesheim (1976), workers in organizations are parochial and selfish and are motivated mostly by their own self-interest. Some writers contend that the workers are "bought" through salary, fringe benefits, and other

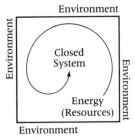

Figure 9–8.   Closed system

perquisites. Workers seek to meet their needs through the organization and they are in a constant competition to secure power. If necessary, they form coalitions which seek to dominate the organization (Figure 9–9). This theory views the informal power structure as paramount. The influence of the environment on organizational goal setting is considered to be much less than the influence of the dominant coalition inside the organization.

Exchange theory. Levine and White (1961) used *exchange theory* to describe the relationships between work organizations. They defined *exchange* as "any voluntary activity between two organizations which has consequences, actual or anticipated, for the realization of their respective goals or objectives" [p. 583]. For an agency to achieve its own objectives, it has to *possess* three elements—clients, labor services, and other resources. An agency that lacks some needed resources must *exchange* resources with other agencies or groups to achieve its goals and will seek to acquire more resources than it cedes away. Certainly, if an agency has a long-term net loss of resources, at some point its existence will be jeopardized.

Blau (1964), writing on the relationships between individuals and groups, stated that social exchange theory "can be considered to underlie relations between groups as well as between individuals; both differentiation of power and peer group ties; conflicts between opposing forces as well as cooperation; both intimate attractions and connections between distant members of a community without social contacts" [p. 4].

Units of exchange can be tangible (for example, money or gifts) or intangible (political "pull" or feelings of gratitude). Parties in the exchange are concerned about receiving the rewards dispensed by the others. The exchange should be reciprocal and provide benefits to both parties. Inequalities develop, however when one person or group possesses more power (resources) than the other. The person or group thus empowered can make the distribution of resources contingent on the other's compliance with its example or dictates (Thompson, 1968). The weaker entity is then dependent on the stronger one.

What immediate inferences from exchange theory help to clarify the staff/ organization relationship? First, from the bureaucratic conceptual framework, direct service practitioners enter an organization at the bottom of the formal

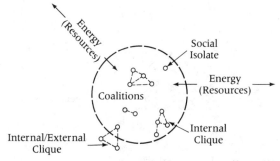

Figure 9–9. Social System

power structure, as depicted in Figure 9–10. Entrance at the bottom means that they are in dependent, resourceless positions, a status evidenced by most positions having probationary periods of six months to one year. (In academia, the probationary period is usually five years, which tells us something about the strength of the formal bureaucratic structure in such settings). Since right of appeal and grievance procedures usually are not extended to probationary employees, they quickly observe the pivotal role of their supervisor, who will make the initial off-probation or termination decision. Few new employees choose to "make waves" by not handling their clients well or by suggesting changes in organizational operations which could threaten the supervisor and administrators.

It is during this high-anxiety, initial employment period that the process of *organizational co-optation* starts, when the organization's behavioral patterns of norms, rules, policies, procedures, and goals tend to supplant one's own. Not only is this natural process not necessarily malignant but a certain degree of co-optation may be absolutely necessary for a suitable fit between the individual and the organization. We must be aware of the structure and processes of our organizations in order to feel relatively comfortable and to help our clients. But the process may continue to the point that the worker becomes estranged, detached, dehumanized, and functions as a "resigned bureaucrat." The need for supervisors to understand the anxiety-laden, resourceless position of the new (and perhaps young) worker is evident.

Continuing to speak in terms of the formal power structure, we must keep in mind the total range of resources the possession of which adds up to power. As indicated in Figure 9–7 (p. 160), money, human resources, physical plant, equipment/supplies, clients, information, technical/professional expertise, time, and "political" support are all part of this. With regard to this list, the direct service worker should enter the job with technical/professional expertise and, in the end analysis, determine how his or her time will be spent. As time goes by, the worker will acquire clients, information on clients and the environment, and "political" alliances, and the possession of these resources will exemplify a growing reciprocal dependency of organization and

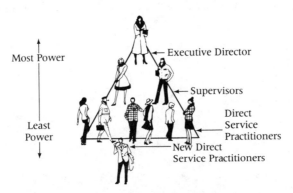

Figure 9–10.   Formal Power Structure

worker. Perhaps an awareness of this interdependency is seen in deciding that the new individual is a valued employee who should be given permanent status. Indeed, as one increasingly demonstrates competence in managing resources, one becomes a candidate for promotion.

More authority and resources are granted as an individual moves up the power hierarchy, though dependence on organizational superiors is clearly indicated in job descriptions and everyday decision-making responsibilities. The new supervisor now has an additional resource to command—the power of assigned staff. Also, a secondary resource is now granted: the more workers one supervises, the more prestige is associated with the position. At each level of the organization, then, one looks upward to one's superiors from a dependent position and downward toward one's subordinates from a more powerful position. (Note that this discussion has been aimed at the formal organization; the informal power structure will be described later.)

What inferences can we make about direct service practitioners in relation to open systems and exchange theories? First, direct service practitioners are the primary organizational *boundary spanners* who relate to clients. Clients move from the environment into the organization's domain of services through the gatekeeper of the agency's resources—the direct service practitioner. Accordingly, in terms of the clients, the direct services practitioners are seen as having primary control (power) over agency benefits or services.

The virtual monopoly over client benefits and services may lead to problematic experiences with dissatisfied clients. The management of one's caseload, with as few problematic situations as possible, becomes a direct service practitioner's major resource. But clients represent another resource as well. They provide information on their needs, problems, and goals to the practitioner, giving the worker a better picture of the clients, as a major environmental force, than those held by supervisors and directors. The immediacy of this information is important for the organization's adaptation to the environment.

If clients' needs change and the organization does not adapt to the change, it may find itself with few referrals or clients. Without clients to justify its existence, the organization will be in an untenable position. Thus, the organization's dependence on the direct service practitioner to provide intelligence information on client problems and needs heightens worker power. (Exceptions to this formulation can be found in county social service departments or mental health agencies which have monopolies based on statutory mandates and therefore no competition.)

Open systems theory enhances our understanding that organizations have two levels of goals—formal and operative (Perrow, 1961). All social service agencies were set up by either a political unit (city, county, state, federal governments), by a specific constituency (church, elderly citizens, parents of mentally retarded children), or by a combination of both. If asked, agency developers would say that the purpose of the organization is to provide certain services to a specific needy client group. Though it would be written into the law, this formal goal should never be thought of as constituting the sole purpose of the organization.

As we have noted, the primary goal of any organization is *survival;* the individuals and other resources of the organization should be envisaged in a dynamic state of exchange with their environment in the interest of survival. The intrinsic drive toward entropy (a wasting away or tendency to disorganization) is countered by the goal to import more resources than are exported. Other operative goals include day-to-day and short-range goals which the organization's members set to enhance the organization's power and the individual's status within it. The operative goals themselves may be manifest or latent. Usually the goals of program development, maintenance, or expansion are open, whereas the individual's goals would tend to be less visible. The social service practitioner has to be knowledgeable about all goal types (formal and operative) and levels (manifest and latent).

Goals should be conceptualized as "pullers" rather than "pushers." Goals and motives are not the same. The anticipated enjoyment or reward of goal attainment pulls one in their direction, but the desire to attain the goals reflects one's motivations. The desire (motivation) to earn money (goal) is related to the need for food, lodging, clothing, and so forth. Since organizational members, not the organizations themselves, set the formal and operative goals, the members will try to meet their personal goals within the context of setting the organization's goals. Thus goal setting at both the organizational and personal levels entails interactions and relationships with other staff and people outside the organization (clients, other agencies, constituents). Such interactions, if negative, could cause goal displacement—that is, if achieving desired goals is impossible, substitute goals are sought.

ORGANIZATIONAL FUNCTIONING AND PRACTITIONER RELATIONSHIPS

Specialization versus generalization

Bureaucratic theory posits an inevitable drive toward increasing the specialization of worker functions in the organization in order to enhance efficiency and effectiveness. Movement toward specialization is found in all professions, not just in social services. As Chapter 11 will show, specialization may also have a negative effect on the worker's emotional functioning.

Specialization has a significant impact on the practitioner as well. Specialization usually determines the work groups which we are assigned. For example, child welfare workers in a county social service department are grouped together under their own supervisor and usually their own work space; the same applies to income maintenance workers and social service workers in other settings. Since work groups determine our primary interactions with other workers, they play a central role in our job efficiency, effectiveness, and indeed our emotional functioning. We experience all the facets of intragroup dynamics as we perform out daily work routines.

Although assignment to specific work groups meets the needs of formal organizational structure, work groups determine to a considerable extent the nature of the informal power structure which exists in all organizational settings. Homans (1950) hypothesized that interactions lead to the development of sentiments, such as liking the other person, which can serve as the basis for informal clique or coalition development. The harsher and more crisis-laden the organizational structure, the deeper will be sentimental attachments. In wartime military service, for example, strong cliques are formed for mutual physical and emotional survival. Likewise, in the crises of college life, attachments to friends become very close. A further description of work group dynamics is included in a later section; but here, specialization, as a force, must be seen as an aspect of organizational environment.

Generalization is the opposite of specialization. Especially in newer, developing agencies with less specialization, the workers tend to have a wide range of responsibilities and duties. As the agencies become older, especially public agencies that are accountable to political constituencies, goals of efficiency and effectiveness may lead to specialization, although conscious efforts can either prevent or reverse this trend. The medical profession, for example, has become so top-heavy in specialists that medical schools have developed "family practice" educational tracks. The family practitioners are generalists. Social service agencies have also been caught in the generalization versus specialization dilemma. Voluntary, nonprofit agencies have retained more of a generalist focus, which may be a reflection of their small size and focus on one profession, namely, social work. The burgeoning, private, family counseling groups tend also to reflect a generalist orientation.

The impact of specialization on the practitioner's job satisfaction and emotional functioning has come under increasing scrutiny during the last two decades. At a Volvo factory in Sweden, for instance, it was found that dull, routine, unchallenging work on the automobile assembly line led to worker frustration and estrangement. In assembly-line production, the workers didn't see the important contribution of their work to the car as a whole. To counter these problems, workers were reorganized into new work groups, with each group cooperating to build each car practically from start to finish. Worker satisfaction and productivity improved, but each worker had to learn a variety of skills to perform a wide range of tasks. In other words, he/she had to become a generalist.

How are these concerns transferred to social service work settings? First, why do agency controllers (such as politicians, executive directors, and community elites who serve on voluntary agency boards) think that progress is measured by further bureaucratization, or in this case, specialization? Though the need for accountability of fiscal expenditures, for efficiency, and for effectiveness cannot be denied, surely there are limits; at some time we reach the "point of diminishing returns" as regards specialization.

As an example, when one of the authors worked in a county social service department in 1959, he had a caseload that included clients from all four of the Social Security Act categories (needy blind, disabled, elderly, and families without breadwinners), general assistance, and child welfare. Although pressed for time, he believed that he was helping his needy clients. Job satisfaction in the agency was fairly high and the burnout rate was correspondingly low.

An assessment of present-day county social service departments would show the opposite situation. Applications for Aid to Families with Dependent Children, which, previously had only two pages, now have ten or more pages.

Supplemental Security Income (needy blind, elderly, and disabled) is handled at the federal level; the AFDC program remains at the county level. In the county office, there is a split between income maintenance workers and service workers; this latter group may be further split into child welfare and adult services workers. Job dissatisfaction is rampant and the turnover rate is alarming. Organizational structure has caused such public agencies to have become overspecialized. Who are the losers?—alienated practitioners, inadequately served clients, and, ultimately, the taxpayers who support such a dysfunctional system.

Formalization

Formalization denotes the degree to which an agency has written rules, policies, and procedures to guide (or to control) practitioners' behaviors. Generally, informal functioning characterizes a new, developing organization; but as time goes by, rules, policies, and procedures proliferate to secure uniformity of behavior and to save time. Slowly, the worker's discretionary area (freedom) is diminished. As the privilege of discretionary judgment decreases, so does perceived autonomy (Figure 9–11).

Agency policies and procedures manuals, though outlining behavioral constraints, also serve to instruct newer, less knowledgeable professional workers. Another factor leading to their development is the impossibility of memorizing all the rules, policies, and procedures promulgated by federal and state welfare agencies. The manuals are needed for information retrieval.

The diminution of practitioner discretion and autonomy is an important consideration. Not only does organizational formalization constrain our behavior but there are societal expectations for appropriate behaviors, such as those of professional, religious, family, and agency organizations (see Figure 9–12). How does a worker with little discretion and autonomy feel? Referring to transactional analysis, we may speculate that he/she feels like a child and probably resents it. With little autonomy, don't we also feel dependent? Referring to *exchange theory,* won't this perceived dependence create a sense of powerlessness and estrangement? Agency controllers might well be asked such questions.

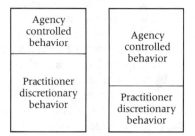

Figure 9–11. Practitioner versus agency control of behavior

Figure 9–12.   Types of role expectation constraints on individual practitioner

Centralization versus decentralization

Centralization versus decentralization is an aspect of organization functioning comprising several components. One component can be conceptualized in geographical terms: service delivery to clients can be in one central location or out where the clients are. The latter approach was well known to our 19th-century counterparts: the Charity Organization Societies (1870s) and the Settlement Houses (1880s) were founded on it. In the 20th century, the Social Security Act (1935) *required* states to develop social service departments in each county (with a few exceptions). After that, the approach received less attention until development of the New Frontier and Great Society programs, such as community mental health centers and antipoverty programs, in the mid-1960s.

Moreover, the location of decision making may be either centralized or decentralized. The authoritarian style of organization permits little practitioner input to decision making, but the democratic and collegial organizations encourage it. Figure 9–13 shows the various types of practitioner involvement in decision-making processes.

Organizational behavior norms, or "informal policies," play an important role in the life of the worker. Rapidly learning "the ropes" and "how things are done here" can prevent the worker from engaging in behavior considered to be inappropriate. Both the informal and the formal power structure will

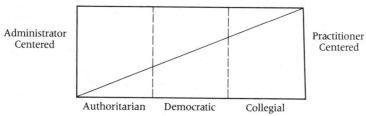

Figure 9–13.   Leadership styles

place heavy role expectations on the worker. At times, their differing expectations will lead to role conflict and their unclear expectations to role ambiguity. Both can create seriously handicapping anxieties. One deeply felt norm requires the worker not to encroach on the "turf" or job responsibilities of other workers. The informal power structure may be the best informational resource for precluding such incursions.

Agency policies and rules

Formal, written policies, as guidelines for action, can constrain our behavior or provide a small measure of freedom. A visualization of policies (Figure 9–14) will often indicate that the worker's behavior must fall within certain limits. Deviations through "fences" would require corrective action, but staying within the "fences" permits the practitioner a small measure of autonomy and direction.

Rules also provide structure; they tell workers specifically what they may or may not do, and they are inviolate: No Smoking!, Coffee Breaks Are Only Fifteen Minutes! Frequently found in agency manuals, written rules orient new workers to the job and provide behavioral constraints on all workers. Although the intent in enacting rules is to diminish worker discretion (autonomy), experienced practitioners often find ways to circumvent rules for their own and their clients' advantage. The other side of the coin, of course, is the practitioner who "lives by the book."

Organizational uncertainty

There are two dimensions of organizational uncertainty—internal and environmental (client behavioral uncertainty will not be addressed). Practitioners who wonder what is going to happen to them in the organization are showing *internal uncertainty.* New employees on probation look forward to receiving tenure so that they no longer have to worry so much about negative evaluations of others. Indeed, the very foundation of such uncertainty relates to the quality of intrastaff relationships. The relationships may be practitioner-to-practitioner or to-supervisor or to-administrator. To a considerable extent, these relationships determine what happens to the worker in securing permanent status, promotions, work group acceptance, and formal structure acceptance. Acceptance (and thereby reduction of uncertainty) depends on the practitioner's meeting the behavioral expectation of the formal and informal power structures.

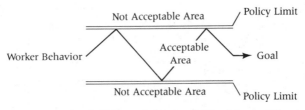

Figure 9–14. Policies as behavior guides for practitioners.

Another element of uncertainty for the practitioner relates to that caused by the *environment* external to the work organization. As indicated by open system theory, organizations are resource-dependent on other organizations and groups, and these other groups and organizations (such as local, state, and federal agencies) will affect what happens within the practitioner's agency. Federal and state laws that relate to funding and regulating community agencies greatly influence agency functioning—indeed, whether the agency will have a future.

In a broader sense, the general economic-environmental condition readily crosses agency boundaries. In the private sector, businesses may fail for lack of sales. In the public sector, agencies may have to cut back on staff or to close because of lack of taxpayer funding. Research has indicated a close relationship between unemployment and the development of psychosomatic-related problems, such as alcoholism. Uncertainty about job retention can have major debilitating impacts on practitioners, negatively affecting the practitioner-client relationship.

Other sources of uncertainty that heighten a practitioner's anxiety level may include deteriorating relationships with one's own family or other loved ones. It is not possible to compartmentalize our lives so that each segment exists in a vacuum from the other. An unhappy family life will have a negative effect on the practitioner in the work organization and vice versa.

Communication patterns

Communication patterns within an organization have both formal and informal levels. In the formal power structure, the quality and direction of communications generally reflect the organizational administrative style. In democratically and collegially administered organizations, however, communications must be two-way. Although written communications exist, the emphasis on mutual involvement in problem solving dictates greater reliance on spoken and face-to-face communications. Certainly, this minimizes the issuance of rules and changes from the top down. Both communication styles involve more committee work to accomplish tasks, to solve problems, and to seek organizational and personal goals.

Size

An organization's size has a direct effect on the practitioner, on his relationships with other practitioners and with his supervisor. Systems theory suggests that as an organization grows larger, there is a drive to differentiate into more and more work groups, partly to make labor more efficient. As Figure 9–15 shows, the proliferation of subunits places more social distance between each and may result in growing levels of supervision.

With each division, as from Program A2 to subprograms A2*a* and A2*b*, the functional and probably spatial distance increases, reducing the likelihood of face-to-face interactions. Each subunit will develop its own informal power structure. As certain individuals perform a linchpin function in the formal organization, so certain individuals also perform this function between subgroups of the informal power structure. These interactions and communications create bonds between the groups.

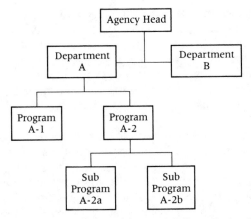

Figure 9–15. Organizational differentiation into subunits.

Chapter 9 has focused on the facets of bureaucratic organizational structure that can impact negatively on the practitioner. Autocratic, democratic, and collegial administrative types were explicated. The "reality shock" that inevitably accompanies a student about to enter the labor market can be lessened considerably if the student is knowledgeable about agency structures and processes. Finally, each practitioner should have a specific career advancement plan. To actualize the plan will entail demonstrating one's technical expertise and the ability to understand and to work within an organizational setting. Chapter 10 will discuss the various practitioner relationships with other practitioners, supervisors, and others within the context of the theories introduced here.

STUDY QUESTIONS

1. Select any organization of which you've been a nonpaid member, such as a church or a YWCA. Which organizational model did it follow? What was the degree of bureaucratization?
2. Select an organization of which you were a paid employee. Within which organizational model was it operated? What was the degree of bureaucratization? What were the similarities to and differences from the organization you chose for the first question?
3. Why might an employee become a "resigned bureaucrat"?
4. What do "lumping" and "dumping" mean?
5. What are the underlying values in McGregor's Theory X and Theory Y?
6. If an employee is operating in an adult ego state but is treated as if in the child state, how is the employee likely to feel?
7. What are the advantages to the practitioner of using an open systems perspective in analyzing a client's or an agency's environment?
8. Differentiate formal and informal power structure in organizations.
9. Why is it important for practitioners to understand their "boundary spanning" and "gatekeeping" roles?
10. What are the purposes of policies and rules?

REFERENCES

Behling, O., & Shriesheim, C. *Organizational behavior: Theory, research and application.* Boston: Allyn & Bacon, 1976.

Berne, E. *Transactional Analysis in Psychotherapy: A Systematic Individual and Social Psychiatry.* New York: Ballentine Books, 1961.

Von Bertalanffy, L. *General systems theory: Foundations, development, applications.* New York: George Braziller, 1968.

Blau, P. M. *Exchange and power in social life.* New York: John Wiley & Sons, 1964.

Herzberg, F. One more time: How do you motivate employees? *Harvard Business Review,* January-February 1968, pp. 53–62.

Homans, G. C. *The human group.* New York: Harcourt, Brace & Co., 1950.

Katz, D., & Kahn, R. L. *The social psychology of organization* (2nd ed.). New York: John Wiley & Sons, 1978.

Levine, S., & White, P. Exchange as a conceptual framework for the study of interorganizational relationships. *Administrative Science Quarterly,* 1961, 5, pp. 583–601.

Maslow, A. H. *Motivation and personality* (2nd ed.). New York: Harper & Row, 1970.

McGregor, D. *The human side of enterprise.* New York: McGraw-Hill, 1960.

Merton, R. K. *Social theory and social structure* (Rev. ed.) Glencoe, Ill.: Free Press, 1957.

Perrow, J. C. The analysis of goals in complex organizations. *American Sociological Review,* 1961, 26 (6), pp. 855–859.

Seabury, B. A. Arrangement of physical space in social work settings. *Social Work,* 1971, 16, pp. 43–49.

Thompson, J. D. *Organizations in action.* New York: McGraw-Hill, 1968.

Weber, M. [The theory of social and economic organization] (A. M. Henderson & T. Parsons, Trans.). New York: Oxford University Press, 1947.

Weinstein, D. *Bureaucratic oppositions: Challenging abuses in the workplace.* New York: Pergamon Press, 1979.

10

Intraorganizational Relationships: Negotiating the Context

Chapter 9 dealt with the organizational environment in its structural aspect. Chapter 10 highlights the relationships of practitioners with other practitioners, supervisors, executive directors, and boards of directors, both inside and outside the agency. We will focus on various theories relating to the behavior of people in organizations. What sort of treatment can new practitioners expect? What is the importance of the work group and the informal power structure? How do supervisory and practitioner actions relate? How does one survive or get ahead in a formal organization? How can we change organizations and help our clients at the same time? Understanding intraorganizational relationship processes can help to answer many of these questions.

Maslow's hierarchy of human needs

A. H. Maslow's hierarchy of human needs model is still the most used needs model in existence (see Figure 10–1). The physiological needs center on the bodily functions of eating, drinking, sleep, and sex. If these needs aren't met (except for sex) we are in a life-threatening situation. Hence, Maslow's hierarchy rises from the most life-threatening situation (physiological) to the least life-threatening (self-actualization). In another view, we can see the progression from physiological needs which are shared with other members of the animal kingdom to needs that are uniquely human. Stressful situations may bring about a breakdown in human functioning, starting with a concern about self-actualization and decaying downward to security and physiological needs, on which hang physical survival.

Maslow's theory accurately depicts the various levels of needs associated with groups and the work place. Clearly, one must acknowledge that if the lower-level needs aren't met, it is difficult to devote energies to the higher-order needs. For example, when you are hungry or thirsty, is it easy to con-

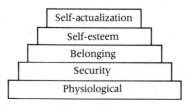

Figure 10–1. Maslow's Hierarchy of Needs

centrate on studying or do you find yourself gravitating toward the refrigerator? Here, each level of needs will be examined in reference to the work place.

In exchange for the practitioner's expertise and labor, the work organization provides a salary and fringe benefits, which meet the worker's physiological and security needs. Keeping in mind that meeting lower-level needs takes precedence over meeting higher-level needs, it can be seen that whatever threatens the former will be viewed as the most anxiety-provoking. For a well known example, anxiety about job retention intensifies among employees in all types of work organizations in periods of national economic decline. The two lower levels of needs, then, can be viewed as essential to the practitioner's survival. Few practitioners will deliberately behave in ways that will lead to their dismissal because lower-level needs must be met for them and for their families.

How do these two needs relate to relationships? Relationships with clients, co-workers, supervisors, administrators, boards, and community agency personnel can enhance or detract from our ability to meet these needs in the work organization. As individuals, we seek to enhance our needs fulfillment in order to diminish personal anxiety. If a great many clients complain to the agency director that we are not helping them, would this not threaten job advancement or retention? If our supervisor gives us a poor annual performance rating or our co-workers in the informal power structure comment negatively about our competence, we may also experience job difficulty.

For job retention and advancement, then, it is paramount that we understand the impact on our careers of our relationships with others and manage these relationships in our best interests. This is not to advocate the development of Machiavellian politicians in the office but only to suggest that an understanding of the "political" nature of relationships is important. For the individual practitioner, for example, poor relationships with other agency employees may hinder securing services or benefits for our clients.

How do the higher-order needs affect us? To start with, we are born into our first group—the family. Later, we affiliate with church groups, attend school, join the Scouts, engage in sports, and eventually we marry and form our own family group. *Human beings are primarily group creatures.* It is partly from group affiliations that we develop a sense of identity and security. Certainly, the peer group meets human needs at all ages (especially those of adolescents in identity crises). Since, as adults, we spend eight hours a day in a work organization, work groups—both formal and informal—have major effects on our lives as well.

Formal work group.   The formal structure shows the practitioner's place in the agency's table of organization. This formal structure meets part, but not all, of our need for a sense of belonging. It clearly defines who is responsible to whom, who has authority over whom, and, on a horizontal plane, who occupy the same level of authority and responsibility (see Figure 10–2). On overt, formal relationships and work groups, such as Supervisor B and practitioners A, B, and C, the expectation is imposed that the various components of the work organization will strive to meet agency goals. What individual practitioners will do, the client groups they serve, and how they serve them will be determined by membership in the formal work groups (which might also be called *program* or *staff teams*). Generally, a job description will indicate the practitioner's responsibilities and duties in these formal work groups.

Practitioners can also meet their self-esteem and self-actualization needs in formal work groups. Recognition, rewards, and opportunities to develop unique individual talents may be provided, depending on the milieu (or cli-

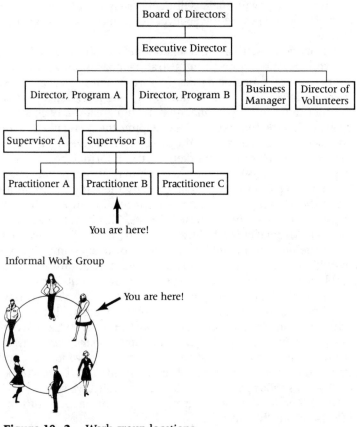

Figure 10–2.   Work group locations

mate) of the particular group. Unfortunately, bureaucratized work organizations may permit little emphasis on meeting these higher-order needs because of the emphasis on hierarchical authority, division of labor, regulation of behavior by written rules, and impersonality of interpersonal relations. These dimensions relate more to the lower-order needs than to those of belonging, self-esteem and self-actualization.

Informal work group.   We also meet our needs in the informal work group (or power structure). Among organizations comprising more than a handful of people, it is virtually inevitable that personal friendship groups or cliques will form. According to Homans (1950), because interactions in work groups are based on similar interests and liking, informal work groups become major sources of meeting individual and social needs. Indeed, merely *not* being a member of such a reference group can engender anxiety. Few people wish to be social isolates.

In such primary (face-to-face) groups, we feel more secure, our needs for belonging and identity are met, and we receive reactions from other members that can meet our self-esteem and self-actualization needs. Primary groups are noted for their informality as compared with secondary groups (such as formal work groups), which tend to be characterized by rules and regulations (DuBrin, 1981). Informality, however, does not mean an absence of clearly defined roles, including those of leaders and followers, within the groups.

Group enforcement process.   Behling and Schriesheim (1976) indicate that informal group membership exacts a price—conformity. To meet affiliative needs, we must be fairly conforming to group behavioral norms. The conformity develops through enforcement processes and the "discomfort" that the deviant experiences. The first such process is that of education (or socialization) by group members. When a new person comes to an agency, the informal group will let him/her know "how things are *really* done around here," perhaps contradicting the orientation provided by the formal work organization. The second enforcement process—surveillance by group members—can lead to warnings (the third process) and to granting of rewards or punishments (the fourth process). Generally these enforcement processes are greatest with new members and taper off after they have demonstrated internalization of the norms. Most of us accept these kinds of "trials" because by the time we join work groups, we have gone through this process many times before. However, one does have a free choice to "buy into" the group or not, at the price of sacrificing the opportunity to meet our affiliation and higher-order needs.

Group conformity processes are paralleled in the formal organization. New staff members undergo a probationary status, orientations to the job, and continuing in-service training, which serve to educate or socialize them into the job. For formal surveillance, a supervisor is assigned. Although the supervisor's overall role is broader than just this, monitoring the practitioner's conformance to agency policies and procedures has the highest priority. The upshot, of course, is that, at least during the initial socialization period, the practitioner has two groups looking over his/her shoulder (see Figure 10–3).

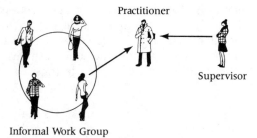

Figure 10–3.   Sources of surveillance

Most practitioners are understandably relieved once they complete their probationary period because the surveillance should now decrease. The formal organization, of course, has many ways of dispensing rewards and punishments. Rewards can range from salary and fringe benefits to acceptance, support, and recognition. Punishments can vary from warnings to negative performance evaluations to dismissal. Being fired can have catastrophic effects on the practitioner's emotional and economic status. Dismissal cuts across all our needs and throws us back onto our other primary reference groups—family and friends.

Herzberg's two factor theory

How does Figure 10-4 concern relationships and practitioners? The so-called hygiene factors, or potential dissatisfiers, show a clear correlation with Maslow's hierarchy of needs and references to relationships. The hygiene factors include our physiological, security, and group belonging needs. Herzberg felt that these factors, if unmet, could serve as great dissatisfiers; but, if met, still did not serve as great motivators. Relationships with subordinates, peers, and one's supervisor, as well as the quality of supervision, if negative, can lead to job dissatisfaction and lessened job performance, which can in turn affect one's standing in relation to raises, promotions, and tenure.

The "motivating" factors relate to group belonging, self-esteem, and self-actualization needs. If unmet, these, too, can serve as dissatisfiers, but, if met, they are the best motivators. Growth, advancement, responsibility, the work itself, recognition, and achievement all arise within the context of our working within groups in the formal work organization. Without the help of others—subordinates, peers, and supervisors—meeting these needs will be very difficult, if not improbable. Accordingly, avoiding job dissatisfaction and meeting our motivational needs both involve a major commitment of time in working with others. Inept, negative, frustrating relationships, whether imposed by the organizational structure or by the individual's lack of interpersonal skills, will constrain a practitioner's effectiveness with clients and functioning within the organization.

Exhibit 1.   Factors affecting job attitudes, as reported in 12 investigations

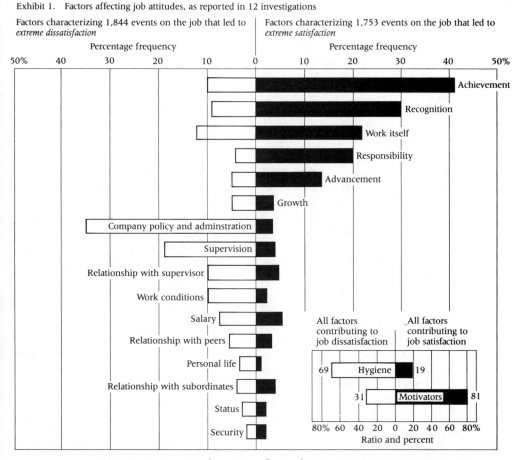

Figure 10–4.   Herzberg's two factor theory. From "One more time: How do you motivate employees?" by Frederick Herzberg. Reprinted by permission of the *Harvard Business Review,* January-February, 1968, 53. Copyright © 1968 by the President and Fellows of Harvard College; all rights reserved.

McGregor revisited

Although Theory X and Theory Y have been previously discussed within the context of the "organizational climate," we are now interested in integrating Maslow's hierarchy of needs and McGregor's Theory X and Y as they relate to motivating workers and meeting their needs (see Figure 10–5).

The traditional, top-down authority, Theory X hierarchical supervisory system does seem to meet the lower-level physiological, security, and some group belonging needs. As Herzberg (1968) suggests these needs may serve as great dissatisfiers but not as great motivators. Obversely, the less punitive, more autonomous functioning in a Theory Y hierarchy better meets the need for group belonging, self-esteem, and self-actualization. This is not to say, of

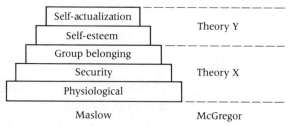

Figure 10–5.   Integration of Maslow's and McGregor's theories

course, that workers might not prefer certain kinds of work settings characterized by the Theory X structure of relationships, but we believe that social service agencies do not fit into this category. The dilemma facing the social service practitioner is that he or she will work in a bureaucratic agency, whose hierarchy of relationships more resembles a Theory X structure than a Theory Y structure. The practitioner should therefore learn the structure and processes in both Theory X (authoritarian) and Theory Y (democratic and collegial) organizations in order to negotiate the structure to meet client(s) needs and for personal self-advancement.

Understanding the structure and processes in organizations should not be thought of as important only to the direct service practitioner. People at all organizational levels have the same kinds of needs and strive to meet them, overtly and covertly (see Figure 10–6). The practitioner must understand that people's needs at each level involve not only their own intrinsic drives but their assigned work roles as well. For example, the practitioners, supervisors, and executive director all perform a "middle" role in the sense that their performance is judged and job rewards allocated on the basis of the behavior of their subordinates. Practitioners are judged by the behavior of their clients. Supervisors are judged by the behavior (competence) of their assigned practitioners. The executive director is judged primarily by the performance of all staff in the organization.

To deal with these expectations, we each try to determine behavioral goals that meet our needs. For example, the administrator tries to obtain resources (money, staff, material) for the agency, to accept the organizational or community power structure, to maintain internal and external stability, and to provide sufficient services to clients to look effective (Perow, 1978). In talking about roles now, we introduce a major theory which helps to explain practitioner feelings and functioning—role conflict and ambiguity.

Supervision

Role conflict and ambiguity.   Katz and Kahn (1966) postulated that *role conflict* (receiving incompatible performance demands) and *role ambiguity* (receiving unclear performance expectations and feedback from the environment) were major difficulties for workers in organizations. What do practitioners do when the supervisor expects them to behave in certain ways, but their clients or their own values indicate engagement in different ways? What

Figure 10–6.   Individuals at each level seek to meet their needs

does the practitioner do when work assignments are unclear? Compounding these problems is the frequent changing of policies and procedures to comply with federal or state mandatory regulations. A benefit we could provide to our clients one week may be withdrawn the next week because of changed regulations or budget cuts. Harrison (1980) has shown that role ambiguity may have more of a negative impact on child welfare workers than role conflict.

Diminishing role conflicts and role ambiguity is a major responsibility of the practitioner's supervisor. This is not to say that the external or internal agency environments will ever be so stable or so certain that the practitioner will never experience anxiety. But since supervisors play such pivotal roles in helping practitioners to solve their problems and to meet their needs, it is appropriate to study this position at this point.

Structure and processes.   The overall goal of supervision is to direct and monitor the work of others. More specific goals are to ensure compliance with agency policies and procedures and to develop the job competence of the supervisee. Since all direct service practitioners (and supervisors themselves) are under supervision, it is well to put its structure and processes into perspective.

Supervisors are involved in all the internal management functions: (a) planning, (b) organizing, (c) staffing, (d) directing, and (e) controlling. Through the work of their supervisees, they play a pivotal role in achieving agency objectives and in ensuring the organization's survival. Their degree of involvement in overall agency management will differ according to the executive director's leadership style—autocratic, democratic, collegial—but in any case they will be held accountable for their supervisees' work performance and outputs.

Planning involves studying problems, setting objectives, and devising suitable activities to achieve them. Organizing resources, including staff, to meet the objectives is next. Leadership and direction must be provided in implementing the plan, and the use of resources, including staff, must be coordinated, monitored, and evaluated in relation to meeting objectives. Providing services to clients is somewhat similar to this.

Supervisors play four relationship roles with their supervisees (Plunkett, 1979): Educator, counselor, judge, and spokesperson/advocate. The *educator* role is especially important for new or beginning-level practitioners. The supervisor usually handles the informal orientation to the agency and in smaller agencies may handle the formal orientation as well. Once through the orientation, the supervisor assigns work, assesses the practitioner's strengths and weaknesses, and arranges for training to overcome the latter. Policies, procedures, and rules will be emphasized. Supervisors may also teach job skills such as relating to certain minority or ethnic groups.

In the role of *counselor*, supervisors can help the novice to think through job-related problems so that the next, similar problem can be handled independently. Personal problems that impinge on the practitioner's work life may be shared with a respected supervisor. Although advice giving may be practiced in the former instance, skilled supervisors will practice restraint in the latter instance. Some writers describe this activity as more of a coaching rather than a counseling role, which eradicates some of the implication that there is something wrong with the supervisee.

In the *judge* role, the supervisor must assess the practitioner's compliance with policies and procedures, assess work performance and outputs, and mediate any disputes the practitioner might have with others. In large bureaucratized agencies, computerized management information systems monitor practitioners' compliance with policies and procedures, such as client eligibility criteria and error rates in filling out forms. In smaller agencies, the supervisor monitors these activities daily. For the sake of uniformity, performance appraisals can be highly standardized, though such standardization does not increase the validity or reliability of such rating forms. With either the standardized or less standardized appraisal forms and processes, the subjective assessment of the supervisor plays a major role.

In the role of *spokesperson/advocate*, supervisors interpret management's viewpoint and actions to the practitioners and vice versa. This role gives supervisors considerable power. Insofar as the supervisor controls the flow of information both ways, both groups depend on him or her to provide the vital information they need to do their jobs and to ensure agency survival.

Since the practitioner's supervisor decides whether he or she will pass probation, receive a merit raise, attend a state conference, or be assigned a better office, practitioners should study their supervisors carefully. There is nothing dishonorable about applying diagnostic skills to determine what makes a supervisor tick. There is nothing wrong with a practitioner's trying to ensure tenure in an agency. Basically, there are two ways to do this—to play the "political game" or to manifest professional competence.

Getting ahead.   "Political game" tactics are not based on professional or technical competence but on the *manipulation of relationships* within the organization. For example, the sycophant or yes-man ceaselessly curries the boss' favor through flattery and agreeing with him or her. DuBrin (1981) describes six other tactics to get ahead, which generally involve the relationship with one's supervisor:

- *Blackmail*—involves finding out something embarrassing or job-threatening about a superior and bargaining one's silence for promotion. Since most practitioners wish to earn promotions and higher salaries, they are in at least mildly competitive situations with their peers.

- *Character assassination*—skillful, low-key, it is one way to decrease another person's ability to compete.
- *Removal of competitors*—although infrequently seen, some people try to get ahead by supporting the transfer or promotion of competitors out of the work unit.
- *Division*—another way is to attempt to break up the cohesiveness of a competitive group on the theory that if they split up or argue amongst themselves, they can't compete very well.
- *Setting a person up*—making someone look ineffective might lead to his or her transfer or demotion.
- *Claiming undue credit*—Claiming the credit for other people's ideas or work accomplishments is a ploy used against peers, as well as by supervisors/administrators against subordinates.

Engaging in any of these tactics can involve compromising or violating one's values and ethics. DuBrin suggests that there are better ways to get ahead within the context of the supervisor/supervisee relationship. First, it is possible to use one's technical or professional competence *to help the supervisor to succeed.* This may be in managing one's caseload with a minimum of disruption or in providing the information the supervisor needs to work toward his or her goals. A *display of loyalty* to one's supervisor or organization in a time of trouble will be noticed. Becoming a *volunteer for assignments,* especially those critical to the supervisor's or the organization's goals, is seen as showing initiative and leadership potential. *Using praise* sparingly toward one's supervisor or peers shows a concern for the feelings of others and an ability to evaluate the performance of others. (If overdone, of course, we gain a reputation for sycophancy.)

Having a sense of humor, whether in times of stress or merely in response to the supervisor's jokes, can help to develop and maintain a valuable rapport. The final technique is *to become a crucial employee.* This means acquiring valued resources, such as professional knowledge, technical knowledge (federal and state laws, rules, and procedures) or other knowledge that can help the supervisor (or organization) to meet goals. By sharing with the supervisor the problems that we see developing in our services to clients, the supervisor may be able to deal with them quickly, before they pose a serious threat to anyone.

Using competence to support one's supervisor may bring about the development of a close personal relationship based on mutual trust, empathy, and respect. Since the author recommends this method for getting ahead and rejects "political" methods, we now turn to value conflicts which most social service practitioners experience.

Value conflicts

Figure 10–7 shows that each social service professional carries around two value systems—the personal and the professional—and most of us experience little conflict between the two. The professional values support us in giving primacy to the client's needs over our own in the helping relationship.

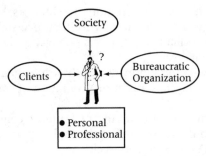

Figure 10–7.   Sources of value conflicts for practitioners

By giving us a framework within which to practice, they reduce uncertainty and ambiguity. But value conflicts experienced by social service practitioners may arise in our relationships with our clients, with society as a whole, and with our bureaucratic organization. Often we find ourselves separated from our clients by such factors as race, ethnicity, gender, rural/urban orientation, education, language, class, and religion. All of these factors contribute to our personal values. Overcoming these barriers is one of the most important tasks in a practitioner's education and practice, requiring a considerable amount of introspection and living through of experiences.

Although not necessarily viewed as a day-to-day problem, the impact of societal values is all-pervasive. Keith-Lucas (1972), who wrote the seminal formulations on societal values in social work, developed three clusters of value systems. The first, called the *capitalist-puritan* (CP) *system,* he summarized as follows:

1. Man is responsible for his own success or failure.
2. Human nature is basically evil but can be overcome by an act of will.
3. Man's primary purpose is to acquire material prosperity, which he achieves through hard work.
4. The primary purpose of society is the maintenance of law and order in which this acquisition is possible.
5. The unsuccessful or deviant person does not help although efforts should be made, up to a point, to rehabilitate him or to spur him to greater efforts on his own behalf.
6. The primary incentives to change are to be found in economic or physical rewards and punishments [p. 138].

In stark contrast to this "cut and dried" system, which places primary "value" on maintaining an ordered society, is the system Keith-Lucas labeled the *humanist-positivist-utopian* (HPU) system, which places a primary value on people.

1. The primary purpose of society is to fulfill man's needs, both material and emotional.

2. If man's needs were fulfilled, he would attain a state that is variously described, according to the vocabulary used by the specific HPU system, as that of goodness, maturity, adjustment, or productivity, in which most of his and society's problems would be solved.
3. What hampers him from attaining this state is external circumstances, which are not in general under his control. This, in various HPU systems, has been ascribed to a lack of education, to economic circumstances, to childhood relationships, and to the social environment.
4. These circumstances are subject to manipulation by those possessed of sufficient technical and scientific knowledge, using, in general, what is known as the "scientific method."
5. Man and society are ultimately perfectible [pp. 139–140].

The *Judeo-Christian* value system focuses on the spiritual nature of humankind.

1. Man is a created being, one of whose major problems is that he acts as if he were not and tries to be autonomous.
2. Man is fallible but at the same time capable of acts of great courage or unselfishness.
3. The moral difference between men is insignificant compared with the standard demand by their Creator, and, as a consequence, man cannot judge his fellow in such terms.
4. Man's greatest good lies in his *relationship with his fellows and with his Creator* [italics added].
5. Man is capable of choice, in the "active and willing" sense, but may need help in making this choice.
6. Love is always the ultimate victor over force [pp. 140–141].[1]

Keith-Lucas's erudite discussion on the interrelationship of these value systems is particularly valuable. Every practitioner should decide to which system he or she subscribes. Since values are beliefs and preferences, there can be no objective judgment that any of the three is "good" or "bad." However, our relationships with clients, other agency personnel, and the general public will be affected in some measure by overall value systems and those with whom we are interacting.

To be more specific, we could observe that many social service practitioners hold the HPU perspective. This perspective, though, may lead to conflicts with members of the business community, who serve on boards and who contribute to the United Way, and with representatives of the political power structure, who also serve on boards and provide public funding for social service agencies. These two groups may hold values more akin to the CP perspective. Indeed, their service on boards may be more aligned with the goal of holding down or decreasing program expenditures than with providing

---

[1]From *Giving and Taking Help* by Alan Keith-Lucas. Copyright 1972 The University of North Carolina Press. Reprinted by permission of the publisher.

services to needy clients. But it is wrong to stereotype the individual members of any group (value perspectives should be individually determined); and it would also be wrong to assume that positive relationships cannot be formed between people who hold different values. Our goal here is simply to point out the role of value systems in contributing to the development of conflictual situations.

Both the formal and informal power structures in bureaucratic organizations have value systems. The formal structure tends to give highest priority to values that help it to attain task and maintenance (survival) goals. An internal and external sense of balance is so important that one becomes careful not to rock the boat. This will never be in writing, of course. To determine what the formal value systems are, one must study the agency's overt goals, policies (task and personnel), and task procedures.

As previously observed, new practitioners should learn the agency's formal and latent values as soon as possible. In addition, the informal power structure—which is usually a clique or coalition of peers (based on friendship) and individuals in certain "powerful" positions, such as long-tenured practitioners and secretaries—can be of help in illuminating the agency and its values. An example of the latter would be an informal standard of work production, such as services provided to clients or pages of typing. The "eager beaver" who violates work norms may be subject to informal correction. The primary resource for learning about formal values is again the practitioner's supervisor, who can prevent the practitioner from violating formal and informal values and behavioral norms.

Supervision revisited

Having discussed the value systems that impinge on all of us and the crucial role of the supervisor in transmitting the agency's values to the practitioner, let's return to the supervisor and his or her functions.

The traditionally oriented supervisor, reflecting the "scientific management" and Theory X approaches, typically does the work assignment planning, makes the assignments, then monitors the supervisee's accomplishment of the tasks. If needed, training is provided so that the job will be done "right". The supervisor is concerned about discipline and about how task accomplishment will reflect on him or her. Performance checking procedures are rigid and, with the advent of computerized management information systems, the paperwork is extensive. Both achievements and failures are pointed out.

The newer human relations-oriented supervisor includes the supervisees in planning, controlling, as well as doing the task, but does not issue dictatorial edicts. Situations are created and monitored so that the novice can learn naturally, as the need arises. Control systems are set up so that the supervisee can check his or her own behavior. A team spirit is developed so that all can share in recognition of good work. Career paths are developed with each of the supervisees. The supervisor attempts to help subordinates to meet their higher needs in Maslow's hierarchy.

What are some relationship principles that skilled supervisors follow? First, each subordinate should be treated with objectivity, impartiality, dignity, and respect. The positive or constructive aspects of the supervisee's work should be recognized and rewarded; supervisees are not just units of production; they should know the explicit and implicit goals of the agency, the performance standards to be met, and their expected technical or professional competencies. Supervisors must keep uppermost in their minds the negative effects of role conflict and role ambiguity on employee job satisfaction and performance. Although they can never ignore their responsibility to ensure practitioner compliance with agency policies, as much focus as possible should be placed on enhancing the supervisee's job competencies and career development. Just as practitioners should remain relatively calm in relating to their clients, supervisors must keep their cool in relating to subordinates. Praise should be given in public, but punishment should only be given in private.

Playing games. The relationship may take pathological directions, however. Reflecting the 1960s use of the "game" concept to explain human behavior, Kadushin (1979) described a number of "games" that supervisors and supervisees play. Games were regarded as conscious interactional patterns designed to provide a predetermined payoff to one of the participants. In the supervisor-supervisee relationship, games may arise to alleviate anxiety, to forestall change, or as resistance to accountability. Kadushin [p. 184] described the first game as "Two against the Agency," in which the supervisee uses the conflict between bureaucratic needs and his or her professional orientation to explain noncompliance with routine agency paperwork. Client needs are reported as being more important than such mundane activities. This type of supervisee can't accept bureaucratic controls and tries to enlist the supervisor's aid to subvert them.

Supervisees may also play "Be Nice to Me Because I Am Nice to You" [p. 185]. By disarming the supervisor with flattery, they make objective assessment of their work difficult. Kadushin called the next game "Treat Me, Don't Beat Me" [p. 186]. By exposing all his or her problems, the subordinate attempts to lessen performance expectations and demands. Attempting to make friends with the supervisor, the subordinate may play the "Evaluation Is Not for Friends" game [p. 186]. Getting the supervisor to view the supervisee as an equal may complicate the authority dimension of the relationship. In a similar game called "Maximum Feasible Participation" [p. 187] the supervisee shifts the roles to peer levels and attempts to assert an equal right for work-related determinations, such as supervisory discussion agendas.

In a game called "If You Knew Dostoyevsky Like I Know Dostoyevsky" [p. 187], a literary-minded practitioner compares his clients' behavior with that of characters in the classics, thereby seizing control of the supervisory discussion. A similar ploy is seen in "So What Do *You* Know about It?" [p. 188]. By claiming that only those with direct client contact or personal life experience can understand a situation, the supervisor is placed on the defensive. In "All or Nothing at All" [p. 189], the supervisor is made to feel that he or she has sold out to the Establishment and is poorly motivated to help clients.

Additional games designed to manipulate the supervisor include "I Have a List" [p. 189], in which a list of questions is used to set up the agenda;

"Heading Them Off at the Pass" [p. 190] which involves confession of one's mistakes and self-flagellation; "Little Old Me" [p. 190] which involves controlling through dependence; "I Did Like You Told Me" [p. 190], or blaming the supervisor when things go wrong on a case; "It's All So Confusing" [p. 191] when the supervisee shops around for inputs from different people and then blames their inconsistencies for his or her confusion; and "What You Don't Know Won't Hurt Me" [p. 191], or manipulating information given to the supervisor.

Kadushin points out that supervisors also play games. The first was "I Wonder Why You Really Said That?" [p. 192], in which honest disagreements are defined as resistances. Another game was "One Good Question Deserves Another" [p. 192] in which the supervisor avoids admitting personal knowledge limitations by turning questions back onto the supervisee. For either party, in Kadushin's view, the best defenses were to refuse to play, to use gradual interpretation of the other's behavior, or to express one's feelings about the situation honestly. Playing such games interferes with the open, trusting relationship needed to help clients and to provide for mutual growth of supervisee and supervisor.

Hawthorne (1979), too, noted the negative character of the interactions between the supervisor and supervisee. The first game was called "They Won't Let Me" [p. 198], in which the authority of superiors is used to back up a negative response to a supervisee's request or stated need. In "Poor Me" [p. 198], the supervisor seeks the sympathy of the supervisee, inducing a role reversal. In "I'm Really One of You" [p. 199], the supervisor joins the supervisee in complaining about the agency but does little about the complaints. Hawthorne described another game as "Remember Who's Boss" [p. 200], in which the supervisor assumes a dictatorial demeanor. In another power game, listed as "I'll Tell on You" [p. 201], the supervisor controls by threats. "Father/ Mother Knows Best" [p. 201] cloaks control under paternalism/maternalism. Finally, in "I'm Only Trying to Help You" [p. 201], control is disguised as help.

The author contends that we all—supervisees and supervisors alike—are the victims of such game playing at one time or another. Moreover, in either role, we may unconsciously slip into game playing ourselves. Such game playing does not help us to serve our clients better nor does it help us to develop job competencies that will advance our careers. We must recognize when others are using these techniques with us and when we are slipping nto such roles to relieve our own anxiety.

POWER, CONFLICT, AND CHANGE

Though *power* can be described in many ways, we believe that "the possession and control of resources" is one of the simplest, most fruitful definitions. Based on exchange theory, resources are money, workers, physical plant, equipment, clients, information, professional expertise, and political support. To possess or control such resources is to have power; to lack them is to be dependent on others to provide them to you. This dependency makes you less powerful than the other person. To receive the needed resources, you must do the other person's bidding.

At least initially, before new practitioners have proved their expertise, they are extremely dependent on, and vulnerable to, the dictates of the formal and informal power structures. As time passes, the practitioner learns the ropes, which lessens the dependency. In time, the practitioner may become a technical specialist, making other practitioners and the organization itself dependent on him or her, and thereby increasing his or her power. Emerson (1962) identified the inverse relationship between power and dependence, and his formulations apply to the relationships between individuals or between organizations. Between two entities, he asserted, there are four possible dyadic relationship patterns.

1. The first involves a high-balanced power relationship between the two entities. Each would have sufficient resources to meet its own needs, and neither would have a power advantage.

2. In the second relationship, involving low-balanced power, neither would have sufficient resources; hence, neither would have a power advantage.

3. The third alternative involves an unbalanced power situation favoring one entity.

4. The fourth situation also exhibits unbalanced power but favoring the other entity. For example, supervisor-subordinate relationships are unbalanced in the sense that the former generally has more power than the latter. But having demonstrated professional competence in managing caseloads and keeping problems under control, the power balance starts to shift.

Max Weber (1947) believed that power involved the use of force or coercion in the sense that the awarding or withholding of resources could be used to impel desired behavior. Asserting that the most frequent use of power arose from the concept of authority, in which the less powerful voluntarily responded to directives and expectations, he developed a three-part typology that is still useful today.

The first type is *traditional* authority as exemplified in the leadership of long established social institutions such as the British monarchy or the Vatican. The second type of authority is *charismatic,* based on the magnetic personal characteristics of a leader such as Martin Luther King, Jr., certain U.S. presidents, Mahatma Gandhi, Winston Churchill, and General George Patton. Weber termed the third type of authority *legal,* based on the office a person holds in an organization. The director of a bureaucratic agency can hire, determine the work activities of, and fire subordinates. The subordinates defer to this authority because the director occupies the higher position. Weber's view of authority is limited in recognizing only the formal and not the informal power structure.

French and Raven (1968) developed a five-part power framework based on the relationship between the more and less powerful. In *reward* power, the more powerful person has a resource desired by the less powerful. In *coercive* power, the more powerful has the resources to force the less powerful to do something. In *legitimate* power, the more powerful person has the acknowledged right to wield power over the other. *Referent* power occurs when the less powerful person tries to emulate the other, which resembles the "role model" conceptual relationship between two people. In the fifth power type, labeled *expert,* special knowledge is attributed to the more powerful person.

Finally, Mechanic (1962) cogently described ways in which people at the lower end of the formal organizational structure can acquire and wield power. Mechanic believed that the acquisition and use of power were related to the ability to gain control over persons, information, and other organizational resources. He sharply differentiated formal (positional) power from informal power techniques. Stating that "Organizations, in a sense, are continuously at the mercy of their lower participants . . ." [p. 351], he defined power "as any force that results in behavior that would not have occurred if the force had not been present" [p. 351]. However, he also stated that "power is closely related to dependence. To the extent that a person is dependent on another, he is potentially subject to the other person's power" [p. 352]. This underlines the power-dependence relationship between people based on exchange theory.

To start with, Mechanic asserted that the power of lower participants was related to their access to higher-ups, to information, and to such resources as equipment, supplies, and money. The longer a lower participant remains in an organization, the more such access increases. In this way, experienced lower participants would have knowledge of value to higher-ups, thereby making them dependent. Expert, professional, or technical knowledge makes a person harder to replace and therefore more powerful. Secretaries play pivotal roles in limiting access to higher-ups and in getting things done, which gives them considerable power. The more effort one puts into doing things for the higher-ups, the more one's power increases. The more central a position is to an organization's power centers, the more access, communication, and power there will be. Lower participants can form coalitions, increasing their collective power. The following of rules can at times be a "bargaining chip" in securing concessions from higher-ups. People who are viewed as "attractive" have greater access to other people, including higher-ups, which gives them power not enjoyed by peers. The more a higher-up delegates, the more he/she becomes dependent on the lower participant.

Internal change strategies

The generic nature of the power-dependency relationship—hereafter called the *power-dependence ratio*—must be kept in mind. This foundation of power, or lack thereof, will affect any change strategy in which we are involved. Now, let's look at some internal change ideas suggested by several writers.

Askerooth (1973) has delineated a three-stage strategy. (a) In the *preparation stage,* practitioners increase their interpersonal competence and try to make themselves as useful as possible to the organizational hierarchy. This is similar to our suggestion that the practitioner demonstrate professional and technical competence and then enhance his power base by becoming an expert in an area of critical knowledge or skill. (b) Askerooth's *process stage* involves stressing the benefit to the organization if the change is adopted. A high level of communication may lessen resistances. (c) The *establishment stage* involves gaining acceptance of the change by means of its now being seen as a routine operation. An appeal can be made to professionals' values and competencies to accept the change. The practitioner should attempt to lessen managerial resistance by helping in the implementation process and ensuring that other aspects of the agency, as a system, are not adversely affected.

Based on the work of psychologist Kurt Lewin (1951), Brager and Holloway (1978) have developed a more complex change model:

> Thus, if one is interested in altering an aspect of organizational functioning, he will attempt to influence the force field. This begins with his envisioning an alternate state of affairs, or change goal. With the change goal in mind, the practitioner identifies the driving and restraining forces that respectively appear to support and inhibit movement toward the goal. He then assesses the feasibility of alternate action strategies. Ultimately, he selects a plan which will involve reduction of the restraining forces, the increase of the driving forces, or both. If successful, the plan will alter the field of forces in the predicted manner, facilitating the desired goal [p. 31].

The description of the basic *problem-solving model* in social work is diagrammed in Figure 10–8.

The problem-solving model, based on the work of John Dewey (1933), has received wide application in social work (Compton & Galoway, 1975). An excellent discussion of the relationships between environmental factors (such as political and economic forces), internal organizational structure and processes, and the meaning of the change to participants' values and commitments is provided by Brager and Holloway (1978).

Rothman, Erlich, and Teresa (1976) developed a most helpful step-by-step manual, based on organizational theory and research, to initiate and promote internal and community change. The model, which uses practitioner "logs" to assist in problem and action plan analysis, is based on four action guidelines:

Promoting an Innovative Service or Program:
- By demonstrating it first with a smaller portion of the target population, then expanding to the larger group.

Changing the Goals of an Organization:
- By introducing new groups into the organization who support those goals, or
- By increasing the influence of those groups within the organization who support those goals.

Increasing Participation in Organizations and Groups:
- By offering benefits associated with participation.

Increasing Effectiveness in Role Performance:
- By clarifying the role and obtaining agreement about it among superiors and influentials [p. 7].

A study of these guidelines indicates the foundation change strategy of redistributing power within the organization. Each of the guidelines involves the

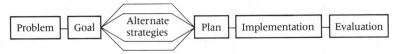

Figure 10–8.   Problem-solving model

practitioner with significant people within or outside the organization to be changed. The need for the practitioner to have acquired the ability to form constructive interpersonal work relationships is evident.

Horejsi, Walz, and Connolly (1977) have pinpointed many of the problems in working in large-scale dehumanizing bureaucracies. Discussing lobbying (advocacy) techniques, they note the central role of face-to-face encounters with legislators (which permit the development of a relationship much more effectively than just phone calls and letters). Further, they discuss the need for social service workers to form coalitions or alliances to humanize organizational working conditions both for the practitioners and for the delivery of services to clients. They accurately highlight the need to raise the consciousness of recipient groups with regard to their rights and the need for reform. Practitioners and recipient groups alike should press for opportunities to provide input into the organization's decision-making processes since both are being dehumanized.

External change strategies

External change strategies generally have at least one of two goals: (a) to advocate help for an individual client or family (such as receiving food stamps) and (b) to advocate help for a class of clients (such as developing a halfway house for alcoholics). Since many of the advocacy and change processes are generic, a description of activities developed by Sunley (1970) shows a mixture relating to the two goals, which also can be applied internally. Studies and surveys of community problems yield information which can be used to deliver expert testimony, to support petitions or to support community educational methods. Case conferences with other agencies, interagency committees, coalition groups and client groups can serve as vehicles for advocacy purposes. Well known individuals and groups can take public positions on issues. Within an organization, an aggrieved staff person or client can seek administrative redress. Program demonstration projects, if successful, can be used to justify advocacy activities. The persistence of demands can eventually have an effect. As indicated by all writers, direct contact with officials and legislators is one of the most effective ways to influence them. If nothing else is successful, groups wishing change frequently turn to demonstrations and other public protest activities.

Although such a description may seem overwhelming, breaking it down into certain components, such as primarily internal strategy (activity) versus primarily external strategy or both, can provide useful discussion topics for students. For example, how would the student fill in Table 10–1 with the above information?

Brager (1968) emphasized the need for constructive relationships: "In an ongoing relationship [among the actors in the process] . . . the dangers of manipulation are significant. For here trust is expected between the parties and [the opposite] discovery between parties may be seriously damaging to the attainment of immediately desired objectives and, more important, to the long-range relationship" [p. 15]. Advocacy situations must be individually assessed in relation to who benefits, to the target, to the goal pursued, and to

TABLE 10–1. Change strategies exercise

	Client Strategy	Shared Strategy	Practitioner Strategy
Internal to Agency			
External to Agency			

the nature of the selected strategies. Brager saw advocacy strategies as "political" acts insofar as it was necessary to "manipulate" others.

Dear and Patti (1981) have suggested seven advocacy tactics for use at the legislative level:

1. Introduce the bill early in the session or, ideally, before the session has begun.
2. Have more than one legislator sponsor a bill.
3. Seek to obtain the sponsorship of the majority party, especially when the majority is Democratic. It is even more beneficial to obtain meaningful bipartisan sponsorship, with the primary sponsor a member of the Democratic majority.
4. Whenever possible, obtain the support of the governor and of relevant state agencies.
5. Seek influential legislators as sponsors of proposed legislation, provided they are willing to exercise their influence in promoting the bill.
6. Press for open committee hearings on the bill and, when such hearings are held, attempt to arrange for testimony in behalf of the bill by expert witnesses.
7. Use the amendatory process as a strategy for promoting a favorable outcome for the bill [pp. 290–294].[2]

Although these tactics seem addressed toward work at state and national levels, they would be just as effective at city and county levels because the processes for passing ordinances at these levels are the same. The Dear and Patti tactics indicate the importance of a face-to-face relationship with legislators. Impersonal tactics, such as letter writing, may be included in the overall endeavor, but personal contact may be the most effective in convincing legislators that our clients need help and that it's in the legislator's best interests to participate.

Proposed advocacy process model

It is wrong to think that only confrontational or abrasive tactics must be used in advocacy endeavors. Maypole (1982) has developed a useful model incorporating systems and exchange theories and power-politics principles.

---

[2]From *Legislative Advocacy: Seven Effective Tactics*, by R. B. Dear and R. J. Patti. Copyright 1981, National Association of Social Workers Inc. Reprinted with permission, from Social Work, Vol. 26, No. 4 (July 1981), excerpt.

Systems and exchange theories, as applied to organizational relationships, were summarized in Chapter 9. Gummer (1978) has described the power-politics approach as involving individuals and coalitions within and between organizations in pursuits aimed at securing control over the organization. Whoever controls the organization controls the resource allocation process, and this control ensures the survival of the winning party. For the sake of simplicity, the relationship model will be described as *dyadic*—that is, involving just two organizations. In reference to Emerson's power-dependence theory, we can see the process as being founded on the relationship between the focal organization (which we will refer to as *ours*) and the other organization in the dyad.

The interdependence of community agencies cannot be overemphasized. Each organization resides in an ecological niche (see Figure 10–9). Dill (1958) has labeled this network as the focal organization's "organizational set." Since the set as a whole represents a system, any change in structure, processes, client groups, or services in one organization is bound to affect each of the others. Such changes can lead to either favorable or unfavorable ends for any or all members of the set. Changes, of course, can be good for one organization but not the others, which is why any proposals for change must be carefully studied.

Assessment of the relative power-dependence relationship must be an integral part of the problem-study phase of the model. The problem—such as maintenance of an effective program in the face of pressure for retrenchment because of decreased funding—must be clearly identified. The organization calling for our retrenchment, such as another community agency, must be closely studied because it might be a competitor operating a similar program. The *power-dependence ratio* between the two must be determined. To a considerable extent, the goal selected to resolve the problem and the strategies chosen to achieve the goal will depend on this ratio. With the ratio in mind, study the strategies shown in Table 10–2.

Thompson (1967) has suggested that organizations in subordinate power positions will try to adopt cooperative advocacy strategies. This will entail several different nonoffensive strategies, such as bargaining or negotiating exchanges to meet our goals; entering into contractual relationships to lessen the stronger agency's impact on us; securing (or co-opting) the other agency's participation in our operations (such as having a member serve on our board and developing a positive relationship with him/her); entering into coalitions

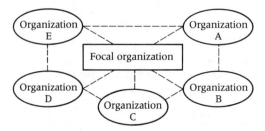

Figure 10–9. Community agency ecology

TABLE 10–2. Advocacy strategies continuum

Cooperation	*Competition*	*Conflict*
Bargaining	Increasing own sources	Blocking competitor's resources
Contracting	Decreasing own needs	
Co-opting	Increasing competitor's needs	Blocking competitor's goal attainment
Coalescing	Decreasing competitor's supplies	
Compromising		

with organizations to increase our power position; and entering into compromises to lessen the degree of penalty to us in the unbalanced relationship. If we were the stronger organization, we would try to maximize the payoff in the relationship through a minimum of investment by avoiding formal arrangements. As the stronger organization in the dyad, we could easily withstand the pressure from the other agency to diminish our programs. An overt or covert threat to respond in kind could destabilize the weaker opponent.

Litwak and Hylton (1962) defined competitive interdependence as one agency seeking to maximize its goals at the expense of another. Because community resources (such as funding) are limited, those claimed by one agency will not be available to another. In competition, then, we see two approaches. In the first, we can seek to increase our sources of supply in order to decrease dependence on the other organization, or we can decrease our need for resources (such as funding or client referrals) from the other organization. In the second approach, we can seek to increase the other organization's need for resources that we can supply, or we can decrease the other sources of supply to the other organization (Behling & Schriesheim, 1976). If cooperative strategies don't work, the stronger organization is clearly in the more competitive status. But resources range from referrals and information to "political" support, and it may be that the weaker organization has resources necessary to the other organization, which it did not take adequately into account during the ratio-assessment process. If the prospect of losing the competition may threaten the organization's survival, however, we see a shifting of gears into conflictual strategies.

Schmidt and Kochan (1972) identify the necessary antecedents to conflict as perceived goal incompatibility between the organizations, plus the opportunity and capacity to interfere with the other organization's resource acquisition and goal attainment. Whereas cooperative strategies permit a *win-win* experience for both parties insofar as they can achieve at least part of their goals, and the competitive strategy results in a threatening *win-lose* experience, conflictual strategies may result in extensive damage to the loser. A careful assessment of the power-dependence dyadic relationship may prevent an organization's getting into a *can't-win* situation. The dangers of a less powerful organization's attempting to block the resource acquisition and goal attainment activities of the more powerful are apparent. The retribution costs may be very high. But even a more powerful organization may lose in the long run if it uses such strategies unnecessarily, so that losers will bear grudges and seek revenge in some fashion in the future.

For the focal organization, cooperative strategies may lead to a maintenance of the status quo or to an expansion of responsibilities, clients, and services (referred to as *domain*). Competitive and conflictual strategies may produce either of the same payoffs, but, in the case of a serious defeat, the focal organization may undergo a retrenchment in its domain, which can have long-lasting negative effects on its future operations.

Viewing the communities in which we work (and including state and federal levels as "communities") as political arenas helps us to choose strategies most likely to meet our clients' needs at the lowest cost. We have all seen people so frustrated by political and bureaucratic structures that they have angrily challenged people in the systems. What has been the usual result? Quite often, it has been very little because they haven't adequately analyzed the problems, the power-dependence relationships between the actors, and the appropriate strategies to achieve their ends! In their failure they set themselves up to become "burned out," after which they either become resigned bureaucrats or leave the organization. In a way, even a knowledge of the intricacies of the advocacy planning process is power, the possession of which enhances the probability of attaining our goals. Within this context, a deeper discussion of intraorganizational conflict is indicated.

Intraorganizational conflict

Few individuals in any kind of organization escape conflict of some type. Whether we are speaking of families, associational groups, informal or formal work groups, conflict is an ever-present fact of life. Indeed, its absence might signal a group in which members are merely going through the motions. Even so, however, though little conflict may be shown overtly; covertly, the opposite may be true. In any event conflict should not necessarily be regarded in negative terms. If it is not of crippling proportions, it may lead to better problem definition, search for alternative solutions, and problem resolution.

Schmidt and Kochan (1972). As stated previously, Schmidt and Kochan (1972) identified the antecedents of conflict as perceived goal incompatibility between two organizations (or people) and the opportunity and capacity to interfere with another's resource acquisition or goal attainment. Clearly, if neither party perceives goal incompatibility, the chances of conflict are negligible. As it becomes clearer that one party will attain its goals or resources at the other's expense, the chances of conflict escalate. At least to some degree, however, the development of conflict would depend on the opportunity for the two parties to do something about it. If the opportunity and capacity existed, then overt interfering with, or blocking, resource or goal attainment could occur. The pivotal role of the power-dependence ratio helps to explain why some conflict is overt and some covert. The more powerful party would be inclined to meet conflictual challenges head-on and to apply its superior power; the weaker party would be more likely to use indirect strategies to avoid head-on confrontations.

Pondy's overall conflict model.   Pondy (1967) developed an overall conflict model with three dimensions. The *bargaining model,* which involves conflict among interest groups for scarce resources, is appropriate for labor-management analysis, budgeting processes, and staff-line conflicts. The groups have identifiable boundaries, and in attempting to meet their own needs they compete for mutually exclusive goals, such as funding or control.

The second model, labeled as *bureaucratic,* demonstrates vertical conflict between the individual practitioner's need for autonomy and self-actualization and the organization's need for practitioner control, feedback, and working toward organizational goals. In an immediate sense, the practitioner-supervisor relationship and the potential for conflict fall within this dimension. If the supervisor's control is met by practitioner resistance, the typical response is to impose written, impersonal policies and procedures.

The third model, *systems,* involved lateral conflict between parties to a functional relationship. Two different work groups, programs, or departments may have to work together to serve clients or to meet organizational goals. Conflict is manifested in difficulties in coordinating or sequentially meshing activities. In institutions, the housekeeping department staff may feel that clean floors and walls are more important than the therapy provided by social service personnel. Nurses and aides, whose responsibilities include maintaining control over patients, may sabotage therapy programs that foster less inhibited self-control. The interrelatedness of the two groups is manifested in the necessity of their interacting sequentially with their patients. Aides may have to make sure that patients get out of bed to go to occupational therapy programs in the morning or arrive at the dining hall in time to receive their noon lunches. Such sequential interdependencies enhance the prospect of conflict.

Steiner's conceptual framework.   Steiner (1977) proposed a somewhat similar conceptual framework for understanding conflict. *Ideological* conflict is generated when there is a wide discrepancy between what an agency claims it does and what it actually does. Individuals and groups may have vastly different ideas about the characteristics of a given problem and what should be done to resolve it. Likewise, members of leftist groups and of the Moral Majority may have conflicting ideas about what should be the relationship between a government and its people.

Structural conflict has its basis in the organizational context. Differential divisions of labor, roles, power, and allocations set up conditions for conflict. Higher-ups seek to control practitioner performance. The structure of a formal work group and the work itself may contribute to job dissatisfaction, reduced performance, and vertical conflict. *Functional* conflict relates to the specific purposes and activities of one's formal work group, as when a budget department is seeking to minimize expenditures while service departments are more concerned about helping clients. In short, different goals and activities may lead to conflict. Whether or not the two parties' activities are sequential, their goals may be mutually exclusive.

The fourth overall category, *jurisdictional,* was further subdivided into three categories. In *turf disputes,* individuals and organizations attempt to expand their responsibilities at the other party's expense. Any perceived incursion into one party's responsibilities will encounter resistance. *Client conflict* has two dimensions. In the first, organizations compete for clients because having a sufficient number of clients tends to ensure adequate inputs of funding and survival. *Client/agency conflict* reflects the struggle between meeting the clients' needs and the agency's ability to ration allocations to meet their needs (see also Gummer, 1979). Differing expectations may lead to hostility, distrust, and damaged relationships.

Steiner's last jurisdictional category, *battle for resources,* represents an organization's need for other resources, whether money, manpower, equipment, information, or prestige. The staffs' perceived deprivation may be absolute (not enough money) or relative (other agencies have enough, why don't we?). This struggle is seen most overtly in the annual budget planning processes in agencies.

Murray's interpersonal relationships.   Murray (1974/1975) has reviewed the central role of interpersonal relationships in conflict situations.

> The element of interpersonal trust and liking in a relationship as a critical factor in shaping the emergence and manifestation of organizational conflict is one of the most thoroughly studied, or at least written about, in the literature. . . . The erosion of trust, the breakdown of communications as the precursor of zero-sum conflicts, and the use of coercive conflict manifestations are well-developed themes in explaining conflicts between individuals and groups in both vertical and lateral relationships. . . . The relative power the parties in conflict have over one another is another factor which is well recognized in the literature [p. 47].

Resolving conflict.   This section looks at ways to resolve conflict, particularly within the frame of reference of the practitioner. Table 10–2 (p. 199) has utility for conflict resolution. Here we will integrate these strategies into the conflict resolution model (Figure 10–10) developed by Stepsis (1974).

As a strategy, *avoidance* of conflict has survival value. It is frequently adopted by a party that has little stake in the goals or resources in question or in resolving any problems related to them. The weaker party may deliberately adopt this strategy to avoid the heavy costs in competing with the stronger party. According to Stepsis, a residual fear persists that conflict cannot always be avoided and that the weaker party will have a no-win situation imposed on it.

Stepsis states that *defusion* of the conflict is essentially a delaying tactic to cool off the situation. Resolving minor points, pushing major issues into the future, claiming that problems are the result of "personality clashes" within the agency rather than of major structural or functional problems, or appointing a committee to study and arrive at recommendations for resolution—all

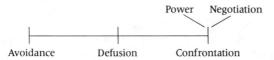

Figure 10–10.   A continuum of responses to conflict situations

are ways of avoiding open conflict. Again, however, failing to resolve the issues means that they may resurface in the future.

Stepsis further divided the confrontation strategy into *power* and *negotiation*. Power plays involve threats, coercion, physical force, bribery, and punishment. Such a win-lose strategy may secure the more powerful party's immediate aims but at the long-term cost of the weaker party's undying enmity. Negotiation, the more favored strategy, should produce a win-win situation enabling both parties to reach their goals. Stepsis noted, however, that:

> Successful negotiation . . . requires a set of skills which must be learned and practiced. These skills include (1) the ability to determine the nature of the conflict; (2) effectiveness in initiating confrontations; (3) the ability to hear the other's point of view, and (4) the utilization of problem-solving processes to bring about a consensus decision [p. 52].[3]

The Maypole model in Table 10–2 involves cooperation, competition, and conflict strategies. The cooperation strategies of bargaining, contracting, co-opting, coalition forming, and compromising are closest to Stepsis's negotiation strategy. The conflict strategies of blocking competitors' resources and goal attainment are closest to Stepsis's power strategies. The competitive strategies of increasing one's sources of resources or decreasing the competitor's, or decreasing one's needs or increasing the competitor's, would fall between Stepsis's polarized model. The Maypole model would seem to provide a wider range of strategies. Whereas Stepsis applied the problem-solving process model (see Figure 10–8, p. 195) to only the negotiation strategy, Maypole applied it as the base for each of the strategies to determine which to select at the outset. If a cooperative or negotiation model were selected, the problem-solving model would be jointly accomplished with the other party.

Filley (1975) has developed a very useful conflict resolution model on the theory that cooperation can be enhanced when conflicting parties share each others' likes and dislikes, associate with each other, become identified with something of value to the other party (such as a church or union), acknowledge help provided by the other, and dissociate themselves from situations disliked by the other. Filley developed a number of guidelines, asserting that as complete a problem analysis as possible be made. Since, in a conflictual situation, our own prejudices and biases may negatively affect our feelings and views, we should strive to be as objective as possible and to depersonalize the problem. Once we understand the problem (and we will never have "perfect" information), we can set the goal in resolving the conflictual situation.

[3]"Conflict Resolution Strategies," by J. A. Stepsis. Reprinted from: J. W. Pfeiffer and J. E. Jones (Eds.), *The 1974 Annual Handbook for Group Facilitators.* San Diego, CA: University Associates, 1974. Used with permission.

The next step is to make as complete a list of potential solutions as possible to be examined by the conflicting party as well as by ourselves. For each potential solution, what are the potential costs and benefits to us and to the other party? Is there some win-win solution? Can a can't-win situation be avoided? Can a win-lose situation be molded to our benefit? If not, can we arrange a minimal loss to ourselves?

Filley argued that the criteria for resolving the conflictual problem should be mutually agreed on in the decision-making stage. Without this agreement, either party could claim "foul" if it didn't agree with the end solution. If sufficient trust can be generated in the relationship, each party could review the position and recommended solutions of the other. In any event, at this stage, without at least some evidence of a constructive relationship, resolving the problem will be very unlikely. In wishing to use negotiation strategies, then, feelings of openness, trust, warmth, empathy, and genuineness must be developed. Even their partial attainment can aid in problem/conflict resolution.

SUMMARY

This chapter has covered a wide range of issues related to intraorganizational structure and processes. Maslow's hierarchy of needs, Herzberg's two factor theory, and McGregor's Theory X and Theory Y help to illuminate motivations to action within the organizational context. Problems associated with role conflict and role ambiguity within the work context were noted. The central role of the supervisor was discussed in relation to several theories and practical frameworks. Ways of relating to the supervisor without game playing were suggested to allow mutual growth in job and professional competence. Change strategies, both inside and outside of the agency, were enumerated and their role as motivators and as conflict producers were described. Maypole's goal-attainment model, based on organizational theory, was related both to advocacy and to problem/conflict resolution strategies.

But what happens to practitioners who fail to negotiate through the bureaucratic context very well? What if the work environment is that of Theory X? What happens if we try and fail to meet our clients' needs or try and fail to change our organizational context? These questions are dealt with in Chapter 11 on the phenomenon of "burnout".

STUDY QUESTIONS

1. How does Maslow's hierarchy of needs theory help us to understand human motivation?
2. Why are human beings said to be primarily "group creatures"?
3. From which source is a new practitioner most likely to learn the "regular" way of performing an organization's required tasks—from the formal or informal power structure?
4. What are the *hygiene* and *dissatisfier* factors in Herzberg's two factor theory? How important are relationships?
5. What part does one's supervisor play in problems of role conflict and role ambiguity?
6. What roles should supervisors play with practitioners?

7. How should a practitioner deal with other people's game playing?
8. What are the risks in a practitioner's engaging in political game playing?
9. Describe a plan that could help you to get ahead in your first social service job.
10. Summarize the three types of societal value systems to which Americans may subscribe.
11. Discuss the types of power that individuals hold at various levels in organizations.
12. What are the similarities between the problem-solving model to plan organizational change and to use with clients in casework?
13. Discuss any six techniques for advocating changes in the community. Which of these could also be applied within agencies? What is the role of "relationships" in the techniques you choose?
14. How is the power-dependence ratio applied in planning for advocacy activities?
15. Think of any conflict you have experienced within the last two weeks. Which aspect of the Stepsis model did you apply?

REFERENCES

Askerooth, G. Advocacy in the organizational society. Minneapolis, Minn.: Minnesota Resource Center for Social Work Education (DHEW grant #46-P-252 33/5-02), 1973.

Behling, O., & Schriesheim, C. *Organizational behavior: Theory, research and application.* Boston: Allyn & Bacon, 1976.

Brager, G. A. Advocacy and political behavior. *Social Work,* 1968, *13* (2), 5–15.

Brager, G., & Holloway, S. *Changing human service organizations: Politics and practice.* New York: Free Press, 1978.

Compton, B. R., & Galoway, B. *Social work processes.* Homewood, Ill.: Dorsey Press, 1975.

Dear, R. B., & Patti, R. J. Legislative advocacy: Seven effective tactics. *Social Work,* 1981, *26* (2), 289–296.

Dewey, J. *How we think.* Boston: D. C. Heath, 1933.

Dill, W. Environment as an influence on managerial autonomy. *Administrative Science Quarterly,* 1958, *2,* 409–443.

DuBrin, A. J. *Human relations: A job oriented approach.* Reston, VA: Reston Publishing Co., 1981.

Emerson, R. M. Power dependence relations. *American Sociological Review,* 1962, *27* (1) 31–41.

Filley, A. C. *Interpersonal conflict resolution.* Glenview, Ill.: Scott, Foresman & Co., 1975.

French, J. R. P., & Raven, B. The bases of social power. In D. Cartwright and A. Zander (Eds.), *Group Dynamics* (3rd ed.). New York: Harper & Row, 1968.

Gummer, B. A power-politics approach to social welfare organizations. *Social Services Review,* 1978, *52* (3) 349–361.

Gummer, B. On helping and helplessness: The structure of discretion in the American welfare system. *Social Service Review,* 1979, *53* (2), 215–228.

Harrison, W. D. Role strain and burnout in child-protective service workers. *Social Service Review,* 1980, *54* (1), 31–44.

Hawthorne, L. Games supervisors play. In Carlton E. Munson (Ed.), *Social work supervision.* New York: Free Press, 1979.

Herzberg, F. One more time: How do you motivate employees? *Harvard Business Review,* Jan.-Feb. 1968, 53–62.

Homans, G. D. *The human group.* New York: Harcourt, Brace & Co., 1950.

Horejsi, J. E., Walz, T., & Connolly, P. R. *Working in welfare: Survival through positive action.* Iowa City, Iowa: University of Iowa School of Social Work, 1977.

Kadushin, A. Games people play in supervision. In Carlton E. Munson (Ed.), *Social work supervision*. New York: Free Press, 1979.

Katz, D., & Kahn, R. L. *The social psychology of organizations*. New York: John Wiley & Sons, 1966.

Keith-Lucas, A. *Giving and taking help*. Chapel Hill, N.C.: University of North Carolina Press, 1972.

Lewin, K. *Field theory and social science*. New York: Harper & Row, 1951.

Litwak, E., & Hylton, L. F. Interorganizational analysis: A hypothesis on coordinating agencies. *Administrative Science Quarterly*, 1962, *6* (4) 395–420.

Maslow, A. H. A theory of human motivation. *Psychological Review*, 1943, *50*, 370–396.

Maypole, D. E. A composite model of interorganizational strategies. *Journal of Sociology & Social Welfare*, 1982, *9* (*1*), 4–18.

McGregor, D. *The human side of enterprise*. New York: McGraw-Hill, 1960.

Mechanic, D. Sources of power of lower participants in complex organizations. *Administrative Science Quarterly*, 1962, *7* (3), 349–364.

Murray, V. V. Some unanswered questions on organizational conflict. *Organization & Administrative Sciences*, 1974/1975, *5*, 35–53.

Perrow, C. Demystifying organizations. In Rosemary C. Sarri and Yehieskel Hasenfeld (Eds.), *The management of human services*. New York: Columbia University Press, 1978.

Plunkett, W. R. *Supervision: The direction of people at work* (2nd ed.). Dubuque, Iowa: William C. Brown Co., 1979.

Pondy, L. R. Organizational conflict: Concepts and goals. *Administrative Science Quarterly*, 1967, *12* (2), 296–320.

Rothman, J., Erlich, J. L., & Teresa, J. G. *Promoting innovation and change in organizations and communities: A planning manual*. New York: John Wiley & Sons, 1976.

Schmidt, S. M., & Kochan, T. A. Conflict: Toward conceptual clarity. *Administrative Science Quarterly*, 1972, *17*, 359–370.

Steiner, R. *Managing the human service organization: From survival to achievement*. Beverly Hills: Sage Publications, 1977.

Stepsis, J. A. Conflict resolution strategies. In J. W. Pfeiffer & J. E. Jones (Eds.). *The 1974 annual handbook for group facilitators*. La Jolla, Calif.: University Associates, 1974.

Sunley, R. Family advocacy: From case to cause. *Social Casework*, 1970, *51* (6), 347–357.

Thompson, J. D. *Organizations in action*. New York: McGraw-Hill, 1967.

Weber, M. *Theory of social economic organization*. New York: Free Press, 1947.

11

Burnout

W. David Harrison

Although apparently a widespread phenomenon, burnout has only recently received widespread attention. Is it really a new phenomenon or old wine in new bottles? Is burnout inevitable in some jobs? To what extent is it a cause, an effect, or both a cause and effect of relationship problems? And, perhaps most important for practitioners, what can be done about it? Chapter 11 examines these questions.

WHAT IS BURNOUT?

Idealism and enthusiasm characterize most people beginning careers as helpers. Burnout is the opposite state. Beginning helpers asked to describe how they expect to feel about their work in the future are not likely to reply apathetic, uncaring, effete, fed-up, tired, or disillusioned. But all experienced practitioners have observed these qualities in colleagues and may even have felt them personally. Whatever else it implies, *burnout* denotes an untoward change in the helper. An assumption in the use of the term is that one was formerly "fired-up." Several definitions from the literature show variations on this theme.

Freudenberger (1975) described *burnout* as a verb, "to fail, wear out, or become exhausted by making excessive demands on energy, strength, or resources" [p. 73]. Note that the verb implies change from a state of presumed or relative well-being to one of inadequacy and enfeeblement. There is an assumption that things go downhill because of an imbalance between what is required of one and what one can deliver.

As a noun, *burnout* denotes a state of exhaustion and reduced effectiveness accompanied by feelings of apathy, futility, reduced quality in social interactions, and dissociation from a commitment one once had (Maslach, 1976).

Burnout as a noun can also be viewed as an end-state or condition resulting from inadequate responses to stressors and to the state of stress itself. This does not necessarily mean that the sufferer is personally inadequate. Stress and its causes vary in frequency, kind, and intensity, and some of these conditions involve individual capabilities, skills, and supports in relation to the demands of the environment. Cherniss (1980) combines several of these elements in referring to burnout as "a process in which the professional's attitudes and behavior change in negative ways in response to job strain" [p. 5].

Burnout may also be viewed as a particular form of work alienation—feelings of estrangement, a sense of being apart from, or not connected with, something else. Usually we think in terms of social alienation (dissociation from society), of which work alienation is one sort. Marx developed the idea that the inability to control the process of one's work and see it through was the major cause of alienation in industrial society. If one assumes that social service systems are fundamentally similar to industries the definition of burnout as a form of alienation is quite persuasive. Every worker in a public agency can attest that the multitude of factors imposed on the helping professions serve to remove professional autonomy or control of the helping process from the worker and client and shape the practice relationship from the outside in many fundamental ways. There is a good deal of evidence for an alienation viewpoint, and we shall examine its role in causing and dealing with burnout, if not actually being synonymous with it.

Maslach and Jackson (1979) have done pioneering research on burnout, including constructing a psychometric tool to measure the phenomenon. The Maslach Burnout Inventory—including scales of emotional exhaustion, depersonalization, personal accomplishment, and personal involvement—has been noteworthy for its role in making burnout a clearer, more empirically sound construct. Research aimed at defining and sorting out its causes and solutions should prove increasingly helpful in the next few years. When a situation such as burnout seems to affect many people in many areas at once, there is a tendency to take the nature of the phenomenon and the similarity of people's experiences for granted. Empirical investigations should provide sounder, more objective knowledge about burnout. Of particular interest is the question of whether it is a discrete entity or something that has only been relabeled.

The term *burnout* is currently so popular, or at least so common, that it has become a convenient receptacle for all sorts of maladies that are somehow related to human service work. Indeed, its widespread use might give one an alibi to avoid one's responsibilities as a developing professional. If it is assumed that burnout will inevitably occur and that the nature of the job and the organization makes it impossible to develop or maintain competence and personal fulfillment, why try?

Public opinion is often highly intolerant when employees of statutory and nonprofit agencies claim to feel burnout; they are seen as whining at the public's expense. Public impatience is understandable in view of the generally low level of public knowledge of just what it is like to take on a helping role. When the setting is a bureaucracy providing the resources to sustain the mind and body of citizens who are often the most difficult to understand and help, public misunderstanding is aggravated. But at least three very important motivations for studying and attacking burnout should be more widely known.

1. *Quality of service.* It is generally assumed that quality of service declines with the development of burnout. Though the precise mixture of cause and effect is uncertain and probably varies from person to person, a worker who is burned-out is by definition not a particularly effective or efficient worker.

2. *Expense.* Turnover, another widely assumed concomitant of burnout, is expensive, both in money and in lost competence. Developing skills in the various helping roles is time-consuming, and it is difficult to find experienced replacements for front-line workers who move on.

3. *Worker welfare.* Workers who are uniquely vulnerable to burnout deserve a better fate than winding up on an ash heap. Worker welfare is an important concern, especially when one considers the number of idealistic, public-service minded young people who are trying to express their concern for the common and individual good through the helping professions. One need only talk to a few of the disaffected to see what an enormous public resource is lost throughout burnout. No one sets out to be an ineffectual bureaucrat, and no one wants this sort of public servant. But it happens, and it should be avoided whenever possible.

Characteristics of burnout

There is likely to be diversity among definitions of burnout until further research and better developed theory reveal more about the variety of experience which the term now obscures. For the present, the best way to understand burnout might be to list characteristics which lead to application of the label. Students and inexperienced practitioners who read the next few pages and wonder what they have gotten into should reassure themselves that these conditions are not inevitable for all social service practitioners. Moreover, these characteristics may each be indicative of other job-related and personal problems as well. For a valuable exercise, ask several practitioners independently to produce lists of the characteristics they see as indicative of burnout. On comparing the lists, a common core and some specific variations are almost certain to appear.

Detachment. Maslach (1976) has identified *detachment* as a dominant characteristic of burnout sufferers. Placing psychological space between oneself and one's clientele is a common way to detach, and it may be done either passively or actively. Since helping requires a certain "attachment" relationship and detachment is the opposite tendency, there is almost always a vague sense of misery involved. Obviously, such important parts of helping relationships as empathy, authenticity, and acceptance are severely hampered by detachment which involves a reduced awareness of the human qualitites of both helper and helped. In this respect, detachment can be thought of as a type of alienation.

Detachment takes many forms, however. In a hospital one sometimes hears staff speaking of "the diabetic in room 222" instead of "Mr. Gray in room 222." The difference in and of itself may be inconsequential, a pattern of identifying service consumers by problem rather than by name can signify some loss of ability to engage in a respectful and empathic relationship. Frequent use of the gross classifications "low functioning" and "high functioning" and the range of official and popularized psychiatric terminology are common variations. This is especially important for vague labels such as "character disorder" or "EMR" which are not usually part of clients' understanding of their situations.

Another version of detachment, which seems superficially innocuous, is using first names for clients who, for their part, refer to the worker by title and surname. While there are some situations in which first names are appropriate, using them can also be a way of maintaining differences and narrowing the basis for respect in a relationship. The related practice of using animal analogies to describe clients reveals a great deal of practitioner difficulty in forming relationships. Improbable as it sounds, it is not difficult to find workers who constantly speak of clients who "live like pigs" or who "have the brains of a flea" or are "just river rats." One particularly problematic version of detachment is the derogatory use of "these people," literally prejudging individuals on the basis of a few characteristics. Worker difficulties in dealing with race and gender issues frequently surface in this manner. Since these issues are so demanding on the practitioner, they are often among the first to emerge in a burnout picture.

Detachment not only involves various ways of belittling the client; it also involves losing basic helping skills, such as listening, accurately perceiving feeling states and problems, and communicating these perceptions. Detachment bespeaks a reluctance to get involved in a feeling-level interchange when one senses that "I've been here before and I cannot help this person." This component of burnout calls to mind the phenomenon of alienation, a state of enmity or indifference where there had previously been positive feelings.

Alienation.   Both large-scale alienation and the individual experience of it have psychological and social causes. In either case, the effects on practice, on the client, and on the practitioner are similar. Karger (1981), while rather simplistically interpreting research on the burnout phenomenon and its causes to fit a Marxist viewpoint, has thoughtfully presented the case for burnout as alientation. These feelings of estrangement frequently lead to a profound sense of anxiety and guilt. The worker who is becoming alienated seldom does so all at once; there is usually a feeling of guilt and of "What's happening to me?" which conflicts with the normal desire to be helpful that led workers into their field in the first place. Consider the following example.

Tom Chevington, a young social worker, had spent a great deal of effort in working on a plan of care for Martha Rothbury, a 90-year-old client. She had begun to grow weak and had twice tumbled down her stairs at night. Tom spent several weeks trying to find accommodations that offered a single living level. After presenting a major case to the Housing Authority, they agreed to adapt an apartment for her. When he jubilantly presented this victory to Ms. Rothbury, she decided that she wanted nothing to do with a move.

Tom realized that he had become so wrapped up in the technicalities of safety and of finding new quarters that he had overlooked the emotional aspects of such a move; he had failed to provide an opportunity for the client to explore the matter. But "to go into all these details with these old people is impossible," Tom said to himself, "They'd talk your ears off if you'd let them." Later that day, in the cozy home of Dan Hepscott, another aged client, Tom found himself mesmerized by the embers in the fireplace. He knew something was wrong. He found himself thinking of his client not as the center of a helping process but as an obstacle. It was unpleasant, even distressful, Tom thought to himself as he ignored Mr. Hepscott's offers to share photos of his grandchildren. "Is this what I went to college for? I wanted to help these people. I'm getting into a state about most of these old birds I get assigned to. There's got to be more to social work than this. I'm going to get nothing but grief from those turkeys back at the office since old Martha won't move, and I wouldn't explain even if they'd listen. What am I doing here?"

One of the most profound signs of detachment and alienation is the worker's change in attitude toward the agency or other sponsor of service. Apathy and indifference, cynicism, and resignation are part of this dimension of burnout. Inefficiency with little attempt to remedy—indeed, a norm of dreary ineffectuality—may take over. Often the difficulty in doing the job well becomes entwined with an individual's sense that it is impossible to do a good job. Thoughts of moving to other, ostensibly better jobs, are replaced by fears that one is simply not good enough to do the job in another setting where the standards of practice are higher and where worker attitudes are presumed to be more optimistic. Workers in some settings also find themselves troubled by a "golden handcuffs" syndrome, unable to risk the economic changes that a move might entail in a time of economic uncertainty. Most human service workers earn modest (hardly "golden") salaries, so that security in the form of tenure, seniority, and the like may take on inordinate significance. One may feel that he or she cannot risk a change.

Turnover. For workers who have not built up to the "golden handcuffs" level, one of the signs commonly associated with burnout is a high rate of turnover. Turnover may mean either an individual's frequent job changes or a high rate of change in certain types of jobs or agencies. While some turnover is caused by a desire for increased income, it is likely that problems with the work and one's ability to successfully perform it are more important causes of turnover among social workers. In one recent study of relatively well-paid child-protective service workers, for example, a significant predictor of worker plans to leave the job was the worker's dissatisfaction with the work itself. Attitudes about pay, promotional prospects, co-workers, and supervision were not significantly related to these plans (Harrison, 1980).

On-the-job resignation.   While turnover is one of the ill-effects of burnout, it may be a healthy, adaptive individual response. Much more problematic in general is the syndrome of on-the-job resignation: spending less time with clients, loss of caring, apathy. Leaving a job may be adaptive in the sense of allowing one to proceed with one's career, but on-the-job resignation is maladaptive insofar as it causes more problems in the future than it solves in the present.

In addition, many workers experience a number of the cognitive characteristics of burnout. Stress, a condition arising from loss or threatened loss of well-being, often includes a state of "rigid" thinking, tunnel vision, and inability to perceive the environment adequately (Fleming, 1981). Thinking and feeling states are both parts of what might be called an individual's *information-processing system*. From an information-processing viewpoint, one would say that the state of stress develops when there is an interruption in the person's normally reliable sequence of receiving information, combining it with other data, and applying it to the situation at hand.

Although both information-processing and burnout are terms borrowed from machines, the subjective, feeling side of stress in the burnout condition is prominent. It involves negativism, cynicism, and an inability to make use of information and other resources. It has even been suggested that in one of the most difficult types of practice—helping neglecting parents who are very poor—one way to tell whether the parent presents the "apathy-futility syndrome" is to see whether a sense of resigned fatalism spreads to the worker (Polansky, DeSaix, & Sharlin, 1972, p. 22).

The interrelated thinking and feeling problems arising from stress can thus be seen in the widely held attitude that "nothing will work" with a given client group. Whether this is principally a rationalization ("I can't seem to help, therefore nothing will help.") or primarily an interruption in the process of thinking logically through possibilities is unclear. What is most important is that when a worker consumes information with the foregone conclusion that it either has little meaning or an undesirable meaning for practice, he or she is almost certain to be both ineffective and acutely miserable.

Burnout behavior

In addition to the preceding theoretical descriptions, there are many behavioral signs of burnout; no one, nor indeed, any specific combination constitutes a sure-fire burnout diagnosis. Some of these behaviors might be adaptive ways of dealing with the problem, especially if they only occur briefly. Usually, however, they interfere with one's work life and frequently make one's personal life unsatisfactory as well. A sample follows of specific burnout behaviors which workers have discussed in workshops.

Communication and participation changes.   The worker who began the job reticent may become withdrawn. The friendly, outgoing worker may become tiresomely garrulous. Wit may change to biting sarcasm. Very often the important characteristic of these changes is that they block discussions of feelings about the work and how one is engaging in it. Most changes are magnifications of existing interaction styles, but it is not uncommon to see dramatic reversals. These may come in the form of emotional eruptions by workers who had formerly been skillful in their handling of the ups and downs of the job.

Closely related is *irritability,* especially the tendency to overreact to situations and problems. There is a sense that the worker's defenses are barely able to contain the turmoil beneath. The armor has grown thin, and potential as well as real rebuffs or threats irritate the vulnerable spots below. The worker responds by saying symbolically "Get away from me! Don't mess with me!" and at times does not wait for an overt irritant. If burnout is severe, a suspicion and conviction may develop that agency policies and practices are designed to threaten the worker; co-workers' actions may likewise be perceived as suspicious. Suspicion may be coupled with detachment strategies in a belief that clients are consciously out to make life hard for the worker—a pattern of dealing with one's own sense of frustration or guilt in being unable to meet the demands of the job.

But one should be cautious in interpreting such perceptions and accompanying behavior because they frequently occur within organizational environments oriented to nitpicking of worker performance, particularly in paperwork, while ignoring worker efforts to be of assistance to clients. In this area, unfortunately, skilled and ineffective workers sometimes act similarly but for different reasons. The competent worker may become "fed up" with constant criticism of details while strengths are ignored. The weaker worker may create a storm over details in order to avoid a close examination of substantive matters of performance. It is important to clarify the different routes to a given behavioral pattern to determine whether they represent processes of adaptation or not.

Excessive consumption. A characteristic that seldom gets much attention in general discussions of burnout is the increase many workers experience in their consumption of food or alcohol and other drugs after a time in a burnout-prone job. Undoubtedly this exemplifies using food and drugs to make work feel less stressful, but it comes as a particularly disarming and worrisome shift for many in the helping fields. Perhaps seeing heavy doses of client vulnerability to alcohol, tranquilizers, and even illegal drugs makes workers feel more alarmed when they see themselves or colleagues developing early signs of dependency. Asked how she maintained her professional commitment, integrity, and apparent effectiveness in a particularly difficult position, one supervisor quickly replied "I overeat. Everyone who's really committed around here winds up fighting the battle of the bulge." Of course, changes in eating patterns can have other meanings as well. The important point is that there are often significant changes which seem to vary with emotional reaction to the job.

Health problems. There is little clarity about just how stress affects health, but workers who say they are feeling burned-out very often have physical problems, too, and see burnout and illness as related. Common psychophysiological maladies, such as ulcers and colitis, are just the beginning when practitioners discuss physical concomitants of the burnout problem. Many other complaints, in which the psychogenic aspects are far less clear, include heart disease, kidney problems, cancer, allergy and hives, sexual dysfunction, headaches, and a heightened propensity to get nagging illnesses such as colds and influenza. The validity of this sort of self-report information from practitioners who admit to feeling acutely burned-out is dubious, of course, and the relation of these conditions to burnout is even more questionable. But it is important that many workers see burnout as something that could plausibly cause these diseases, and they may be at least partially right.

On the other hand, many workers simply deny the problem, refusing to acknowledge any signs of stress or burnout, disagreeing with or rationalizing questions about their effectiveness, efficiency, and so on. Frequently workers talk about the problems of everyone else in the unit except their own. This may be appropriate unless accompanied by an air of superiority and invulnerability, which may signify that deep down it hurts too much to talk about.

Workaholism. Some workers refer to a workaholic condition on the part of burnout sufferers. This refers to the practice of spending inordinate amounts of time with one's work and being constantly preoccupied with it. Although this is an easy pattern to fall into in the social services when one has a large caseload, some workers nevertheless put in too much time on the job, not realizing that efficiency has been overtaken by muddling, and are unable to perceive the point of diminishing returns on effort.

Being preoccupied with their work at home also extends to people who seem to have few friends other than co-workers and few conversations during their "off hours" which do not involve some aspect of the job. An example is the live-in child care worker in group care settings who has great difficulty taking days off, even after two or more consecutive weeks of round-the-clock responsibility for a group of trying youngsters. Work and nonwork lives become inseparable. This is not necessarily a pattern to be avoided by everyone because it is prevalent and apparently functional in many occupations, but in helping professions it is likely to cause problems. The demands for focusing on others and giving oneself in a helping relationship ordinarily have to be balanced by time for rest and recreation. Before attributing this sort of behavior to burnout, the situation should be carefully examined as a way of escaping nonwork problems, a practice usually of limited value. Also, not everyone who spends extra time on the job is ineffective; it is likely that the very best workers put in more than the standard civil service day.

Avoidance. A closely related type of behavior is avoiding the job or components of it. This is not necessarily the same as saying that one is putting forth no effort. The occasional feeling that one simply doesn't want to get out of bed to go to work is a mild form most of us have experienced. Usually, this behavior is a reasonably innocuous form of detachment, whereas avoidance comes on a continuum. For example, Armstrong (1978) refers to practitioners "frequently walking through K-Mart in the afternoon between home visits" [p. 232]; a hospital chaplain describes her increasing use of "mental health days"; and a psychiatric ward counselor describes the tendency of staff to congregate in the lunchroom when particularly angry and demanding patients are admitted. Common practices sometimes indicative of burnout include putting off contacts with clients and coming to work late.

There are several situations that almost always reflect a burnout problem: experiencing growing difficulties in family relations due to work factors, seeking psychotherapy because one's work has convinced one of severe personal inadequacy, systematically "bad-mouthing" other workers, even sabotaging the agency's program. Some workers adopt a sort of "noble savage" attitude about their clients, glorifying certain aspects of a lifestyle that has been shaped by inequality and deprivation. Likewise, workers may envy what they see as a carefree client lifestyle, particularly when it contrasts with their own sense of struggling to meet the demands of their own roles. These are signs of a worker's loss of empathy. Some clients have difficulty filling the roles that society rightly or wrongly assigns them, and workers may be dutifully working to be good family members, professionals, and employees. But professional practice requires a fundamental respect and acceptance of the client and the ability to convey this respect empathically. Thus, a sound helping relationship may be replaced by "I won't hassle you if you won't hassle me" exchanges. The futility of this orientation is obvious.

Another form of avoiding the job is psychological avoidance, especially making a clear distinction between one's work life and one's home life. Once during a neighborhood picnic, a counselor who worked in a state unemployment assistance agency was asked what his job entailed. The response was a quiet, strong "I don't want to talk about it. I never talk about it," which said that he was serious. Many of us face similar situations. When meeting new acquaintances, discussion often shifts to one's occupation. A group of child-protective-service social workers discussed how they reached a characteristic decision point in such encounters. After sharing that they were social workers, they would quickly read the response of the conversation partner. They had learned that simply mentioning their job was likely to set off opinionated broadsides about welfare, chiselers, the evils of "permissiveness," the need for stronger punishment of child abusers, and other matters about which the worker had strong feelings and often held unpopular opinions. Some listeners seemed interested in hearing morbid or sensational details that could be molded to fit their stereotypes. Many sympathetic listeners said "I could never do *that* kind of job," or "I'm glad that there is someone like you working there," or "You must work with a lot of hopeless cases." Either way, the workers found themselves becoming very involved in some of the same dilemmas they faced on the job daily. Many learned how to avoid conversations about their work with anyone who did not show signs of familiarity or sensitivity. Avoiding the risk of getting involved in conversations that bring work-induced stress into the nonwork world does have a certain adaptive value. While it may allow short-term freedom to enjoy a congenial nonwork life, friendships of lasting value often include some discussion of careers.

The outstanding quality about all these states is that few workers can see their way out of them without experiencing a sense of inevitability and futility.

Many workers eventually overcome the assorted problems that may collectively constitute burnout for them. When one is miserable, however, the general feeling is one of helplessness. Not only do workers feel they can do little to help those who ostensibly need it, but they, too, come to feel like victims unable to solve problems themselves. For many, the only answer is to leave the field they started out in so eagerly. For most, a critical understanding of burnout, its causes, and ways to support oneself and one's co-workers will counteract the worst of it.

WHY DO PRACTITIONERS BURN OUT?

Because a construct as diverse as burnout is certain to have a number of different causes, it is important to consider precisely which elements of burnout one is attempting to explain with each causal connection. In fact, however, we have little clear, validated understanding of the term and its correlates, much less of how specific variables actually make burnout occur. So many theories seem to fit. Alienation, role strain, stress, crisis, adaptation, human ecology, postindustrial expectations, and many other phenomena can be used to explain it.

This situation, though providing a rich variety of ways of looking at the problem, also presents us with a difficult job. How do we weigh all the possibilities to find the most helpful in a given situation? Here, we have selected primarily explanations that provide the most direct answers to the question of what to do about burnout. These can be conveniently grouped as social-historical, organizational, managerial, educational, and personal. After overviewing these factors, we will pull them together as they directly affect the practitioner. The result will be a social competence model of burnout.

It is assumed that most social service practitioners want to "do well at doing good." Burnout, from a social competence viewpoint, is a result of frustration of this motivating desire. The most frequently proposed causes of burnout point to one or another of these frustrations, but using the social competence model we can look at them together. Further, this approach shows how burnout causes more burnout. When the practitioner's ability to achieve valued goals is reduced, frustrations and foiled expectations are much more likely. Before we fully develop the model, let us look at the most frequently cited causal systems.

Social-historical sources

Social and historical sources are particularly enlightening when burnout is viewed as a form of alienation. If alientation means feeling powerless to control, affect, or see through the process of one's work, burned-out practitioners share many of the characteristics that Marx attributed to industrial workers in general. Workers who want to do a good helping job may feel that they have only a few of the needed resources at their disposal. Moreover, in many of the institutions and agencies where they work, they have a small, circumscribed role, not unlike that of the worker on an industrial assembly line, with relatively little influence on the end product and often little understanding of how one actually fits into the whole. For example, a relief counselor in a residential treatment program complained:

> No one even seems to know I'm here, just working nights and weekeneds. I never attend the treatment planning sessions because they never schedule them for when I'm around. And usually the kids are the first to tell me when they're going home. . . . I just do the best I can; asking questions just creates more hassles. . . . I really wanted to help kids when I came to work here, but now I leave it up to the shrinks to straighten out these little demons [author's files].

This particular example of alienation can be seen as having both organizational and personal causes, but it is noteworthy that the counselor talked about his work in much the same way as do many employees in industrial, thing-oriented work settings. Depersonalization and detachment are the common threads.

Horejsi, Walz, and Connolly (1977) have pointed out how Daniel Bell's (1973/1975) conception of postindustrial society is particularly pertinent to social welfare workers. Postindustrial society is characterized by high technology and consumption, large-scale organizations, government regulation of the economy, mass communications, redefinition of the family, and a large middle class. At the same time, inequality endures and is felt intensely. Bell notes three major culture-shaping principles of postindustrial society: (a) the economizing mode, emphasizing efficiency and accountability; (b) the participatory mode, in which most people highly value collaboration in decisions and processes that affect them; and (c) the actualizing mode, in which people expect life (including work) to be personally fulfilling in the here and now.

These general characteristics shape our expectations in subtle yet powerful ways. Many people enter helping fields out of interests rooted in the participatory and actualizing modes; they look for fulfillment for themselves and hope to contribute to the fulfillment of others. But in most areas of helping practice, the economizing mode has been very hard to incorporate with the others. Workers feel this in the push for large caseloads, in paperwork that seems more to interfere than to facilitate, and in demands for effectiveness from various segments of the community, each of which appears to define success differently. In effect, the worker is caught in a bind between being able to do the things that seem most important to her or him and society's demands for economizing.

Alvin Toffler pointed out in *Future Shock* (1970) that we usually neither recognize nor appreciate the influence of fundamental social changes as they are occurring and that this common perceptual flaw leads to a particular vulnerability. The conservative mood of the early 1980s has served to illuminate this point more clearly than ever. The helping professions face great and rapid change, which challenges their adaptive ability. Meanwhile, there is an atmosphere of "open season" for criticizing public employees, the poor and sick, and social service workers in particular. Practitioners are criticized for ineffective services, even in programs having no stated goals (a prerequisite of evaluation) and frequently in situations in which relationship-based helping has been treated as a substitute for concrete resources.

Organizational sources

Many broad social patterns show up in society's organizations where they are combined with the specific traits of individuals and groups. For example, many American social welfare organizations fear a high degree of stigma, or presumed personal deficiency on the part of clients or consumers. Frequently, stigma is highlighted by calls for social agencies to assume greater social control over clients who bode potential social unrest and disorder. This attitude is also expressed in the paternalistic notion that clients are defective and in need of some sort of quasiparental protection or social therapy. When this paternalistic attitude is combined with the notion that service consumers have rights and responsibilities of their own, it is apparent that social agencies operate amid rather serious value conflicts, which translated into organizational policies and practices, leave the worker in a state of acute personal value conflict. The beginning worker who has been highly motivated may find it extremely difficult to decide just what to believe about social and personal responsibility, causation, policy, and simply the way society "ought to be."

Specific organizational factors that contribute to burnout include limited time off, inadequate staffing, lack of worker participation in decision making, "red tape" or work that appears useless, and an absence of appropriate training or other support. Each of these in itself can be a problem to the worker attempting to gain competence in effective practice, but it is not uncommon for an organization to exhibit all these factors. These negatives are not only organizational correlates of burnout; the absence of positive factors may be just as problematic as the presence of negatives (Kanner, Kafry, & Pines, 1978). Workers need to know that they are valued and when they are doing well.

Managerial sources

Organizations often develop and pass on characteristics through various managerial positions which link staff, and informal aspects of the organization. One of the functions of managers or administrators is to develop and transmit role expectations—specifications of the behavior the organization wants of its employees. Harrison (1980) found that certain social workers had extremely high levels of role ambiguity (uncertainty about what they were supposed to do) and role conflict (the perception that they were expected to do incompatible things simultaneously). Role ambiguity was clearly related to dissatisfaction with the work and a high propensity to leave the job. Supervisors, the worker's closest managerial contacts, were a particularly strong source of dissatisfaction for workers who had high degrees of role conflict. In even casual discussions of burnout it soon becomes evident that many workers are not pleased with the way their roles are defined (or have been defined), and it is very common to hear complaints that this management function is not fulfilled adequately.

Managers point out that they cannot provide optimum clarity because they have to operate under nebulous, rapidly changing policies and guidelines, and frequently the range of worker skills and motivations is so great that role problems are inevitable. While there is merit in the position that there is almost always someone doing something inadequately in complex organizations, it is also clear that workers respond best to certain forms of managerial leadership (Armstrong, 1978). Experience, enthusiasm, trust, and wililngness to trust others are particularly important qualitites. The ability to handle authority issues calmly and securely is another and is closely related to the ability to resolve conflict constructively. Where these qualitites are conspicuously absent, there is a high risk of burnout. Often staff meetings are particularly important events in regard to manager-worker relations, and their frequency and usefulness can be barometers of burnout and burnout resistance. It appears that there are optimum frequencies for meetings, and the best number and balance between procedural and problem-solving meetings needs to be found not only for each organization but perhaps for each work group therein.

Providing feedback to practitioners is a particularly important managerial function because it is important that workers have a sense of doing well at the work they value. Feedback—the information received from others about how one is doing—is crucial in developing this personal sense of competence. Confusing or ambiguous feedback prevents one from knowing the quality of one's performance. The following list of feedback styles is based on Kramer and Schmalenbergs' work (1977):

1. *Almost nothing.* No news is good news does not hold for long in the difficult business of helping troubled people; it turns out to be ambiguous and either useless or harmful.

2. *Body language.* Frequently a frown is a form of feedback, but one of the important problems with subtle body language is that it is subject to much interpretation, and the burden of clarification is generally up to the receiver of the message, who must take the initiative in getting matters out in the open. Naturally, where there is a sound basis in trust, authority, and respect, body language can provide a valuable form of communication.

3. *The unanticipated snap.* This usually refers to a general negative response to what had been presented as a meaningful piece of information. Frequently one wonders whether the "snapper" is responding to a hard day, to other problems, or to what one has actually said or done.

4. *Clobbering.* This refers to the list of negatives that comes all at once, seemingly out of the blue.

5. *Hidden agenda.* Frequently one is told that one is doing things in such a way that additional responsibilities are in order. The tone may be positive or negative, but the troubling question is whether one is being praised or punished.

6. *The meaningless evaluation.* There is great variability in formal evaluation procedures. Those that are generic for a number of diverse positions are particularly hard to work with. But regardless of the format and the mix of written and spoken evaluations, it is particularly deflating to a worker to receive a document in which he or she is not taken seriously as a developing person and employee. In this case, indifference is a negative.

7. *Trusted co-worker feedback.* A particularly important source of information about how one is doing is the peer network, particularly peers who are seen as competent while employed in similarly demanding positions. This

is probably of such importance because of the quality of empathy that accompanies the information, but it is also subject to too close an indentification by the communicating peer. High on feeling and relationship components, this form of feedback requires the objectivity of each communicator to be monitored.

8. *Ongoing supervision.* Supervision can amount to almost any form of communication and relationship, but it is often an excellent place to learn how one is doing and how to do better. Supervision can be seen as a set of administrative, educational, and enabling roles, the informational and relationship elements within each of which can be powerful in developing or preventing burnout.

Educational sources

Recently, a graduate student in social work commented how much more resistant to burnout she would be after getting her master's degree and returning to work at the department of social services. When the possibility was raised that she might be less resistant than ever, she was dumbfounded. After some consideration, she realized that her *educational* experience had certainly increased her knowledge and skills, that she had clarified and developed her personal and professional value systems at school, and that her expectations had grown by leaps and bounds. But she was sobered by the prospect of trying to apply her new knowledge and skills in the world of feeble public assistance grants, desperate situations of domestic violence, and clients with admirable plans but no opportunities for implementing them.

Professional education has the difficult task of preparing students to be excellent practitioners in systems which often do not support or even recognize good professional practice. This is a special problem for the worker who has been in the excellent settings for practicum instruction but who has to face the realities of employment in less developed settings. Professional schools are usually oriented to ideal practice, and most models or theories of "how to practice" are oriented to optimum conditions. Thus, the student becoming a practicing professional has to adapt to the realities of compromised standards and less than ideal plans while maintaining a sense of competence and self-esteem. When the classroom deals with realities rather than with idealizations, most students are very appreciative.

However, there are some students who attend school merely to "retreat from the trenches" of frontline work with the poor and the powerless. Many of the practice formulations taught are variations on voluntary psychotherapeutic methods which are too narrowly focused for general practice social service work. While these methods are difficult or virtually impossible to apply in many practice situations, practitioners often persistently attempt to do so (Mayer & Timms, 1970; Maluccio, 1979). While the client is interested in solving immediate practical problems, the practitioner wants to ferret out and cure, or at least treat by conventional psychotherapeutic methods, the pathology that is presumed to exist. This is a case of theoretical bias to find and treat the "real" problem, and it poses very significant dilemmas, not only in terms of values such as client dignity and self-determination, but also in terms of effectiveness. Most practitioners can monitor problem-oriented, goal-directed work with some training and skill, but the "cure" or resolution of personality disorders is an unrealistic carrot that professional schools too often dangle in front of their students.

Personal sources

The following exercise shows one way to begin considering the personal sources of burnout. First, prepare separate lists of the positives and negatives associated with your job or prospective job, contacting people who work in a similar capacity. Then carefully compare the two lists. Frequently they will reveal a few positives but considerably more negatives. Indeed, people are often hard-pressed to explain why they stay at a job with a few positives such as "I really do help some people" or "There is more flexibility with my time than in other lines of work" when these are compared to a dozen or more problems. The answer, of course, is that the positives are highly important to social workers and their occupational kin. Especially as they begin their careers, practitioners are generally very highly motivated to help; they are caring, humanitarian, ambitious, and frequently naive. High expectations constitute a desirable characteristic for helpers because they are an important component of hope, which is generally needed for change to occur. And yet there is a catch: the higher the expectation, the greater the vulnerability to crashing when expectations cannot be fulfilled. When the formula

$$(Expectation) - (Experience) = (Attitude)$$

is applied, attitude's low rating can be explained in part by expectation.

Being competent at helping others—in short, having a positive effect and knowing it—is probably the greatest motivation for people in helping fields. When the sense of being the cause of important effects, or the hopes of attaining it, diminishes, burnout is a likely result. An important area for investigation is how some practitioners maintain a realistic perspective on professional goals. How do they determine which goals can realistically be attained? How do they manage to keep up with progress toward goal attainment? It would be valuable if each practitioner were to stop periodically to specify what his/her motivating, really important career goals are and whether they are achievable at the current job.

Another contributor to burnout is the struggle that we all face in mastering the tasks of adult development. In this society, a great many of these developmental struggles are played out on the job. In Erikson's epigenetic formulation, for example, he points out the adult crises of intimacy versus self-absorption, generativity versus stagnation, and integrity versus despair and disgust (Erikson 1959, pp. 95–99). Note that self-absorption, stagnation, despair, and disgust collectively constitute a tidy description of burnout. The question becomes whether an individual's detachment and dehumanization are job-induced or whether they would develop in some form regardless of the situation. Here again is one of the difficulties of using the term *burnout*—namely, it can mask a number of human conditions that are often highlighted or exaggerated by the job and as a consequence get labeled as job problems.

Freudenberger (1975) has pointed out a number of specific personality groupings among the burned-out. It is fairly easy to find examples of the following sorts of people in any kind of work, including social welfare settings:

1. The committed, dedicated worker who takes on too much for too long with too much intensity, attempting to respond to clients, agency, profession, community, and self but being unable to set limits.

2. The worker who is overcommitted due to dissatisfactions in the non-work part of life, who overidentifies with the agency or profession, and loses the rest of himself or herself in the process.

3. The authoritarian who seeks to control virtually everything about the work because of a conviction that he or she alone can do the job. Overextending one's resources for working with people and alienating co-workers lead to a burnout syndrome.

4. The administrator who will not delegate has a special problem in that burnout may be tenaciously self-perpetuating. The administrator sees that many of the staff are burned-out, attempts to do more because he or she distrusts their ability to see through assignments, becomes overextended and burned-out in the process. Dealing with staff problems can often present a special middle-management challenge because of "the foreman's dilemma" of being in allegiance both to top administration and to direct service workers whose work he or she has often done.

Out of these and many other sources, a list of basic personal sources can be developed. Each is best seen as a threat or barrier to the development of the worker's social competence or ability to accomplish the valued job. The following are of particular importance:

1. Not having the knowledge and skills to achieve the tasks that the job demands.
2. Not communicating feelings, or communicating them inappropriately.
3. Not setting limits.
4. Physical and psychological isolation.
5. Political naivete.
6. Being unable to resolve the dilemma of being a professional in an agency that does not really value professionals.
7. Ignoring or not using available positive feedback.
8. Not matching one's personality characteristics with the nature of a specific job.

With few exceptions, social workers are highly motivated to be helpful to their clients when they begin their careers. This force can be thought of as a particular version of Robert White's (1959, 1963, 1979) notion of competence motivation. In White's view, people seek environmental interactions in which they feel themselves to be the cause of desired effects.

Motivation to deal with one's world is goal-directed, and goals are largely determined by individual abilities, needs, and interests. For social workers,

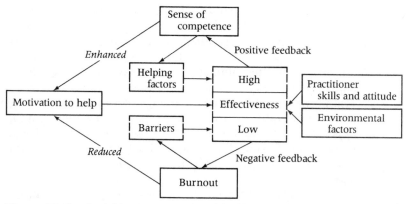

Figure 11–1.   Social incompetence model of burnout

the goal of helping others is a highly valued focus for this kind of motivation. When the worker is helpful and knows it, the sense of competence or efficacy is enhanced. The successes, failures, and learning resulting from one's work ideally crystallize into a pattern of increasing competence. Goals are met, work is more efficient, and a level of challenge is maintained without the worker becoming overwhelmed.

When the overall, motivating goal of being helpful is not attained, the worker reacts with frustration. This can occur whether the reason is lack of ability or judgment, environmental interference, or inadequate resources. It may also occur when the worker misperceives a situation and treats an impossible goal as though it could be achieved rapidly. A state of stress may develop, manifesting itself through behavioral, cognitive, emotional, or physical changes. Though not immediately apparent, these changes are the individual's initial ways of mustering an attempt at adaptation to a new and difficult situation.

When attempts at altering the situation are not successful, long-term adaptive strategies such as withdrawal, apathy, illness, and rigidity may develop. The worker may respond by changing the nature of the motivation to do well, the expectation of being helpful, and the amount of effort applied in future attempts at helping others. The shift may be conscious or unconscious. In brief, the worker is no longer highly motivated to be a cause of the desired effect and burns out in the sense that the "light" or energy of motivation appears to be lost. Most workers have seen clients who have similarly "thrown in the towel," and an extensive literature has developed about them. Nevertheless, for many workers, as for many clients, desirable change can occur given the right conditions to reignite motivation.

Social competence model.   Harrison's (in press) social competence approach to understanding burnout is consistent with the growing interest in the nature of transactions between individuals and their environments within social work and related fields. This approach builds on the work of White, which has been expanded and applied by a number of others (Goldfried & D'Zurilla, 1969; Deci, 1975; Harter, 1978; Maluccio, 1981). The concept of competence has proved valuable in studies of growth and development, as well as in theories of how to practice in the helping professions.

Though White was principally interested in presenting his theory of an intrinsic, self-generated motivation to explain how the individual responds to and shapes the environment, his ideas have been successfully combined with many others which have implications for the study of burnout. For example, cognitive and information-processing theories have contributed to our understanding of problem-solving processes, which represent a fundamental kind of person-environment interaction. A social competence view of burnout offers considerable flexibility and therefore increased likelihood that an individual practitioner can locate particular problem sources and points for assessment and change.

Three additional components of the model should be noted. The first is the attribution of causation. The extent to which workers accurately perceive themselves to cause the outcome of service, whether the goal is attained, whether there is no change in client status, or whether matters get worse— all are crucial for determining the degree to which they can deal with burnout. If one inaccurately attributes success to oneself, there may be a short-term gain in the sense of competence, which can be shattered later when an apparently similar situation arises but does not prove amenable to similar efforts. If a worker perceives that outside factors, such as paperwork requirements, limit his or her competence, a special dilemma arises. The limitations may indeed be externally imposed, but they can lead to a self-deluding pattern: "If only they would get this paperwork off my back, I could help somebody." In reality, both successes and failures are usually caused by a variety of factors, and explaining them in terms too narrow to reflect reality is a problematic but common practice.

The second additional component of the model is the personal cost to the practitioner which a successful piece of work may entail. If "costs" were to be taken literally, workers could help poor clients by giving them a portion of their own paychecks, though for most workers this would be a self-limiting practice: the costs would very rapidly exceed the resources! There are emotional and political parallels, though, which are not so obvious to one who has not experienced them. Although giving of oneself is taken for granted in successful practice, it can occur too much, too fast, and lead to Pyrrhic victories

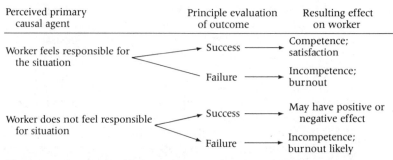

Figure 11–2.   How self-perception as a change agent affects attitude

that will exact a toll later. In addition, most workers are soon wise to the extraordinary costs they can incur when they become advocates for their clients in a hostile environment. At certain points in one's career and around some issues, it is both wise and ethical to take the heat in the client's interest, but there are practical limits and some undesirable consequences of advocacy if the worker is in a truly powerless position.

Finally, it should be pointed out that reward systems will vary for different people. The intrinsic feeling of a job well done constitutes a particularly strong reward for most practitioners; but it can be extremely hard to develop this sense because situations are often vague and the degree of success is hard to gauge. It is valuable to make goals as realistic and as clear as possible and to build processes which make it possible to monitor goal attainment. Extrinsic rewards are also important, but exactly how they relate to burnout is not clear. When there is too little positive feedback, either in the form of comments about one's work, meaningful evaluations, or salary increases to reward performance, the worker is clearly at risk.

WHAT CAN BE DONE?

Burnout is caused by a wide array of psychological and social factors, all of which hamper one from attaining a state of competence. Incompetence or marginal competence lead to defensive strategies which can be labeled as signs of burnout, and defensive strategies can lead to more incompetence. Prevention and solution to the problem must come in both general and specific forms, covering the broad scope of how we think of social services and of what we individually face in our work.

A competence approach to burnout makes several assumptions, one of which is that burnout is not inevitable even in very difficult types of work. While this is a very optimistic assumption, it is based on the image of highly skilled practitioners working in supportive agencies, even if the clients present extraordinarily difficult problems. Obviously, not all workers and organizations are like this, but it is important to isolate the fact that it is not the client's problem that leads to burnout if the worker is prepared and the environment is genuinely oriented to helping. Dealing with burnout should be a matter of improving worker ability, environmental support, and the way the agency and worker use each other's unique resources.

A second assumption is that burnout is best fought by means of some sort of cooperative action. The dismal feelings that accompany burnout are often kept private, and one's self-esteem is often very vulnerable in burnout situations, but it is extremely hard to fight the problem without letting someone in on the situation and sharing at least some of the problem-solving burden.

It is easy to find overconfident instructions on solving one's problems or on improving oneself, but it is very hard to find the motivation to do so. The following suggestions might prove thought-provoking, but they are useless unless one entertains some hope that things can change and realizes that these changes will involve others in one way or another. The suggestions for change must focus on the person who is experiencing burnout, on the environment or situation in which the person works, or on the patterns of interaction between the two. Individuals and small groups can begin with any of these focal points in a given situation. We will begin by looking at social and organizational considerations and then move on to what individuals can do.

Professional organizations and education can provide a sense of order and direction amid storms of social change and public opinion. Social work and other professions that help the powerless and unpopular have survived periods of vulnerability before. Paying attention to historical precedents for dealing with professional uncertainty and turmoil can develop a sense of continuity, contribute reassurance and the knowledge that individuals are not quite so alone with their problems. Professional organizations can fight isolation, provide feedback, and work to increase effectiveness through formal and informal education. Such organizations are particularly helpful when they increase public understanding of their fields and develop comprehensible explanations of what their practitioners do.

Unions have proved valuable in several areas in the human services, although the mention of a union in human services frequently leads to heated debate, often based on the notion that public servants might strike to enrich themselves while leaving the public without needed services. This is rarely, if ever, the case. In some situations, unions have helped in improving services by calling attention to such issues as excessive workloads; to personnel systems that neither encourage nor reward effective practice; and to inadequate resources to meet basic client needs and public interests. There are many factors involved in considering the utility of a union of professionals or semiprofessionals, but there is seldom any question that some form of organization should speak for the collective interests of workers and (one would hope) clients.

Armstrong (1978) has suggested that agencies should be evaluated in terms of their size, complexity, formalization, and centralization to find sources of burnout and to pinpoint areas for correction. In general, the large, formal organizations characteristic of postindustrial life are very difficult to change. It is probably best to begin by documentating the untoward effects of certain organizational characteristics and then to develop a long-range plan for change, the important elements of which are specificity and feasibility. Trying to tackle all problems at once is a task almost certain to cause burnout. If organizational changes are clearly aimed at promoting worker competence, more than one worker should be involved in the process. Administrative relationships, whether adversarial or cooperative, are the keys to change.

Managerial aspects of preventing or remedying burnout can be somewhat more specific. Any efforts by administrative or managerial personnel to eradicate burnout conditions obviously have to take into account the state of the workers affected. Workers sometimes overlook the fact that managers may be suffering from many of the same organizational and social barriers to competence that they are and that frequently they are burned-out, too. Thus, we have the same problem facing the worker with a burned-out manager that the client faces with a burned-out worker! The worker's first task is to try to examine how he or she is coming across to the agency's managers, whether at the supervisory level or higher. It is relatively easy for managers to disregard workers who seem always to grumble, complain, and demonstrate incompetence, just as many workers find it easier to work with clients who behave in certain ways than in others.

Basically, good management practice will help to prevent employee burnout. Clarifying the expectations of new employees and making clear what the agency expects are very important. Ideally, a plan can be developed with each employee to define and monitor his/her career goals and how the agency setting can or cannot meet them at any given time. Of immense value, this sort of openness should be cultivated whenever possible.

Because increased worker skill is likely to lead to increased effectiveness, managers should make improved worker skills a priority. This can be achieved through organized educational schemes, but it is also a crucial element of supervision. To expect clients to change, we have to expect ourselves to change as workers. The direction and degree of change are usually under our control to some degree, and supervisors have crucially important responsibilties for assessing the learning styles and developing the interests of their workers.

One of the hallmarks of burnout is reduced time spent with clients, often accompanied by a sense of guilt. In this case it may be helpful for management to sanction a controlled amount of time away from clients to alleviate destructive guilt elements. Recognizing that one needs a break from continual contact with difficult situations can be built into schedules. A related suggestion for administrators is to look into possible changes in work schedules to get the most productive and satisfying balance between worker interests and agency needs for structure. Limiting the amount of time that some workers put in may also be important.

We do our best when we know what constitutes a good job, which areas need greater mastery, and when feedback informs us that we are doing reasonably well in our tasks. From an administrative point of view, good job design and supervision should provide these elements, which can be developed through the work group. Many agencies are divided into units or teams, the goal of which is to develop skill and knowledge that their work is important, effective, and improving. The role of enthusiastic, knowledgeable supervisors in developing and sustaining this sense cannot be overestimated. Supervisors need to be comfortable with their own authority in order for workers to respond to the structure provided. When authority issues are fairly clear, responsible risk taking can be encouraged and feelings can be expressed.

Above all, communications must be clear for people in states of stress to make use of them, and administrators should pay particular attention to their interchanges with burnout-prone workers. One of the most important dimensions is to cultivate the skill of listening to workers who are trying to communicate about policy and agency structures. They are usually looking for ways to do better jobs and thus to feel better about their work. Since workers often have trouble being clear and specific when they are burned-out, listening is extremely important.

Individuals who want to prevent or alleviate burnout have to struggle with the uncertainties of change. Burnout is miserable, but what would it be like to try to change it? Things could get worse, effort could be wasted for no change at all, or one might become aware of secondary gains accompanying burnout that would have to be forsaken in order to produce change. There is clearly some correspondence between one's abilities to be helpful to others and to take help oneself (Keith-Lucas, 1972). Therefore, engaging in personal problem-solving with at least one other person who can provide empathy and perspective is an ideal way to proceed.

The first step is to determine whether burnout is really the problem and not just a convenient label for lack of skill, frustrations about other aspects of one's life, depression, or other forms of misery. Yet the faddish character of burnout makes it almost fashionable to think of oneself as a victim. It is important to think through the causes and characteristics discussed in this chapter to determine whether a different focus for relief might be more appropriate.

The second step, if burnout is the problem, is to confront it. What could be simpler and more self-evident? Yet nothing is more difficult in actual practice. Risking changes in the way one relates to others, taking responsibility for one's own practice and professional development, making goals and plans clear with clients, and developing mutuality in a relationship with someone who is determined to help you tackle burnout are difficult orders. A great deal of courage and lost hope often have to be mobilized to ease the discomfort. Thinking back to the basic goals that motivate one in the human services is important in starting the process.

The third step is to resolve to act. This inevitably involves developing some sort of a plan of action covering what the problem is, what goals you want to reach, and how you are going to go about it. The best plans are usually simple, and it is particularly helpful to monitor your progress at reasonable intervals. Though making the commitment to yourself is basic, it is probably equally important to share your plan with someone who can provide some stimulation, motivation, and whose opinion matters—in short, someone who has taken on at least some of the components of a supportive helping role. Above all, you have to believe that burnout can be changed, if not eliminated, and that change is best accomplished with the help of someone else.

A note of warning before undertaking a plan to relieve burnout: some of us are compulsive workaholics, and the workaholic-burnout syndrome may require a lot of outside authority to break. Prevention is difficult because there is a fine line between the dedicated worker and the one who cannot limit involvement in the early stages of the pattern. Job addiction is very likely to have significant causes outside the job itself, and it is often important to untangle the patterns and causes of such a predisposition through therapy away from the job. The need for careful self-assessment (which includes the opinions of people one respects) is obvious in determining whether change efforts should focus on the job situation specifically or on what predisposes one to on-the-job difficulties.

An obvious way to deal with burnout in a personal plan is to develop specific methods of looking out for, and taking care of, oneself. These may range from eating properly or exercising regularly to completing a course on assertiveness training. The important component is providing oneself with enough pleasant experiences and restorative activities to balance some of the difficulties of doing a competent job in human services. We have to feel good about ourselves in activities that we choose and control in order to feel better in the pressure cooker of the job. Taking care of oneself is a prerequisite for increasing competence and reducing burnout.

Professional development is the surest burnout antidote. Gaining confidence, acquiring skills, and being able to exercise and stick with one's professional judgment are general goals which greatly enhance the likelihood of doing a good job. Professional development can take many forms, from continuing education to making use of supervisors, consultants, and other knowledgeable people who are available on a case-by-case basis. Ongoing association with peers, such as classmates, former workmates, and other colleagues whom one values, is another important means of continuing development which also involves the important ingredient of working together. Social workers are frequently reluctant to maintain these contacts by phone, but in an age of great mobility, long-distance telephone contact may prove to be a wise career investment.

Next, carefully assess what is needed to do a competent job and evaluate the degree to which you are able to do what is needed. Develop a list of specific goals for improvement, and work out a plan for how to achieve them.

One area of skill development which competent workers usually have mastered is that of learning the system and finding creative ways to use problem-solving skills within it. For example, one group of caseworkers wanted to get some outside help in dealing with burnout, but they encountered considerable opposition from administration to allowing time for any sort of program that focused on workers rather than on services. There was fear of a public backlash against such "selfish" activities. One worker pointed out that this kind of attitude was one of the reasons why burnout occurred and suggested that there must be a way to get around the problem.

The unit changed the terms of their request from burnout to stress management and the focus from workers to clients. They requested a workshop to help them acquire stress management skills to impart to their clients. The result was a successful compromise in which the first focus was how to confront and modify one's own stress in order to teach client's how to do it. Burnout's similarity to stress was emphasized, and the series of workshops and consultations developed into ongoing relationships. The outside consultant clearly helped workers to cope with their own situations through increased knowledge and competence, and workers were able to teach clients many stress management techniques.

An important problem that human service workers can address in a plan of action is that of rescue missions. In this sense, a *rescue* is an attempt dramatically and quickly to put a situation right without regard to the years it may have taken to get the way it is. This sort of activity is almost always going to elicit a sense of floundering incompetence because seldom do social service rescue missions get resolved favorably. Again, the help of a trusted colleague can be invaluable.

A final area for consideration is that of examining one's characteristic thought processes as they concern the job. Many cognitive methods have value in dealing with anxiety, stress, and disaffection with the job. Often, self-defeating thoughts become stereotyped and dramatically color the worker's outlook. Have you ever said any of the following to yourself?

"Here comes another useless staff meeting."
"I don't think I can stand another lonesome, whining kid's con game."
"I just can't get through to these people."
"This damn paperwork is impossible. It'll take weeks to get it up to date."
"Another hopeless case. They're completely unmotivated."
"You must be the new worker. Welcome to Burnout City."

Usually these thoughts, which hop in and out of awareness, become automatic monitors of our sense of mastery and competence. When the automatic can be "reset" to variations like the following, one is much better able to maintain the sense of doing well:

"Well, we finally faced at least one issue a bit more clearly."
"She's likely to give me hell, but I'll have to keep the big picture in mind. There's no sense in taking it personally."
"There have been a lot of these cases lately. I ought to do a bit of background homework and become something of an expert."

Getting this process into an affirmative direction requires motivation and commitment. Two or more workers can discuss these cognitive information shapers and consciously help one another by pointing out how they may be operating.

SUMMARY

In some situations, workers are called on to do more than can be done with any degree of quality. The ethical issue of whether to focus on better service for the few or on some kind of service for all must be faced and resolved. It is important to consider the type of service and the consequences of either strategy for both clients and workers. In this way, workers may begin to develop a sense of precisely which goals they value in their work, and they may begin to search for positions that offer more of what they want or education that enables them to do so.

Chapter 11 has only sampled the nature, causes, and solutions to burnout. It is a complex phenomenon—indeed, it may actually be several phenomena; and though its causes and manifestations are many, the individual can usually begin to carve a path out of the jungle by working with others to develop increased competence and conditions to permit its exercise. Finally, since the causes of burnout are so various and pervasive, one must learn to live with gradual, incremental change in the burnout condition just as in other human problem-solving efforts. One simple test of progress, which is also likely to keep the spotlight on competence, is to ask yourself at the end of each day for an example of one thing, trivial or major, that you have accomplished with excellence. By building on small successes, helplessness can be overcome.

STUDY QUESTIONS

1. What characteristics of burnout have you observed among college students? What factors might explain why this occurs?
2. Burnout appears to be consistent with several theories of human growth and development as well as with theories of social behavior. Discuss how a theory not covered in the chapter might explain burnout.
3. Why did burnout emerge as a matter of interest when it did?
4. What, in your opinion, will be the future of the phenomenon known as burnout? Why do you think that this will occur?
5. Interview at least five practitioners in helping fields concerning their conception of the nature and causes of burnout. Organize your findings and examine the extent to which they fit the social competence model.
6. What does social service work have in common with the work setting of the manufacturing industries? What are the differences? How are these likenesses and differences related to job stress and burnout?
7. Think about the type of work that you would like to do when you complete your formal studies. What elements of the work will be most difficult for you to cope with? How might you prepare now to deal with these difficulties?
8. Consider the foregoing text on practice relationships. Which elements do you consider to be your particular strengths and which are you least competent in? How can you use these strengths and limitations in preparing a plan to deal with possible burnout?
9. Consider times when you have been dissatisfied with the practice of professionals and/or employees in a bureaucracy. From your own viewpoint as a consumer of services, discuss how practitioner burnout may have affected your attitude and ability to use the "resource" in question.
10. If it were your responsibility to design the ideal social agency, what factors would you include to minimize burnout? How would they affect the cost of operating the agency? How would cost and effectiveness of services balance out?

REFERENCES

Armstrong, K. How can we avoid burnout? *Child abuse and neglect: Issues on innovation and implementation* (Vol. 2). U.S. Department of Health, Education, and Welfare Publication No. (ODHS) 78-30148, 1978, 230–238.

Bell, D. *The coming of postindustrial society.* New York: Basic Books, 1973.

Bell, D. *The cultural contradictions of capitalism.* New York: Basic Books, 1975.

Cherniss, C. *Professional burnout in human service organizations.* New York: Praeger Publishers, 1980.

Deci, E. L. *Intrinsic motivation.* New York: Plenum Press, 1975.

Edelwich, J. and Brodsky, A. *Burn-out: Stages of disillusionment in the helping professions.* New York: Human Services Press, 1980.

Erikson, E. H. Identity and the life cycle. *Psychological issues* (Vol. 1). New York: International Universities Press, 1959.

Fleming, R. C. Cognition and social work practice: Some implications of attribution and concept attainment theories. In A. N. Maluccio (Ed.), *Promoting competence in clients.* New York: Free Press, 1981.

Freudenberger, H. J. Staff burnout. *Journal of Social Issues*, 1974, 30, 159–165.

Freudenberger, H. J. The staff burnout syndrome in alternative institutions. *Psychotherapy: Theory, Research & Practice*, 1975, 12 (1), 73–82.

Goldfried, M. R. and D'Zurilla, T. J. A behavioral-analytical model for assessing competence. In Spielberger, C. D. (Ed.), *Current topics in clinical and community psychology* (Vol. 1). New York: Academic Press, 1969.

Harrison, W. D. Role strain and burnout in child-protective service workers. *Social Services Review,* 1980, *54* (1), 31–44.

Harrison, W. D. A social competence model of burnout. In B. A. Farber (Ed.), *Stress and burnout in the human service professions.* New York and London: Pergamon, in press.

Harter, S. Effectance motivation reconsidered: Toward a developmental model. *Human Development,* 1978, *21,* 34–64.

Horejsi, J. E., Walz, T., & Connolly, P. R. *Working in welfare.* Iowa City: University of Iowa School of Social Work, 1977.

Kahn, R. Job burnout: Prevention and remedies. *Public Welfare,* 1978, *36,* (2), 61–63.

Kanner, A. D., Kafry, D., & Pines, A. Conspicuous in its absence: The lack of positive conditions as a source of stress. *Journal of Human Stress,* 1978, *4,* (4), 33–39.

Karger, H. J. Burnout as alienation. *Social Services Review,* 1981, *55* (2), 270–283.

Keith-Lucas, A. *Giving and taking help.* Chapel Hill: University of North Carolina Press, 1972.

Konrad, G. *The caseworker.* New York: Harcourt, Brace, Jovanovich, 1974.

Kramer, M., & Schmalenberg, C. *Path to biculturalism.* Wakefield, Mass.: Contemporary Publications, 1977.

Maluccio, A. N. *Learning from clients.* New York: Free Press, 1979.

Maluccio, A. N. *Promoting competence in clients.* New York: Free Press, 1981.

Maslach, C. Burned-out. *Human Behavior,* 1976, *2* (9), 16–22.

Maslach, C., & Jackson, S. E. *The measurement of experienced burnout.* Unpublished manuscript, University of California, Berkeley, 1979.

Mayer, J. E., & N. Timms. *The client speaks: Working class impressions of casework.* Boston: Routledge & Kegan Paul, 1970.

Pines, A., & Aronson, E. *Burnout: From tedium to personal growth.* New York: Free Press, 1980.

Pines, A., & Kafry, D. Occupational tedium of social service professionals. *Social Work,* 1978, *23* (6), 499–507.

Polansky, N. A., DeSaix, C., & Sharlin, S. *Child neglect: Understanding and reaching the parents.* New York: Child Welfare League of America, 1972.

Toffler, A. *Future shock.* New York: Random House, 1970.

White, R. W. Motivation reconsidered: The concept of competence. *Psychological Review,* 1959, *66,* 297–333.

White, R. W. Ego and reality in psychoanalytic theory. *Psychological Issues* (Monograph 2). New York: International Universities Press, 1963.

White, R. W. Competence as an aspect of personal growth. In G. Albee & J. Joffee (Eds.), *Primary prevention of psychopathology: Social competence in children* (Vol. 3), Hanover, N. H.: University Press of New England, 1979.

12

The Future of Practice Relationships

The social and economic factors affecting historical trends in human relationships will continue to exert their force in the future, and as human relationships are affected, so also will be practice relationships. In addition, advances in our knowledge and perspectives on human behavior and the social environment, as well as recent advances in plausible solutions to personal and social problems, will affect theory, practice, and practice relationships.

TRENDS

The processes that have generated fragmentation of the family and the atomization of human relationships will continue. The philosopher Hegel saw society moving toward greater order and rational organization. Today, government and corporations are fulfilling his predictions by building ever larger and more complex bureaucracies. The large-scale organization has begun to supplant the previous functions of the family in child socialization, in care or "processing" of the old, the deviant, the poor, and the handicapped, even in the management of leisure time. Hegel saw that there would be periodic protest against these trends to rationalize our lives. Examples of *romantic protest*, both positive and negative, may be seen in the retreat of Henry David Thoreau to Walden Pond, in the writings of Solzhenitsyn, in the regressive political movements of prewar Europe, and in the political conservatism of the early 1980s. Each reflects a fundamental desire to regain control of one's life, individuality, or values from the advance of impersonal formal organizations. History teaches us that charismatic leaders can play on these needs in people to overthrow or to reinforce the political status quo. Regressive movements can forestall the government's taking responsibility for victims of ailing economic and social systems for whom families no longer have sufficient resources. But apart from its potential for exploitation in the interests of the few, other important concerns motivate romantic protest. If large-scale organizations are a future reality, how can they be rendered responsive to people?

Social work practice which, in part, aims to connect people with the resources and services of organizations, stands at a critical juncture between the individual and the organization. In some ways social service practitioners are the human face of private and public organizations. Practice relationships in the future may be propelled toward structure, efficiency, task focus, accountability, codifiability, and brevity. At the same time, practitioners will almost certainly continue to protest the loss of caring, the loss of concern for individual differences, the diminishing freedom of choice and control, the acceleration of paperwork, accountability for *quantity*, and the concomitant disinterest in the *quality* of relationships that comprise our helping practice.

Economic and environmental crises

The general trends of formal organizations will be exacerbated by two other forces in the next half-century—the economic and environmental crises (for a discussion of these, as related to practice, see Keefe, 1979).

In 1928 an East European economist, Kondratieff (Shuman & Rosenau, 1972), postulated that there are 50-year cycles of economic growth and decline in capitalist countries. Some contemporary economists dismiss the long-cycle theory, others have a wait-and-see attitude. If we accept the Kondratieff hypothesis for the purpose of discussion, we can envisage a problematic future ahead for human relationships and practice relationships.

The last long-cycle expansion began with World War II and peaked in 1974. The next 25 years would be the period of economic contraction. The negative aspects of business and trade cycles would be amplified. Economic slowdowns would become recessions, and recessions would become depressions. Pressures for profit would necessitate more and more efficiency. Corporations would continue to replace skilled, usually unionized, workers with robot machines and systems requiring fewer workers. Deskilled industrial workers would take minimum-wage jobs or face unemployment. The effect on people would be increasing job instability and all the human costs of unemployment.

As corporations increase control of the marketplace, prices once set through competitive market forces will be increasingly administered or set by managers. When demand for a commodity slackens, the traditional response of the manufacturer used to be to lower prices to beat out the competition. As the competitive dynamic is lessened in monopoly control, the response to less demand is to increase prices to keep profit margins up. Hence, inflation becomes a permanent factor in the economy led by monopoly or near-monopoly control of energy, food, and basic goods. When compounded by resource shortages and governmental expenditures for weapons and war that create no new wealth, inflation sometimes becomes rampant.

Expedient political "solutions" to rampant inflation will include high interest rates to slow the demand for goods. Resulting unemployment will lower productivity and create multiple social and personal problems. Cuts in social service delivery systems in an attempt to lessen governmental expenditure and borrowing at high interest rates will exacerbate the plight of the economically dispossessed. The need for social service practitioners will accelerate while federal governmental commitment will slacken until people convert their needs to demands in the political arena.

A very important trend related to the economic marketplace is the exhaustion and degradation of the physical environment. While oil cartels dictate prices that drain industrial economies of their capital, other energy resources, such as coal, grow more precious and come under more centralized control. Opting for nuclear power will create problems of finding sufficient money to build, maintain, and later decommission nuclear power plants. The transportation and indefinite storage of radioactive wastes present vital problems for the environment, health, and safety. Decentralized, clean, and popularly controlled solar energy generation seems increasingly less a hope as government support has diminished and profit by means of control or cartel propel corporate interests in the energy business. Water and air pollution and other forms of environmental contamination will exacerbate pollution related health problems.

Figure 12–1 shows the interrelationships between industry, the environment, the workers, and government programs. In the past, industry felt little responsibility for polluting the environment and for workers' income maintenance. Through the intervention of state and federal governments in the 1920s and 1930s, income maintenance programs were set up for displaced

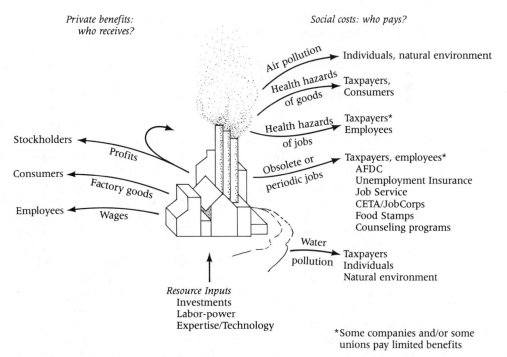

Figure 12–1. The concept of social costs

workers (such as workman's compensation and unemployment compensation). In the 1960s, the federal government extended its interventions with industries through the implementation of the Occupational Safety and Health Act and pollution control acts. The purpose of the former was to enhance worker safety and of the latter to save our natural resources from further degradation and to improve public health. Unfortunately, under the popular banner of reducing federal "red tape," the current federal administration intends to diminish the impact of these latter laws on industry. Accordingly, one can predict the further degradation of our natural resources, continued industrial involvement in threats to public health, and increasing needs for public health income maintenance programs. Understanding the limits of our natural resources will be lost in deference to political-economic processes.

In an exhaustive analysis of different perspectives on the impact of advancing technology on society, Gendron (1977) postulates that, as technology becomes more complex in capitalist society, it becomes more costly for individuals to meet basic needs. Trends that add to that cost include: (a) increasing urbanization with its health and safety hazards; (b) growth of ghettos, which compound city hazards, stresses, and expense; (c) expansion of monopolies, which increase real costs of goods through planned obsolescence and in other ways; (d) expansion of the "welfare state," the costs of which have fallen most heavily on lower income groups; (e) technological growth, which upgrades job requirements and deskills some jobs; and (f) continued income inequality. This latter factor is continuing for minorities and widening for women vis-à-vis white males (Thurow, 1980).

These trends are likely to persist and engulf politically indicated regressive monetary policies attempting to turn back the economic clock with the consequences suggested earlier. Before we address the implications for practice and practice relationships of these trends and of regressive attempts to deal with them, we must note that there are economic solutions that, though complex, are straightforward and viable and hold very different implications for practice.

For example, M.I.T. economist Lester Thurow (1980, p. 211) suggests that four decisions are necessary to create economic equity and productive competitiveness for the future. These are (a) an economic floor for individuals and families (recall the advocacy by the social work profession for a guaranteed adequate income); (b) a full employment system with incomes equivalent to those of white males; (c) elimination of the corporate income tax and an equitable individual tax system on all income, including dividends and interest; (d) a generous system of transitional aid to individuals—but not to corporations. When unprofitable industries are allowed to fail, capital and labor can shift to profitable endeavors. Thurow's ideas aim at economic solutions to economic problems. Like some Japanese managers, he sees that what is best for the economy in a competitive world market is also good for people.

Given Thurow's approach, social service practice would add to its concerns the displaced and inconvenienced, as well as the dispossessed and the injured. Ours would be more a practice of hope and adjustment than of despair and survival because human relationships in general would be more secure without the pervasive threat of devastating economic stresses. Indeed, Michael Harrington (1976) has observed that full employment would strengthen the collective bargaining position of employees and help to force more equitable redistribution of wealth. It is likely, though, that the trends will persist and that sound, sane, democratic solutions will await the growth of critical consciousness and solidarity among people toward gaining control of the forces shaping their lives.

Consequences for human relationships

Economic decline, permanent inflation, and environmental deterioration present bleak prospects for human relationships in the years ahead. People will be forced to migrate at the behest of the energy resource search. Out-migration will leave some areas destitute of a tax base and the means to meet the needs of the poor. In-migration will create problems of splitting families between residence and temporary work sites. Schools will be stressed to provide for the educational and socialization needs of children during year-round sessions with oversized classes and insufficient funds. Health and welfare institutions will be similarly inundated.

Impermanence and insecurity will further stress families with two parents working out of necessity, often in unrewarding, alienating jobs. Family violence, divorce, and separation will be the predecessors of problems for children subject to the mobile, insecure lifestyle necessitated by economic trends. Extrapolating from statistics related to unemployment in recent years (Brenner, 1973, 1976), suicide, alcoholism, hypertension, and mental hospitalization will accelerate.

Directions for practice relationships

In this atmosphere of troubled human relationships, practice relationships may move in two distinct directions: toward prevention and control at the level of practice with individuals, families, and groups, and toward more democratic control at the policy and political levels.

At the level of practice with individuals, families, and groups, the need to repair the injured and support the vulnerable who seek a therapeutic relationship will increase. Current trends find a growing private clinical practice sector in social work. Private practice at a clinical level will probably expand. Social service practitioners may provide more services to a client population drawn from the middle class because the middle class will be experiencing more economic difficulties. Social service professions will be required to become innovative in establishing preventive, as well as supportive, clinical programs for this group.

This trend may represent a movement away from serving the lower income classes or it may reflect the high stress of public social service work. Of course, another important factor could be the economic incentive in serving the middle and upper classes. In public social service positions, salaries usually reflect our society's belief system, which values private industry over public service. Accordingly, there is differential pay for the two areas, regardless of education, technical competence, or quality of work. This movement could lead to a more formal acceptance of social service personnel as professionals by our society.

B. L. Bloom (1978) writes of a paradigm shift in primary prevention of mental disorder from attention to long-term predisposing factors in individual histories to more immediate precipitating factors. The personal history is less implicated in mental disorder, and social conditions are seen as more the concomitants of mental disorder. After observing that studies showing 50% of marriages end in divorce and after noting C. W. Mills' equation of personal troubles and social issues, Bloom deduces: "The clear implication of this line of reasoning is that any intervention that stops short of a throughgoing examination of social conditions that are producing this much disruption may very well fail" (Bloom, 1979, p. 188).

Attempts to enhance professional status by imitation of an archaic medical model will forestall needed new perspectives, as will traditional methods of third-party payments for services on the part of the insurance industry. Because of retrenchment in federal funding, the need for the private (insurance) companies to change drastically their benefit policies will only increase. To continue to fund expensive in-patient systems (controlled by expensive medical staff), while ignoring the efficacy of alternative community care systems, contributes to social injustice. It may be necessary for states to follow Wisconsin's lead in mandating insurance coverage for nonhospital mental health and alcoholism programs.

Models of prevention (see for example: Bloom, 1978), new techniques for individual and family stress management, and approaches focusing on social networks (Mitchell & Trickett, 1980) rather than on individuals and families, will become invaluable for practitioners. Relationships with clients, their friends and relatives, client employers, allied professionals, industrial consultants, and others involved in establishing prevention and treatment programs will become important. If, as seems to be the case, prevention programs are the most vulnerable to the public budget "axe," there will be no lessening of need for direct service programs to clients.

The need for preventive social service intervention in the workplace has been known since the late 1800s and early 1900s, when a few of the larger companies hired "welfare secretaries" to assist workers. Unfortunately, workers viewed these "secretaries" as agents of control for the company, and their use was terminated (Popple, 1981). The re-entry of social workers into industry is a new phenomenon.

Two examples of preventive social services in industry are alcoholism prevention programs and occupational stress groups. During the last three decades, the number of occupational alcoholism programs in industry has increased from 50 to 5,000 (Schweiker, 1981), and management generally views them as being cost-effective. Of course, the programs vary in their degree of sophistication and use of professional social service personnel; but in the course of time they will receive more legitimization and adopt more formalized attributes.

M. P. Lerner (1980) has described Occupational Stress Groups and Family Support Groups. Because the term *stress* does not carry the stigma of the term *therapy,* and because a group focus on stress in the workplace can avoid viewing problems as an individual matter implying blame, stress groups can attract people without fear of being seen as at fault. Common problems of the work environment, individual responses, and work-life sources of private problems can be addressed in a supportive atmosphere. Stress management techniques can be taught without a hidden assumption that problems arise exclusively from individual deficiencies; economic and structural sources of personal problems can also be addressed. Such groups, as Lerner describes them, can have occupational unions rather than companies as their resource and referral base. This would help to avoid perception of the groups as instruments of management exploitation and control contrary to the participants' interests.

Thus, social service intervention in the workplace represents an expanding opportunity for primary prevention (reducing the incidence of problems) and secondary prevention (early case finding and treatment) as well as tertiary prevention (reducing handicap severity). The success of such programs will depend to a considerable extent on the quality of the practitioners' relationships with the workers, unions, and management. New negotiating, advocacy and consulting skills may have to be learned.

At the policy and political level, practitioners will become involved in movements to alleviate the stresses of the overall trends in society. Feelings of lost control—which are closely tied to personal stress and depression—will engender efforts to regain control of political and economic decisions affecting people's lives. Movements for democratic control of the economy will be mirrored in democratic control of the workplace and employee participation in decision making. These latter movements will be particularly apparent in failing industries whose profits cannot keep pace with inflation. In the social services, practitioners will be increasingly unionized to mirror the management-labor model in industry. The effects on practice relationships will probably be mixed.

Practitioners may begin to develop a stronger identity with their clients as part of the same socioeconomic class of employees because of the potential for more equality in client-practitioner relationships, for more dialogue, and for more mutuality of experience and concern. Practitioners with strong status needs may find this potential shift uncomfortable; others may find it liberating.

The objectives for practice that envisage people with similar troubles empathizing with one another and addressing their problems in support, consciousness raising, and action groups will come into play in practice. As people look for sources of stability, support, and solidarity once available in the family, networks and formal groups will become increasingly valuable.

Racism, sexism, and ageism represent fissures or breaks in solidarity. Objectionable in themselves and counter to practice values, this fragmentation of people into factions hinders the process of finding common cause in solutions to common problems. Ethnic-sensitive and minority-sensitive practice will be increasingly in demand. Spanish, our country's second most commonly spoken language, must become a part of the repertoire of practice in most parts of the country.

Through all this, we can expect the social environment to become more apparently politicized. Just as social workers became involved in the rank-and-file movements of the 1930s (Leighninger & Knickmeyer, 1976), labor and political involvement may become increasingly important for some practitioners. For others, our relationships should uphold professional values and ensure their influence through the practice of dialogue and the mutual development of critical consciousness in ourselves, our colleagues, and our clients. Many of the ideas that meet the serious challenges of the near future will be advocated or damned from political positions. Critical consciousness will require that we assess their consequences for people in keeping with our values of individual worth, self-determination, opportunity, quality of life, equality, and meeting basic needs.

As the social workers in the charity organization societies and settlement houses knew in the late 19th century, merely providing direct services to clients is insufficient to deal with their, or the overall, societal problems. Following in the footsteps of social work pioneers, such as Jane Addams, Bertha Reynolds, Lillian Wald, and Paul Kellog, social service practitioners will have to enhance and to use their *advocacy* skills. We believe that the 1980s will see increased involvement of social service practitioners in advocacy activities at all levels—from individual cases, to agencies, to communities, and even to national policies. Their motivations will be to help their clients to resolve their problems and to ensure the survival of the delivery systems in which such services are provided.

Opposing forces will claim that practitioners are only interested in protecting their own jobs. But if there is no service delivery system (networks of service agencies at the community level), there will be no practitioners available to help the poor and other vulnerable groups. As indicated earlier, we project that the incidence of social disorganization and social problems can only increase in relation to the deteriorating economic, social and physical environment.

Regardless of the level of advocacy activities, the practitioners' relationships with others in the change process, including the target individuals or groups, are paramount. Thus, while a letter to a congressman is worthwhile, face-to-face discussions are apt to be more positive. This is not to say, however, that only "positive" relationships will be effective. Saul Alinsky (1946), an effective advocate, built his strategies on confrontational principles, but he did spend considerable time building up his community organizations internally so that they would function as a unified whole. This entailed developing positive relationships among the members and with other groups which formed alliances with them. Openness, honesty, and trust among group members seldom happen by accident; they require careful nurturing by skilled professionals, who know that the expressive (emotional) activities of groups are just as important as the instrumental (task-accomplishment) activities.

Working in formal organizations and society

It appears inevitable that most social service practitioners, like most workers in advanced industrial society, will work within increasingly bureaucratized organizations. Small voluntary private practice or industrial settings, if not engulfed in larger organizations, will remain the exception. It becomes apparent that the study of bureaucratic organizations should be a mandatory feature of professional education. Some excellent written materials are available for use (for example see: Presthus, 1978; Horejsi, Walz, & Connolly, 1977; Bennis, 1966; Hanlan, 1971; Brager & Holloway, 1978). Practitioners must be prepared emotionally as well as cognitively for the reality within such organizations.

Of course, practitioners should not merely accept the social or bureaucratic status quo. We feel that the need to "humanize" relationships with our clients and the operations of bureaucratic organizations (as well as society) must have a higher priority within the social service professions. Walz has convincingly argued that:

> As we enter the 1980s perhaps it's again time to experiment with the administration of public social service. Managing welfare as if it were an industry made it into an industry. Even more seriously, the model did not reduce caseloads, did not improve our relationships with our clients, policy makers or the general public, did not improve working conditions within the agency and did not produce worker loyalty towards the organization (Walz, 1980).

Dedicated, committed practitioners equipped with knowledge of change strategies will have to carry to agency administrators and legislative levels the message of the need to humanize our services.

Stewart (1981) has summarized possible directions for the social work profession in response to recent conservative federal policies:

1. Move into the mainstream of American life by attracting middle-class clients.
2. Turn to the private sector, including industry, churches, and foundations, for funding.
3. Try to maintain present programs.
4. Heighten general public awareness of the need for social programs and social justice.

To these four directions we would add four of our own: (1) foster critical consciousness among colleagues and clients, (2) increase our economic advocacy and political participation, (3) cultivate our own vision of what our society can become, and (4) work to realize that vision in our professional and personal lives.

CONCLUSION

The forces shaping human relationships and thus practice relationships will continue to reflect tension, change, and crisis. Rigid, impersonal, formal organizations and mindless regressive social and political protest will sit like threatening giants on each side of the narrow gate to a humane social future. The humane values, skills, and practice relationships of dedicated, caring professionals are partial keys to that future. Through history there have always been threatening giants. But regardless of their specter and power, people of tolerance, compassion, and vision have helped to strengthen human ties and have worked, struggled, and persisted toward a better life for their fellow human beings. For people in crisis or in need, social service practitioners help to preserve and repair those human ties that will create a viable society and a future worth living.

STUDY QUESTIONS

1. Much contemporary social policy and political rhetoric suggests that there are no solutions to the conditions that give rise to problems with which professional social service practitioners grapple. Here we have identified several concrete solutions. How might you help to bring about these solutions in your practice?
2. Problems of high geographic mobility, insecurity about the future, and other phenomena will shape the kinds of clients we will work with and the problems they have. What kinds of clients do you think will become more populous in the future? What kinds of problems will occur more frequently?
3. If there will be a shift from personal history to social conditions in mental disorder and working toward its prevention, how will this affect therapeutic practice? Does it hold implications for a stress-management approach to prevention?
4. Current trends suggest an uneven future in the delivery of services to people among the United States. Do you believe that more political and social activism is required to achieve the values and goals we work for in everyday practice?
5. Given a continuation of current economic and social trends, more basic needs will go unmet and more people will need the services of professional practitioners. What activities will you have to engage in to see to it that human needs are met and that those needing services and restorative, growth-producing relationships will receive them?

REFERENCES

Alinsky, S. D. *Reveille for radicals*. New York: Vintage Books, 1946.

Bennis, W. *Beyond bureaucracy*. New York: McGraw-Hill, 1966.

Bloom, B. L. Prevention of mental disorders: Recent advances in theory and practice. *Community Mental Health Journal*, 1979, *15* (3), 179–191.

Brager, G., & Holloway, S. *Changing human service organizations: Politics and practice*. New York: Free Press, 1978.

Brenner, H. M. *Mental illness and the economy*. Cambridge, Mass.: Harvard University Press, 1973.

Brenner, H. M. Estimating the social costs of national economic policy: Implications for mental health and criminal aggression. *Achieving the Goals of the Employment Act of 1946—Thirtieth Anniversary Review*. Joint Economic Committee, Congress of the United States. Washington: U.S. Government Printing Office, 1976.

Emerson, R. M. Power-dependence relations. *American Sociological Review*, 1962, *27*, 31–41.

Gendron, B. *Technology and the human condition*. New York: St. Martin's Press, 1977.

Grummer, B. A power-politics approach to social welfare organizations. *Social Services Review*, 1978, *52* (3), 349–361.

Hanlan, A. Casework beyond bureaucracy. *Social Casework*, 1971, *52* (4), 195–199.

Harrington, M. *The twilight of capitalism*. New York: Simon & Schuster, 1976.

Horejsi, J. E., Walz, I., & Connolly, P. R. *Working in welfare: Survival through positive action*. Iowa City: University of Iowa School of Social Work, 1977.

Keefe, T. Radical change and solidarity: The future of practice. *Social Development Issues,* 1979, *3* (2), 63–81.

Kovel, J. Therapy in late capitalism. *Telos,* 1976/1977, *30,* 74–91.

Leighninger, L. & Knickmeyer, R. The rank and file movement: The relevance of radical social work traditions to modern social work practice. *Journal of Sociology and Social Welfare,* 1976, *4* (2), 166–177.

Lerner, M. P. Stress at the work place: The approach of the Institute for Labor and Mental Health. *Catalyst,* 1980, *8.*

Litwak, E., & Hylton, L. F. Interorganizational analysis: A hypothesis on coordinating agencies. *Administrative Science Quarterly,* 1962, *6,* 395–420.

Maypole, D. E. An interorganizational strategy model. Unpublished manuscript, 1981.

Mitchell, R. E., & Trickett, E. J. Social networks as mediators of social support: An analysis of the effects and determinants of social networks. *Community Mental Health Journal,* 1980, *16* (1), 27–44.

NASW Ad Hoc Committee on Advocacy. The social worker as advocate: Champion of social victims. *Social Work,* 1969, *14* (2), 16–23.

Perlman, R., & Gurin, A. *Community organization and social planning.* New York: John Wiley & Sons, 1972.

Popple, P. R. Social work practice in business and industry, 1875–1930. *Social Service Review,* June 1981, *55* (2), 257–269.

Presthus, W. *The organizational society* (Rev. ed.). New York: St. Martin's Press, 1978.

Schweiker, R. S. Schweiker discusses worksite prevention. *NIAAA Information & Feature Service,* August 28, 1981, p. 2.

Shuman, J. B., & Rosenau, D. *The Kondratieff wave.* New York: World Publishing, Times Mirror, 1972.

Stewart, R. P. Watershed days: How will social work respond to the conservative revolution? Letter to the editor. *Social Work,* 1981, *26* (2), 271–273.

Thurow, L. C. *The zero-sum society: Distribution and the possibilities for economic change.* New York: Penguin Books, 1980.

Walz, T. An opinion: It didn't work. *Human Development News* (U.S. DHHS), October 1980, opinion page.

Warren, R. L. *Social change and human purpose: Toward understanding and action.* Chicago: Rand McNally & Co., 1977.

Index